D0706719

American Maritain Association Publications

1988   *Jacques Maritain: The Man and His Metaphysics*. Edited by John F.X. Knasas. ISBN 0-268-01205-9.

1989   *Freedom in the Modern World: Jacques Maritain, Yves R. Simon, Mortimer J. Adler*. Edited by Michael D. Torre. ISBN 0-268-00978-3

1990   *Philosophy and the Future of Civilization* (tentative title). Editor to be announced.

Freedom in the Modern World:

Jacques Maritain, Yves R. Simon, Mortimer J. Adler

Edited by Michael D. Torre

American Maritain Association
Distributed by University of Notre Dame Press

Distributed by University of Notre Dame Press
Notre Dame, Indiana 46556

American Maritain Association
Anthony O. Simon, Secretary
508 Travers Circle
Mishawaka, Indiana 46545

Contents

Part III
Jacques Maritain

Abbreviations[1]

Mortimer J. Adler

CS	The Common Sense of Politics
IF	The Idea of Freedom
PL	Philosopher at Large
TP	Ten Philosophical Mistakes

Yves R. Simon

CDM	"Charles Dunoyer, memoire"
CF	The Community of the Free
FAC	Freedom and Community
FC	Freedom of Choice
GT	A General Theory of Authority
MV	The Definition of Moral Virtue
NF	Nature and Functions of Authority
PDG	Philosophy of Democratic Government
TLT	Trois leçons sur le travail
WSC	Work, Society, and Culture

Jacques Maritain

AS	Art and Scholasticism
CI	Creative Intuition in Art and Poetry
DK	The Degrees of Knowledge
FMW	Freedom in the Modern World
IH	Integral Humanism
MS	Man and the State
PH	On the Philosophy of History
RA	Reflections on America
RC	Religion and Culture
RMNL	The Rights of Man and Natural Law
RR	The Range of Reason
RT	Ransoming the Time
TR	Three Reformers
TRA	The Responsibility of the Artist

---

[1]For complete reference to these works, see the Select Bibliography.

Michael D. Torre

Introduction: Reading between the Lines

Nineteen hundred eighty-eight marked three anniversaries: the 55th year since the French publication of *Freedom in the Modern World*; the 30th year since the appearance of the first volume of *The Idea of Freedom*; and the 20th year since work was completed for the posthumous publication of *Freedom of Choice*. The year also marked the 50th anniversary of their authors' first joint meeting, at a symposium held at the University of Notre Dame. It is most fitting, then, that the American Maritain Association should have returned to that university to celebrate and assess their achievement, then and now. This book is the result of that gathering.

The works' authors need no introduction and shall receive none. Perhaps a word is in order, however, regarding the order of the essays in this volume, as well as the implied conversation between them.

The authors are given in the title according to the genesis of their work (Simon's appearing in French the year before Adler set up his Institute for Philosophical Research). Their presentation is reversed in the book, however, to follow the order of logic and learning. The proper way to begin an examination of freedom is to approach it dialectically. We begin, then, with essays devoted to the work of Mortimer J. Adler. With the essays on Yves R. Simon, we move into concerns proper to the philosophy of man, ethics, and politics. These continue in the essays centered on Jacques Maritain, which conclude with considerations proper to metaphysics and natural theology. In the brief compass of our work, therefore, we have sought to do some measure of justice to the full range of issues raised by the idea and reality of freedom.

Our work is introduced by Donald Gallagher's recollections of these three philosophers. He reminds us that philosophy does not take place in an ideal realm, but is the work of men. In their case, it is the work of men who were *friends* and who stimulated and encouraged each other. Has not the greatest philosophy ever been the product of such a collaborative effort? (One thinks of Socrates, Plato, and Aristotle or Albert, Bonaventure, and Thomas.) Gallagher also offers us a glimpse of these men and their in-

1

fluence upon American Thomism when in its formative stages: a glimpse particularly precious for those of us with little or no experience of them in the flesh. He thereby serves to remind us that philosophy is a living tradition, passed on from one generation to the next.

I. Mortimer J. Adler

Fortunately for us, generations overlap. We were thus privileged to be addressed by Adler—himself a living tradition—who made his presence felt throughout the symposium. In his criticism of Allan Bloom's *The Closing of the American Mind*, he urges a strictly dialectical approach to texts—as the one appropriate to undergraduate liberal education—and sharply distinguishes it from a doctrinal approach. Clearly, the nature and importance of a dialectical education still remain vital issues today. (For a contemporary effort to appropriate Adler's great books approach to learning, see Robert Royal's essay in the section on Maritain.) In his address, Adler also implies that modern, egalitarian democracy is the ideal and "only perfectly just" form of government. This view was not to go unchallenged. Indeed, whether Simon and Maritain themselves were unqualified supporters of modern democracy and its institutions, and—if so—whether they should have been, are questions that run through several of the later essays.

We begin, however, with the dialectical approach to freedom. Desmond FitzGerald gives us a rare inside look into how Adler's massive study was achieved, together with a summary of the main types of freedom it distinguished. As he notes, this book marked a turning point in Adler's career: at Maritain's urging, he then devoted his energies to presenting his own philosophical views. FitzGerald lists for us the fruits of this truly amazing period of creativity—one that, remarkably, is still going on. Perhaps, as FitzGerald intimates, Adler's achievement will finally rest even more upon his own philosophical work than upon the dialectical projects that occupied his earlier years.

With Otto Bird, we turn to the dialectical task. He gives us an elegant synopsis of how to go about constructing a dialectical controversy, using the idea of justice as a model. He thus helps us see precisely how to *use* the dialectical method that produced *The Idea of Freedom*. In his conclusion, Bird notes the Aristotelian parentage of this method, but also indicates the different way it is used by Adler and his associates: not to prepare a doctrinal exposition already envisioned, but accurately to present opposing positions. Such a groundclearing aims to further a better meeting of minds and a more reasonable debate than the history of philosophy has often witnessed.

And yet, as Ralph McInerny notes in his essay, for such an aim to succeed, philosophers must avail themselves of the dialectical work accomplished. Disquietingly few have. The state of the question established by Adler's work seems largely ignored. The scandal remains. McInerny wonders whether we would be justified in seeing Adler's dialectical pursuit as "quixotic," as an heroic effort that has failed, because the philosophical world did not take it seriously. Yet, like FitzGerald, McInerny also points to the present achievements of Adler's own philosophy, and calls *The Time of Our Lives* "better than anything else done on the subject in our day."

John Van Doren, in his illuminating comparison of Adler and Matthew Arnold, raises a similar question. Like Arnold, Adler has attempted to place his entire discipline on firm ground, by clarifying "the ideas on which it stakes its claims." Such an effort supposes a reasonable audience, one that will appreciate the work achieved. Yet Adler himself has been unremittingly critical of established academe, of "the professors." Van Doren ends by pointing to this anomaly, of finding "such trust in reason on the part of a man who finds so little of it going on about him." Is Adler unduly optimistic in what he expects from his "truly democratic system" of education?

For his part, George Anastaplo judges Adler to have overestimated the virtues of modern democracy and underestimated its classical critique. He argues that modern egalitarianism renders the democrat insensitive to natural differences among men; and he questions the improved awareness of justice attributed to modern sensibilities. Is the common man as wise as Adler sometimes leads one to believe, or were not the ancients more correct in judging the opinions of the many to be as likely wrong as right? If so, one should not expect from them (*inter alia*) a just appreciation of that rarity, the true philosopher. Perhaps this would in part explain the lukewarm reception accorded Adler's own dialectical project.

Anastaplo here extends his criticism to Simon's views as well. A similar tack is taken on Simon by John Hittinger, and a contrasting one by Joseph Califano, in the essays devoted to Maritain. Their pieces also contribute to our interpretation of Simon's thought.

II. Yves R. Simon

Turning to those essays devoted entirely to Simon, we begin with Catherine Green's careful analysis of the basis for man's freedom of choice, as Simon expounds it. In particular, she highlights for us two of his most valuable distinctions: between habit and *habitus* and between the passive indetermination of indecision and the active one proper to free choice. She indicates how, for Simon, man's natural desire for the comprehensive good endows him with a "surplus actuality," through which he can determine himself to one good over another and consciously seek it as a means to his final end. These distinctions remove some of the misunderstandings that have so often stood in the way of a convincing defense of man's freedom.

S. Iniobong Udoidem's essay should be read in tandem with Green's, for he applies a similar analysis of freedom to the social sphere. From it, we can see that the requirements of true law and the common good, far from limiting an individual's freedom, actually empower and support him. The superdetermination and autonomy proper to freedom is in fact perfected through man's internalization of law. For that man is most free and self-governing who recognizes and accepts the exigencies of his being, and hence directs himself to goods that will truly fulfill him. Thus, in invoking the authority of its laws and demanding obedience to them, a just society does not bind its citizens, but directs them towards activity that will truly liberate. Whatever may be the fact of social reality, in theory there is no opposition between law and liberty.

The relation between our first two essays pertains also to our next pair: the second applies to the political realm an idea first worked out as it bears upon the individual. In his article, Robert J. Mulvaney shows that Simon recovers a proper appreciation for the ancient virtue of *phronesis* or *prudentia*: a virtue that has been degraded by the modern concept of "prudence" as a technique for getting on in the world. He reveals how sensitive Simon was to the difference between theoretical and practical knowledge: one signalled by the fact that practical thought ends not in an idea but in an *external action*. Again, practical truth is finally determined not by conformity to a state of affairs, grasped through a rational deduction, but by conformity to right appetite. Thus, the possession of virtue is essential if one is to go beyond the probabilities of practical deliberation to terminate it surely in a right decision. Simon here fights against the prevalent intellectualism of modernity, and returns us to a just recognition of the true union of moral and intellectual virtue in practical reasoning.

For her part, Marianne Mahoney argues that only an elaboration of true prudence, along the lines laid down by Simon, can ground a public philosophy that will safeguard the full range of human goods. She criticizes the "justice-dominant" theories of contemporary thinkers such as Rawls, Gewirth, and Nozick; given the unity of the moral good, unless the virtues of temperance and courage are properly defended, justice itself will be undermined. She questions, furthermore, the sharp public-private distinction drawn by theorists of liberal democracy; insofar as this suggests the existence of two separate realms, it is a false dichotomy, and fails to do justice to those "sub-regime" communities (e.g., the family) between the individual and the state. She argues that Simon's theory looks very good in comparison to the fare offered up by contemporary political theorists. For it is precisely the role of prudence to discern and defend the full range of human goods and to give due weight to the particular and the common good. In an age marked by relativism and moral uncertainty, only a public philosophy based on prudence can protect the legitimate rights of the common good from being eroded in the name of individual autonomy and the toleration of individual differences.

David Koyzis continues the argument begun in Mahoney's article. In particular, he shows how Simon's defense of the full range of human goods allows him to occupy a middle position between the predominant modern tendencies of individualism and collectivism. For example, his nuanced view of the different types and functions of authority in securing the common good permits him to defend political authority without becoming authoritarian. Again, his recognition of communal goods narrower than those of the state undergirds his defense of the principle of "subsidiarity." His vision of a healthy society is one in which individuals engage creatively in the activities of diverse sub-communities. Notable here is Koyzis' insistence that Simon primarily defends the "political" regime of Aristotle and the "mixed" regime of Aquinas. He sees that the modern democratic state can itself become tyrannical, and thus he "is at pains to emphasize the value of nondemocratic elements" within it. Does this not suggest that there is a real difference in Adler's and Simon's assessment of modern democracy? . . . and that perhaps Anastaplo's remarks are better aimed at the former than the latter?

For any political philosophy to be complete, it must come to grips with economic realities. As Ralph Nelson's essay demonstrates, Simon sought to do so from the beginning of his philosophical career. Not surprisingly, we again find him charting a middle course between modern positions; in this case, the views of economic liberalism and state socialism. With the former, we find him arguing that property "functions as a support of freedom" and a protection "against governmental arbitrariness." On the other hand, the development of modern technical culture under the free enterprise system has led to the formation of a working class that merely executes the designs of others. Unable to participate in the direction of his labor, the worker becomes a mere operative, a person "deprived of free expansion." Simon therefore defends the necessity of labor unions to secure workers' freedom of autonomy. Yet Nelson sees Simon as wishing to go further, to create structures through which workers can participate in the direction of their labor: a development that seems to be occurring today in European workers' movements. Simon saw this development not only as directly furthering freedom in the workplace, but also as developing the virtue of self-governance, thereby benefitting the worker's entire social and moral life. Nelson concludes by urging that we now need to apply Simon's principles to the changed conditions of agriculture.

Finally, John Gueguen compares Simon's views on work with those of John Paul II in his encyclical *On Human Work*. The striking thing here is the numerous correspondences between them, even though one is nourished on Aristotelian philosophy and contemporary experience, while the other develops primarily from a meditation on Scripture. In particular, both men share a sense of the high dignity of work. Both see work as being *for man*, as developing and expressing his humanity; for this reason, they both defend the good of private ownership. Yet both also see work as creating fellowship and solidarity among men; thus, both see it as deformed when reduced to a mere item of merchandise. Again, Gueguen sees John Paul as substantially agreeing with Simon's views over against those Josef Pieper develops in *Leisure, The Basis of Culture*: work in its full range of activities, not leisure, is its truer basis. In conclusion, Gueguen notes a difference in the way the two men treat the mysterious "irksomeness" of work. Simon sees the onerous character of work as not essential to it; John Paul, however, accepting that this condition exists in man's fallen state, sees it as an opportunity to develop courage and to participate in the Cross of Christ. We see here how practical philosophy finally arrives at a mystery that can be grasped only if one passes beyond it.

In reading these essays, one cannot fail, I think, to be struck both by the extraordinary depth and breadth of Simon's practical philosophy, and by its contemporaneity. Now that its full riches are being made accessible through translations and posthumous publications, it is beginning to be given the attention it so obviously deserves. One can only hope that this renaissance of Simonian scholarship will continue to flourish.

III. Jacques Maritain

The essays centered on Jacques Maritain break into four pairs. The first three discuss matters of political philosophy. (As befit the title of our symposium, we predominately discussed *political* freedom.) In each case, there is a discernible tension between the two essays. Our final pair turns to the higher reaches of metaphysics and to God, from whom all created liberty flows.

We begin with essays on the philosophy of education. Through his original research on the Ecole Nationale des Cadres d'Uriage, John Hellman offers us a fascinating look at an attempt to develop an educational program in Vichy during World War II. He implicitly raises this troubling question: to what extent was Maritain truly responsible for engendering its rather authoritarian educational philosophy? Certainly, the men of Uriage saw themselves as following the lead of Maritain. And, as

Hellman reminds us, Maritain had supplied them with much ammunition against modern individualism and "bourgeois man."[1] Did Maritain's Thomism, and his call for a "new Christendom," help undermine the defense of modern democracy when faced with fascism? Here and in his introduction to *The Road to Vichy* (which should be read as a companion-piece to this essay), Hellman indicates that Simon was himself willing to pose this question. He sees Simon, and then Maritain, shifting to a positive defense of modern democracy in light of the Vichy experience, which saw many of their former friends become compromised by their acquiescence to the Vichy regime.

Yet this rather dark picture should be set beside Robert Royal's piece. For he also attempts to construct an educational program inspired by Maritain's writings, and it looks nothing like Uriage! Admittedly, his is a creative and original effort, yet its point of departure lies in a reading of Maritain. (For this reason, it is put in this section, even though its central discussion of the great books makes it equally relevant to Adlerian concerns.) Furthermore, several of his key references are to *Education at the Crossroads*, which Maritain worked out as Uriage was establishing its own program. Even more telling is the central place Royal assigns *intuition* in the creative process and in the re-creative encounter that describes true education. This emphasis on intuition is quintessential Maritain, a hallmark of his writings from first to last. It contrasts sharply with the regimented discipline of Uriage. True, Royal himself sees the necessity of authority to establish an educational canon. Yet surely he is close to Maritain's own educational philosophy in insisting that a true canon is one hospitable to any modern work capable of "better understanding and enriching human life": a view requiring a style of authority different from that found at Uriage.

This first pair of essays raises the question of Maritain's final assessment of modern democracy: the topic of our next pair. Michael Novak presents the later Maritain (of *Reflections on America*) as a wholehearted supporter of American democracy. He groups him with John Courtney Murray, S.J., as a defender of the "American Proposition": the assertion, in Murray's words, that just government is founded "on a certain body of objective truth, universal in its import, accessible to human reason, definable,

---

[1]Hellman had earlier detailed this assault in "The Humanism of Jacques Maritain," his contribution to *Understanding Maritain: Philosopher and Friend*, ed. Deal W. Hudson and Matthew J. Mancini (Macon, GA: Mercer University Press, 1987), 117–31.

defensible." Thus, as Murray again argues, underlying American government is the belief in "the tradition of natural law as the basis of a free and ordered political life." Maritain, himself a great defender of that tradition, came to see this, and hence became a defender of the American form of democracy. Its founding documents secured God-given human rights and rendered possible a practical cooperation among men of diverse conviction. Novak presses upon us Maritain's challenge to articulate "the ideology of this American civilization," and himself offers an eloquent defense of it, including the economic creativity and enterprise so typical of the American experiment.

Yet, on this last point at least, it may be wondered whether Novak's thought quite reflects that of Maritain. For, as Matthew Mancini points out in his brilliant discussion of Maritain's final essay—"A Society without Money"—he always was an outspoken opponent of modern capitalism. True, it is principally the practice of capitalism and not its theory that Maritain condemns. Yet how not see that condemnation as including within its sweep the American pursuit of the almighty dollar? Would not Maritain see the economic enterprise that Novak lauds as at best equivocal: under the bewitchment of the "magical sign" of money? Furthermore, as Mancini points out, Maritain really condemns the theory of capitalism as well. For he is unswerving in his condemnation of loaning money on interest: an economic practice essential to modern finance capitalism. To Maritain's eye, the Church's medieval condemnation of usury was set "at the threshold of modern times like a burning interrogatory as to the lawfulness of its economy." His positive judgments of modern democracy are balanced by this negative judgment on its dominant economic structure.

Did Maritain really think, then, that there had been a progress in moral and political sensibility in modern times? And are his views on this subject beyond criticism? Our next pair of essays answers these questions rather differently.

For Joseph Califano, Maritain (and Simon) has "a balanced and fertile view of human progress," one that avoids both the false optimism of the eighteenth and nineteenth centuries and the debilitating pessimism of the twentieth. Their philosophy of history grants that man's moral insight does mature over time, yet this progress always runs the risk of misuse and deformation. Califano cites the women's rights movement as a good instance: a just recognition that women must not be treated as property or as less than adults has become tied to an unjust demand for absolute power over the unborn. Thus do good and evil advance together in history. Such a guarded optimism (or "authentic pessimism") is completely opposed to the simplistic ideologies of our day. It counsels a constant vigilance over current events, knowing full well that "what has been won by sweat and blood can easily be lost," and that each generation must struggle to preserve and advance the cause of liberty, justice, and truth.

John Hittinger approaches the subject from a different angle: the egalitarian principle in modern democracy. He shows that Maritain opposes both false claims to absolute superiority (e.g., as made for Aryans by the Nazis) and the doctrinaire denial of natural inequalities (common to the levelling spirit of modern egalitarianism). If, by their common humanity and natural sociability, men are fundamentally equal, that same sociability requires social differentiation and inevitable inequalities. Yet, Maritain subordinates these latter to the principle of equality: they must never obscure the foundational equality of men, nor must they impede the progress in social equality that is the aim of any just society. Maritain appears to leave this future progress open-ended. Here (in a way that echoes Anastaplo's remarks on Adler), Hittinger criticizes Maritain for failing to acknowledge sufficiently the "presence of intrinsic limitations" on political progress. His prospects for democratic achievement are too optimistic. Unless the real differences and inequalities among men are frankly faced and given value, his own egalitarianism dooms modern citizens to being discontent at the equality that eludes them and too ready to grant excessive power to the state to remedy their situation. Hittinger thinks the same criticism, albeit to a lesser degree, can be made of Simon. And he interestingly contrasts their work with the more conservative political ideas of Aurel Kolnai. Hittinger, then, does not agree with Califano that Maritain (or Simon) has found the perfect mean between optimism and pessimism.

The contrasting views of the last six essays—all of which essentially involve Maritain's approach to modernity—indicate how rich his thought is, how difficult it is to capture whole or place in a neat category. At root, the question remains whether Maritain has fully succeeded in transposing Thomas' social thought to the modern world. Certainly, the issues raised above will continue to be debated, no doubt as early as the 1989 symposium on Maritain's 1939 lecture, *The Twilight of Civilization*.

Despite Maritain's constant attention to the political realities of his day, his mind was instinctively metaphysical, and he ever sought to root his thought in the first principles of reality. It is fitting, then, that we should conclude our entire discussion of freedom with two essays on its ultimate foundations.

Raymond Dennehy helps us face up to this apparent difficulty in Maritain's doctrine on freedom: since man's terminal freedom (of independence and "exultation") requires internalizing the moral law, it looks as though man only achieves this freedom at the expense of his individuality. The common moral law appears opposed to the unique self. In a closely reasoned argument developing the implications of the identity of being and unity, Dennehy shows the opposite to be true. He reminds us of Aquinas' dictum that "the higher a nature, the more intimate to that nature is the activity that flows from it"; that is, the higher the nature, the more its action comes from its interiority, expresses its uniqueness. (Contrast the reflex actions of a plant—proceeding automatically from outside stimuli, and common to the entire species—with the deliberate movements of a man—neither automatic nor common.) In God, this identity of being and action is complete: His action comes entirely from Himself and expresses who He uniquely is. And man, in seeking to internalize the moral law, is in fact seeking to participate more in the being of its author; that is, he is seeking to become his own "unique, concrete embodiment of that law." Man's freedom of exultation not only possesses a plenitude of being; but that very plenitude grounds its expression in a way unique to each person. Contrary to appearances, then, following the moral law does not oppose but furthers man's desire to be his unique self.

My own work, rather than creatively developing a particular insight of Maritain, seeks to synthesize the doctrine on freedom common to all three of our philosophers. Seeing their careful distinctions helps us sort out some of the pseudo-problems that have plagued discussions of man's freedom before God. In particular, I observe that freedom of choice and freedom of spirit (Maritain's freedom of exultation) have diverse foundations: man's inclination to the comprehensive good and to the moral good. If one is attentive to this, as Maritain is, one can go beyond the Molinist-Bañezian controversy that has plagued Catholic philosophers since the early seventeenth century. For, with the Dominicans, one should hold that man chooses the moral good only because God inclines him towards it; but, with the Jesuits, one should grant that man is free to turn from that motion. Put differently, the perfection of spiritual freedom does not require that one be able to turn from God's inclination; but the state of fallible freedom that is our earthly lot does bring with it that terrible possibility. And this raises the great, existential question of freedom, one implicit to every choice we make: whether to place our final end in God or ourselves. For, however illusory its goodness may be, the possibility of being the first cause of our own destiny remains attractive. Indeed, it exercises an attraction beyond our power to resist for long. We need an aid beyond ourselves. Philosophy, at its limit, requires that it be surpassed. Part of Maritain's greatness in philosophy lies in his ever calling our attention to this truth.

Finally, Donald Gallagher's 1987 telegram to the American and Canadian Maritain Associations is included, as an appendix. Regrettably, it missed inclusion in our previous volume.[2] In his address, Gallagher urges us to go forward in our work, in the confidence that we can produce something of lasting importance. Perhaps it is not too pretentious to see the two volumes now published as advancing us a little way towards that goal.

Several people helped with this volume. In particular, my thanks to Tony Simon, for his constant insistence upon quality; to Mike Aquilina, for generously volunteering to proofread the text; to Donald Gallagher, for helping to cover the book's cost; and especially to Mike Mollerus, for his incisive editorial suggestions and the professional quality of his typesetting. The book is better, in numerous small ways, for all their work. The defects that remain are to be laid at my door.

---

[2]John F.X. Knasas, ed., *Jacques Maritain: The Man and His Metaphysics*, (American Maritain Association, 1988).

Donald A. Gallagher

Recollections of Three Thinkers: Adler, Simon, and Maritain

In my mind's eye, M.J. Adler stands forth as the Demonstrator and Remonstrator of our time, Y.R. Simon as the Argumentor and Distinguisher of our period, and Jacques Maritain as the Synthesizer and Prophetic Voice of our age.

In this presentation, I view Adler, Simon, and Maritain from the perspective of personal recollections moving back in time to the 1930s and 1940s and in terms of the impact they exercised on young teachers and students in that period. It is then obviously not a philosophical evaluation, even though I recognize that recall involves selection and a sort of implicit evaluation.

I refer to these thinkers by their last names, not out of disrespect but out of regard for their stature and status among the Great Ones. One does not denominate Hegel as Professor Hegel but quite simply as Hegel because he is one of the Great. Let me proceed to a conspectus of each of three philosophers and then to my concluding remarks.

I. Mortimer J. Adler

I did not have the privilege of knowling Adler as colleague or friend. I did enjoy several meetings with him, especially in the 1940s, usually in a group situation. In Saint Louis and other cities, he delivered lectures I attended. His books and articles, which were published in a regular and rapid rate and which I read avidly, exerted a lasting influence upon me.The first lecture by Adler I ever attended I recall vividly. It was given in 1938 at a Catholic women's college in Saint Louis. He contended, in a theme developed at length in his *How to Read a Book*, that, in an exacting sense of reading, few people including scholars ever read a book, even those who devour hundreds of tomes. It was above all in the middle ages that the mental atmosphere was conducive to thorough reading. Few ancients and hardly any moderns have really *read* a book. The medievals did read books.

The exceptions to Adler's rule fortify his thesis. The Cistercians of the Strict Observance, the Trappists as they came to be called from the monastery *La Trappe* in Normandy, were in Rancé's day allowed only one or two books for pondering and digesting during the Lenten season. Abraham Lincoln, from what we know of his youth with little formal schooling, had only a few books at his disposal. These he mastered along with the language he spoke so eloquently. The tradition of *Lectio Divina* in European monasteries scattered far and wide from the patristic era to the middle ages and continuing into modern times promoted *reflective reading* (which is in reality Adler's "reading"; after all, one does not really read if reflection is lacking) of every work handled.

At the present time, it surprises me to realize that Adler was in his late thirties in 1938. To me in my early twenties, he seemed mature and knowledgeable.

In those days, there was much talk about Catholics being in a ghetto and having a ghetto mentality. (The English Catholic writer Wilfrid Ward spoke of Catholics beginning to emerge from their "siege mentality.") The ghetto notion, wrenched out of its original context, has always seemed somewhat ambiguous to me and so I hesitate even to refer to it here. At the risk of digression, let me point out that in the 1930s and 1940s when I was studying and teaching at Catholic universities in the Middle West of our country, there was, at least as I recall the situation, little or no mention of Catholics being confined to ghettos. (Of course, I say half-seriously that one may be so immured in a ghetto that one does not even realize it!) It was only when I was teaching at Boston College in the 1960s that I heard talk about Catholics in the ghetto. Perhaps in that environment, they had been in or were just breaking out of one. Some Irish-Americans, Irish in a distinctively Bostonian style, had received higher education at Ivy League schools and were inclined to disparage the basic values of their culture as well as its narrownesses.

On the one hand, there was in the 1930s to the 1950s (at least) a certain narrowmindedness, a defensive mentality inherited from immigrant forebears who huddled together for protection and guidance. On the other hand, Catholic intellectuals were making contact with their great traditions going all the way back to the middle ages, expanding their horizons, and were thus less provincial than many of their secularist contemporaries.

This seeming digression serves some purpose if it helps us the better to understand the value and the impact of Adler's writings and speeches in the period of which I speak. The scholar who had come from the secularistic world, who repudiated it, and who now championed the Great Tradition that we Catholics were beginning to assimilate and appreciate, was a friend in a time of need.

In *Philosopher at Large,* his autobiographical work, Adler acknowledges that he was sometimes too brusque and brash in his criticisms of the "moderns." In "God and the Professors," a piece he wrote around 1940, he argues that the most serious threat to democracy is the *positivism* of the Professors, the central corruption of modern culture. Democracy has more to fear from the mentality of its teachers than from the nihilism of Hitler. (All this at a time when the hordes of Hitler were conquering Europe and terrifying the peoples of the world.) Adler's logic in these accusations was perhaps irrefutable but his rhetoric (as he admits) was not calculated to influence the people he intended to persuade. Of course, it is arguable that Adler's procedure was necessary at the time, and was aimed at shocking those entrenched in their own secularist ghetto into sanity.

One is reminded of Maritain, shortly after his conversion to Catholicism, writing *Antimoderne* (in the book itself he says it should perhaps have been entitled *Ultramoderne*). It is one of the finest books written by the youthful convert. It contains a scathing denunciation of modern trends as well as a recognition of values brought to light in this time.

In retaliation for his attacks upon the Professorial Estate, some critics called Adler a "dialectical typewriter," a species of heartless logic-machine. Even some Catholics began to be critical of Adler. They were irritated at his criticism of Catholic mediocrity and of the failure of Catholics to appreciate their own priceless tradition. Some persons could not understand why he did not become a Catholic. It was reported that a religious sister who questioned him on this matter was given the simple answer, "I have not received the Gift of Faith!" There was admittedly something paradoxical about a man who accepted much of Aquinas' theology as well as his philosophy and did not go further. (It should be mentioned that Adler himself treats this sensitive topic in *Philosopher at Large.*)

Adler would readily acknowledge that he was more interested in human thought than in human beings. At the same time, his capacity for friendship presents us with another paradox about his personality. On the occasion of his sixtieth birthday (a time much later than that to which we devote attention here), the roster of those who paid tribute to him reads like a roll-call of the leaders in the gallant fight for the Great Tradition. Buchanan, McKeon, Barzun, Fadiman, the Van Dorens, Rubin, Mayer, and many others: these persons he calls *friends.*

Pride of place is reserved for his friendship with Jacques Maritain. Over and over in his writings and early and late in his career, he refers to Maritain as his close personal friend. In *What Man Has Made of Man* (1937), he praises *The Degrees of Knowledge* (1932) as constituting "the outlines, at least, of a synthesis of science, philosophy and theology which will do for

us what St. Thomas did for philosophy and theology in the middle ages."
In *Philosopher at Large* (1977), Adler praises Maritain and conjoins him with
Aristotle and Aquinas as the ones from whom he has learned the most and
as those who are the great champions of living Tradition.

Adler the arch-intellectual does not disdain the common man. On the
contrary, he esteems him. In his later period, one of his books is entitled
Aristotle for Everybody and he says it is intended for the Professors. It
should be emphasized that one of the distinctive insights of Adler resides
in his respect for and his appeal to the judgment of the common man. He
maintains that the so-called "common man" is able to grasp basic truths
(for example, certain of the Great Ideas, especially those in the moral
order). The "common man," an appellation often used and much abused,
is in the final analysis the "uncommon man." It seems to me that, in this
view, Adler in his own way is at one with Pope John Paul II, who names
each human person "this unique individual," and with Jacques Maritain,
who refers early and late to the basic dignity of each person. (In a somewhat special reference bearing on the same theme, Yves Simon argues that
intellectuals and landed proprietors should not have more than one vote,
but one the same as every other individual. Simon argues this way *because
he trusts the good judgment of the average citizen.*)

Furthermore, I find an affinity between Adler's perspective on the uncommon common man and Maritain's idea in his educational philosophy
that emphasis should be placed in liberal education (from high school
years and the following, or from what in many countries are called the
lycee or *college* years) upon what he terms *natural intelligence.* Only later on
does the student, with his intelligence fortified by intellectual virtue, tackle
advanced stages of knowledge. It should be noted that Maritain emphasizes the importance of educating the "natural intelligence" and at the
same time devotes attention to advanced students, who are led to develop
the *habitus* of philosophy for themselves by way of a more formal and
rigorous discipline. In my view, while he makes percipient observations
on *habitus* in *What Man Has Made of Man,* Adler does not bring out these
distinctions as clearly as does Maritain.

At this point, I should mention the influence that the reading of Adler
had upon me in the 1940s and 1950s. Every book and article Adler put
forth was an event for me. Of his plentiful writings, of which I still retain
records and jottings from the text, I take as example a book already mentioned, *What Man Has Made of Man.* This important study of philosophical
and empiriological psychology as well as of psychoanalysis I read over
and over and found it (as I still do) of exceptional value in my teaching of
what was then termed "Rational Psychology" and later "Philosophical
Psychology" or "Anthropology." The book was presented in outline form,

which threw some people off, but even in that shape I regarded it as immensely serviceable.

In this period, Adler co-authored with Father Walter Farrell, O.P., a study of democracy. Well thought out and closely reasoned, it nevertheless became a subject of controversy. In fact, I disagreed with some aspects of the authors' thesis and published a critique of it. I hasten to add that one does not lightly disagree with Dr. Adler. One hesitates to engage in disputation with the Great Disputant. One needs the argumentative skill of a Simon and the insight of a Maritain to fare well in any such encounter.

Yet, when all is said and done, Adler welcomes debate. In his *Idea of Freedom* (vol. II), he praises *rational debate*. His complaint is that there is so little of the rational in the interminable arguments about philosophical and related issues. In medieval times, he points out, the Schoolmen in their disputations and other intellectual jousts afford an example of truly rational debate. Most moderns, including some classed as great thinkers, lunge past each other and assail strawmen.

An unfortunate example of a debate lacking rationality was supplied on the occasion of Adler's study on *The Problem of Species*. An uncalled-for attack was launched on the work by Professor B.J. Muller-Thym of Saint Louis University. He was my thesis mentor at the university and I held him in esteem. In his critique, he not only countered Adler's thesis but questioned his scholarship and competence. I can never forget how Maritain rebuked Muller-Thym and, though he did not agree altogether with Adler's ideas, defended him against what he considered outrageous charges.

I trust I have provided some understanding of what Adler meant for young scholars at the time of which I speak. In a period when Catholic colleges were laboring under material handicaps and certain intellectual disadvantages, the example and inspiration of Adler were heartening. Even when one did not agree with every particular proposition he maintained, his dedication to defending his position was conducive to our appreciating all the more our own traditions.

For those reasons, I consider Mortimer Adler one of the outstanding teachers of our time. I call him the Demonstrator and Remonstrator. Even at my present age, I regard Adler not as venerable but as surprisingly active and thought-provocative for a man of his years.

II. Yves R. Simon

Yves Simon I regarded as a respected senior colleague and cherished friend. It is not an easy task to speak of him in brief. Here I wish to present recollections of and observations about his lectures, his writings, and the books that influenced me, and reflections about his significance as a Christian philosopher, particularly for the period of the 1940s and 1950s.

Vivid in my recollection is the very first lecture I heard Simon deliver, the annual Aquinas Lecture at Marquette University on March 3, 1940. It was entitled *Nature and Functions of Authority*. Vivid in my recollection is the voice of Simon intoning bell-like, "Freedom is the splendor of being."

In subsequent years, I heard him lecture on a number of occasions at Marquette University and at various professional meetings and gatherings and at the University of Chicago, where he taught in the Committee on Social Thought from 1948 to 1961. The most memorable and profitable occasion for me was 1946, at which time Simon gave a summer graduate course, "The Critique of Scientific Knowledge," at Marquette University. (From 1938 to 1948 he was Professor of Philosophy at the University of Notre Dame.) I recall that in the 1950s I arranged a reception for and a lecture by him on his recently published book, *Philosophy of Democratic Government* at the Cardijn Center for Catholic Action in Milwaukee.

In his lecturing and writing, Simon displayed an excellent command of the English language, one he learned not in his youthful but in more mature years. I recall reflecting at the time that his prose was not particolored, as it often is even in expository writing in our tongue, but rather argentiferous. When he spoke, there was a slight French accentuation to his tone, but he spoke English fluently and idiomatically. Sometimes he would even politely correct native English speakers on subtle points of grammar.

On the visits he would make to Milwaukee from time to time (usually for lectures), our acquaintanceship developed into friendship. On occasion, he would stay at our home, and I recall his saying that the apartment we lived in near the university reminded him of one in which he and his family had lived in Lille. A correspondence between us developed as time went on; his letters to me are brief but pithy, full of interest in my activities and full of thoughtfulness.

Vivid in my recollection above other recollections is my last visit to Yves at his home in South Bend, Indiana, not long before he passed away. He never spoke to me about his illness, but we knew without speaking that this was most probably the last time we would see each other. I knew from my friend, Father Leo Ward, C.S.C., of the University of Notre Dame, as well as from other friends, about the religious spirit and the courage with which Yves accepted his suffering. Despite a certain somberness, the visit was, as sometimes such occasions are, a companionable and pleasant one. His sister Therese from his native city of Cherbourg was there, and I can still hear in my memory's eye (or ear!) her beautiful French ringing out like the chimes of a bell.

I turn now to the influence the books, studies, and lectures of Simon had upon me in the 1940s and 1950s. As I have said, I am not providing an evaluation here, but confine myself to expressing how much I benefitted and derived from these works.

It is somewhat difficult to characterize the difference between the influence of Simon upon my thought and that of Adler, already mentioned. When I began reading Simon I was older (by a few but important years!) and more mature, so his work was perhaps not as influential a force as was Adler's. I was pondering and assimilating the great classics of ancient and medieval philosophy, above all the works of Saint Thomas Aquinas, and here was a Thomistic philosopher who provided me with the key to many a complicated question. (In philosophy, as I put it, questions verge on mystery, and Simon respected that mystery while shedding much light upon the matters in question.) At the same time, he was philosophizing about the same things that I was in my own way, and he taught me much of great value for my own intellectual development and for use in my courses. I delved deeply into the books of Simon, from his early works in French, *Ontologie du connaître* and *Critique de la connaissance morale* to his later works that appeared in English and French, such as *The March to Liberation, The Community of the Free, Prevoir et savoir,* and *Philosophy of Democratic Government.* Studies, sometimes not as well-known as they should be, were original and thought-laden in my eyes, such as his "Essay on Sensation." I had done some thinking on this topic myself and this study afforded me invaluable leads and assistance. Above all, vivid in my recollection is the course referred to above, "The Critique of Scientific Knowledge," at Marquette University in the summer of 1946. I admired Simon's "depth of insight, clarity, ease in expounding intricate questions and firm grasp of principles," as I wrote at the time. The course, compressed though it was in a few weeks, was indelibly impressed on my memory and of lasting value to me. In a note I jotted down in the 1940s for a *Notebook on Readings,* I say upon reading Simon's *Prevoir et savoir* and his *Par dela l'experience du desespoir,* "I am profoundly moved and stirred. To read these books means so much more after contact with the living author."

In another note I have at hand, from an introduction I gave to one of his lectures, I write: "Personally, I have so much admiration for and owe so much to the philosophical work of Professor Simon that I could not begin to express how much all his thought and the inspiration of his philosophical life mean to me. Let me confess I stayed up until the wee hours the other morning reading *Philosophy of Democratic Government.* Once again, I marvelled at the author's firm grasp of principles coupled with a grip on the concrete facts of experience, and above all, his burning belief in freedom and democracy and his faith that the philosopher can and should assist in their preservation. It is better, doubtless, to thirst and struggle for justice and freedom than merely to be able to define them. Here is a man who does both."

I continue, "He has a rare understanding and love for American life and democracy" and is proud of his American citizenship. I spoke of his work as a significant contribution to philosophy, something precious from the pen of one who will be reckoned as one of the most original thinkers Catholic culture in our country claims, one it cherishes even if it did not produce him.

Father Gerard Smith, S.J., of Marquette University, a master in philosophy himself and my mentor, who tended to become impatient with lecturers treading familiar ground, once remarked following Simon's lecture at a philosophical gathering in Chicago, to this effect: some men you congratulate upon a fine performance; with Simon, even if he is going over familiar territory, you learn something new every time. This was the way many of us in those days felt about the efforts of Simon. He was the philosopher's philosopher, able to teach even those competent in their chosen field (yet remain a colleague and attentive to the thoughts of others).

The title of one of Maritain's greatest books, if not indeed the greatest, is *Distinguer pour unir ou les degres du savoir.* Concerning the principle *distinguir pour unir* (distinguish *in order to* unite, or, as I would amplify it, let us analyze and clarify the components of a question so that we are able to work out a synthesis), Yves Simon more than once remarked to me that "Maritain stresses the unity and I stress the distinguishing." This pithy statement contains a truth that calls for elaboration. Of course, it goes without saying that each scholar performed both functions well, but it is unquestionable that each gave a certain priority in his actual work to either uniting or distinguishing. It is for this reason that I have called Yves Simon the Distinguisher as well as the Expositor.

Simon's expository style and analytic bent of mind were due in part to the formation he received, as he told me, in his student days at the *Lycee* in Paris. At that time, and no doubt still at present, the student received his real intellectual formation at that level. Among other things, students had to break down or analyze and then put back together in their own words the sermons of Bourdaloue, Fenélon, Bossuet, and other masters. Perhaps of greater importance, at least for Simon's task in philosophy, for his approach to and handling of difficult questions, was the influence of the Dominican theologian, philosopher, and commentator John of Saint Thomas (1589–1644). Maritain also acknowledged his debt to this great master. John's life span closely parallels that of Descartes (1596–1650); yet he seems to have worked in his environment free of concern for the power-

ful tides surging on the shores of philosophy. At the same time, he is un-
questionably one of the great Thomistic masters. Here, too, the question
was one of learning, clarity, analysis, and patient exposition.

Simon's characteristic way of handling problems, his analytic trend,
was sometimes misunderstood. I recall a noted scholar, noted for his wisdom in the *philosophical* history of philosophy, remarking that Simon
tended to drag things out and even to belabor the obvious, that is, what
everybody in the field already knew. I think that what was overlooked
here (and I realize I am referring to a scholar's remark in a brief conversation) was the intent of Simon. That which a number of those in our tradition knew and of which they stood in no need of full-blown expositions, he
considered was precisely what needed to be expounded, clarified and
demonstrated, so that nobody could mistake what was at stake or claim
that important matters were being taken for granted.

Things people (or some of them) already knew or accepted required
demonstration, as Simon saw it, that is, demonstration according to his exacting conviction about it. These things also demanded clear exposition,
which some eminent scholars did not always provide, and of this procedure Simon was an ardent and able follower. Furthermore, while remaining close to the Scholastic tradition and to some extent even to its
terminology, Simon excelled in presenting his thought in clear-cut contemporary language. The philosophical character of Yves Simon's work is
rendered distinctive by this habit of philosophizing cogently and
demonstratively. It is this quality that confers permanent value upon his
work.

The religious and the philosophical are not intertwined in Simon's
work as they are in that of Maritain. (It is true that Maritain carefully distinguishes the two realms.) *Simon is preeminently the philosopher adhering
closely to philosophical argument.* At the same time, his is truly a Christian
philosophy, though he rarely uses the term. What Simon himself says of
Maritain's thought may be applied appropriately to his own. In a tribute to
Jacques Maritain given at the Sheil School of Social Studies in November,
1948, Simon refers to Maritain's illuminating the *disinterestedness*, even, if
you will, the *uselessness* of philosophy. In Maritain, he says, charity is
paramount. The Christian philosopher should be ever ready to set
philosophy aside and rush to succor his neighbor. He is referring in his
tribute to his master, but I refer this thinking to his own attitude to
philosophy and to life.

I would like to add that Simon's views may be put, in my opinion,
more precisely if we adapt Maritain's language to the matter at hand. The
philosopher steeped in the speculative (theoretical) order should be ready
to set it aside and devote himself to the speculatively-practical order (e.g.,

the moral and even the political) and treat the burning questions of the day (e.g., racism and totalitarianism), and then, as an individual, along with other Christians and religious-minded persons, rush to the aid of his neighbors. The question is not merely one of helping your immediate neighbor, the neighbor, so to speak, in your neighborhood. The question is whether one should surrender philosophy and similar pursuits and succor those in need wherever they might be. The question was debated in the Catholic Worker movement and in other lay apostolates in the days when I was actively involved in them. Some held that everyone was bound to give up "higher pursuits" and directly help the poor and the suffering. Maritain, from a somewhat different perspective, held that the philosopher is of best service when he does not adhere to any party (save as a "private citizen," as it were) and *remains the philosopher,* concerning himself with the social, political, and cultural problems of the day.

This does not mean that Maritain did not rush to help a neighbor immediately if needed. (We know that he did.) Nor does it belie Yves Simon's emphasis upon charity to the neighbor. The apparent digression is intended to show that behind the plain and undeniable exhortation to dutiful service to the neighbor next door there lurk delicate questions that have been debated ever since apostolic times.

Let me return to the principal theme occupying us here, the place of Yves Simon in philosophy in the period I recall well. I do not hesitate to say that he should be appropriately called Christian philosopher and not simply the Expositor and Argumentator.

III. Jacques Maritain

Maritain and Simon appeared on the North American scene during a period when European scholars were effecting not an invasion but an incursion upon our shores. During the tumultuous Thirties and the war-torn Forties of this century, scholars and artists from a number of European countries, experts in various fields of higher learning and in various arts, were fleeing from the dictatorships of the Old World. Some of these men and women settled in the USA and Canada permanently; some remained for longer or shorter periods. Every one in his or her way made an important contribution to the maturation of American cultural life. North American Catholic Scholars and intellectuals were ready for such an "incursion," as I call it, and were disposed to welcome the newcomers with admiration and affection. Among the latter were Allers, Boehner, Mueller, von Hildebrand, and a number of others. Of course, Gilson and Maritain came as lecturers; Simon became a regular professor at Notre Dame. These were the three who influenced me most deeply at this intellectually impressionable time of my life.

As is well known, Etienne Gilson and Jacques Maritain were instrumental in the establishment of the Pontifical Institute of Mediaeval Studies in Toronto, Canada. Gilson was undoubtedly one of the founders of the Institute and a permanent force in it until his demise. (The authoritative work on Gilson by Lawrence K. Shook should be mentioned here.) A number of scholars, alumni and others, some to become distinguished in their own right, were deeply influenced by the teachings of this school. There were other important Catholic centers of higher learning (among them the Catholic University of America). Maritain lectured at Notre Dame; Simon, as mentioned, taught there. It is, then, against this background that we are able to appreciate more completely the impact of Maritain and Simon upon American Catholic scholarly life as well as their significant roles in regard to the so-called secular or "non-denominational" university world. As further background, it should be noted that in Europe, as Pope Pius XI had declared sorrowfully, the working classes were being lost to the Church. And the intellectual "elite" were in many instances disaffected. Europe excelled in outstanding scholars but conditions were, it seemed, more propitious for their labors in North America.

Every generation, even if it faces extraordinarily difficult times, such as severe depression or warfare, looks upon itself as ready for the challenges confronting it. Whether it be mere luck or, as some fervently believe, Divine Providence that brings one to the fateful crossroads, every youthful generation stands at the ready. And so with those of my own age: I felt, without being too conscious of these matters at the time, blessed by the opportunity I had to derive inspiration and learning from our European confreres and masters.

In 1933, Jacques Maritain crossed the Atlantic Ocean for the first time in order to give lectures in North America. His association with the New World was to last, with only a few interruptions, for over thirty years. The Maritains dwelt in the United States for seventeen of these years, including the period of World War II.

Jacques Maritain means so much to all of us that you appreciate how difficult it is to speak of him in a few words. As for myself, I can hardly refrain from a kind of adolescent fervor when I refer to his inspiration in my youthful years and to his continuing presence as revered master in my later ones.

In these recollections, I focus upon his books, his lectures, our meetings, and our friendship. With a kind of adolescent fervor, I represent books, lectures, "encounters," and personal associations as winged messengers, as golden moments, as Beautiful Moments, and as Love-in-Christ. I employ poetic language as I am not writing a scholarly study, but trying to recapture the livingness of these relationships—particularly as they were experienced in the 1930s, 1940s, and 1950s.

There are notes in my possession, as already pointed out with respect to Adler and Simon, affording valuable information on my personal reading of Maritain's books. The writings of Maritain, like *magical winged messengers*, introduced me to the mystery of being and the wonders of the human being as illuminated by one I came to revere as the Prophet-Philosopher. (I hasten to add that my first philosophy professor at Fordham University [1933–34] paved the way for this intellectual adventure and gave me my first soaring experience in philosophy.) My notes indicate that I acquired first of all his *Petite logique*, in 1933. Books arrived regularly from the *Librarie du Cerf* in Paris, and I continued to add to our collection. To go beyond the scope of the present essay, I gathered Maritain's books in Spanish and Portuguese on trips to South America, beginning in the late Sixties and on into the Seventies and Eighties; Rome was fertile soil for picking up his works in Italian. My notes indicate further that I began my first reading in Maritain during 1934 and 1935, undergraduate years at Saint Louis University. By 1936–37, I was reading *Les degres du savoir* in the original and presented a lecture and a paper on its themes in a graduate course at the same institution. I return later to the subject of reading the books of Maritain and the influence they had upon me.

Maritain delivered a lecture at Marquette University in 1941, and this was the first one of his I ever attended and the first time I saw him. (There was a brief meeting in a group situation.) In 1949 and 1950, I was the principal figure in organizing and chairing two lectures he gave on contemplation and the spiritual life in Milwaukee. In the 1950s, I drove frequently to South Bend (a distance round-trip of almost 400 miles) and to Chicago to hear him lecture at the University of Notre Dame and at the Committee on Social Thought of the University of Chicago. (So great was the enthusiasm for the leaders of "the revival," *le renouveau catholique*, that a group of professors and students from Marquette University filled several cars on a trip to the University of Chicago just to hear the great Anglo-Catholic poet and critic T.S. Eliot.)

There were meetings with Maritain at lectures, receptions, and similar occasions in a variety of places, but the first personal meeting, or what I would call *un rencontre*, was in 1949, at his home on Linden Lane in Princeton, close to the university, where he was a professor. I took notes of our conversation. Among other things, I recall his urging upon young American Catholic scholars the importance of studying and evaluating the leading American philosophers of the day. In a similar vein, around the same time, Etienne Gilson was propounding the same message to Catholic philosophers at a convention of the American Catholic Philosophical Association in Cleveland in the early 1950s. He himself was a recognized authority on French philosophy, particularly that of the "Founder of Modern Philosophy," René Descartes.

In 1952–54, I studied Contemporary French Philosophy at the Catholic University of Louvain in Belgium on a Fulbright Award and then at the Sorbonne in France. Jacques Maritain and Yves Simon willingly wrote letters of recommendation for me.

In the late 1950s and early 1960s, when I was teaching at Villanova University in the Philadelphia area, I visited Maritain at Princeton on many occasions. It was during this period, I would say, that we became friends. I still venerated him as a Master, but with extraordinary *gentilesse* he put me at ease.

The last encounter in the United States was upon the occasion of his last visit to this country in 1966. Idella and I drove from Boston, where we were teaching at Boston College, to see him in Princeton. It was a wintry day. I recall he insisted on taking us to dinner at a French restaurant near Princeton University. He proved to be a charming host.

In meetings with Maritain, one was struck by his attentiveness to his interlocutor. He listened with care to your thoughts. In the manner of the truly great who are often truly humble, he looked upon you as though you were the most important person in the world. He concentrated upon you as an individual person present with him and gave no sign of thinking of his next appointment. During this period, and even more so later on in his life, Maritain suffered bouts of extreme fatigue and even of illness, and yet remained affable and self-giving to friends and visitors.

Of his attentiveness and courtesy I have already spoken and of these qualities and of his humility and humanity I received over the years many confirmations. I recall that one of my students at Villanova University who came from Princeton remembered as a child in a Catholic grade school seeing this elderly gentleman with a scarf closely wound around his neck at the parish Mass every morning. His simplicity and devotedness deeply impressed the youngster, who dimly remembered the old gentleman referred to as a great professor or philosopher. I recall his considerateness, his grave attention to young students at a Marquette University reception, while *very important people* waited their turn to greet him.

On one occasion, my father and I visited the Maritains at Princeton. We had traveled from northeastern Jersey that day. My father, an average intelligent American of Irish descent (who did not refer to himself as an hyphenated American but was proud to call himself simply an American), was, as I realized, a kind of "specimen" for the Maritains and Raïssa's sister, Véra. They usually consorted with academic or scholarly types, "rarefied beings." Véra said, "Il est formidable!" We sat at tea in the small dining room decorated with the lovely work of the Maritains' artist-friend, Andre Girard, five of us: Jacques and Raïssa Maritain, Véra Oumançoff, my father, and I. With the utmost courtesy, they listened to my father's ideas, and his helpful suggestions about practical problems facing the Maritains were gratefully received. Later, my father always referred to the Maritains with great respect as "very fine people."

At Toulouse in Southern France not far from the Pyrenees at the Community of the Little Brothers of which he was already a professed member, my final *rencontre* or "encounter" with Jacques took place in January, 1973. It was to be only a few months before his passing away in April of that year. Jacques was occupying a cottage or hut in the compound. I recall that the Little Brother who escorted me to his door warned me, "Il fait très chaud dedans." ("It's very hot in there.") It was indeed extremely warm, and Jacques was sitting there with his scarf, as was habitual with him, around his neck. He seemed pleased to see me and pressed me to stay, when I prepared to leave after a while, not wishing to fatigue him. He was ninety years of age and told me that the doctor had informed him that he was in good shape for a man of his age. He added simply, "I know that at my age I can go at any time." He added something which astounded me at the time, although it does not now that I have attained the proverbial three-score-and-ten. He said that even a lifetime of study and writing seemed little or nothing in comparison to the task to be accomplished in philosophy. He had simply prepared the way, he was still a tyro, another lifetime would be required to develop the thoughts as they matured. He was not thinking only of himself; he was thinking of Saint Thomas and of his own twentieth-century compeers. Their work was merely in a preparatory stage; it clamored for completion. On another theme, Maritain remarked how important it was to follow faithfully the teachings of the Holy Father. It was unwise to rely too much on the Bishops, at least many of those in France.

Maritain was grateful for the personal message I brought him from Pope Paul VI, whom he had known for many years and with whom he was closely associated during the time he was French Ambassador to the Holy See and resided in Rome (1945–48). In his chamber, there were two photographs: one of the Pope and the other of his wife, Raïssa. He spoke of his beloved departed partner as though she were present—she was verily to him a presence—and of his longing to be reunited with her. The ninety-year-old's voice broke as he spoke of her with unswerving youthful love.

Shortly before I visited Jacques in Toulouse, my associate in foundation work and I had the special privilege of a very private audience with Pope Paul VI at the Vatican. Five persons were present: the Holy Father, his interpreter, an American priest of Italian descent, my associate, and I. The conversation, if that is the appropriate word, turned to Maritain, and the Pope's eyes brightened. He spoke warmly of the one he had revered and still regarded as a Master from the time he was a young priest. He even mentioned that he had long ago translated *Three Reformers* into Italian. At one point, the Holy Father paused, and reflecting on his friend Jacques Maritain for a moment, he said simply: "*È un santo.*" Later, on the occasion of Jacques' death, Pope Paul VI referred to him as the master of those who know and love.

I mention this audience, even though it is beyond the period that mainly concerns me here, to illustrate the regard and affection in which Maritain was held to the end of his days. I do not know whether I am more impressed by the tribute paid him by the Pope himself, or the veneration he aroused in young people, even children. In a way, each regard speaks volumes, and one is incommensurable with the other.

There is a sheaf of correspondence between Jacques and the two of us, Idella and me. It is treasured, even though it may not be very significant in itself. (I do hold that every letter, particularly from a famous person and no matter how brief it may be, sheds light upon or brings out a new aspect of the personality.) As time went on, the correspondence became more friendly and Jacques Maritain would conclude by saying, sometimes in French, sometimes in English, "with affection and love, your old Jacques" or "votre vieux Jacques." Even though Maritain was old at the time he signed himself thus, I believe the connotation of *vieux* is not merely "old" but implies a sort of comradeship, as when one Frenchman calls another, "*mon vieux.*"

Let me return to the topic of reading Maritain. In my undergraduate years at Saint Louis University (1934–36), I was busily reading *The Angelic Doctor* and wrote a study on Saint Thomas Aquinas, depending upon Maritain, for the university's literary magazine, *The Fleur-de-Lis.* I have already mentioned the report and paper I gave on *Les degres du savoir.* The notes on my readings contain numerous references to reading Maritain's work in the 1940s and 1950s and there are comments either short or lengthy on these books and articles. In my teaching years at Marquette University (1939–58), I was strongly influenced by Etienne Gilson in my approach to the history of philosophy, and, with him as a guide, I strove to present it as a *philosophical* history, not a mere recital of names and themes. However, I continued to study and to derive much from the writings of Maritain, and his work was of great aid to me in my courses in what was then called "systematic philosophy." In subsequent years, at Boston College and other universities, I gave graduate courses in "Contemporary Thomism" with much attention devoted to Maritain, and, on one occasion at least, I gave a course on *The Degrees of Knowledge.*

Permit me to mention my meditative reading and rereading of Maritain in the 1980s, even though those years go far beyond the period upon which I am focusing. No longer a full-time philosophy professor, though I did lecture occasionally, I began in 1981 to read something by Maritain every day, along with the Jerusalem Bible (often in French) and Saint Thomas Aquinas (in the Latin). No longer bound to prepare lectures or to write scholarly articles (and the pressure to accomplish these tasks was intense, as many of you know; I would hesitate to record how many undergraduate and graduate courses I taught in my active years), I was enabled to read Maritain (as well as Saint Thomas) slowly and reflectively. Sometimes I would select a study more or less at random; for a long while, I proceeded methodically through the first volume of Henri Bars' two-volume edition of the *Oeuvres*, but always in a leisurely fashion. Recently, I began moving through the *Oeuvres completes*, of which a number of volumes have already been published. Freed, as I have said, from the demands of teaching, I was able to enjoy the words of Maritain as never before. Insights into the mystery of being and of man as he expounded them came to me as never before. I had the privilege of reading "pages" and not "texts." I was, in short, able to savor the mind-and-thought of Maritain and came to revere him all the more as one of the greatest philosophers of all time. And this appreciation was aroused after a period (the last decade or so) of my teaching career in which I had read widely and deeply in the contemporary philosopher, and in the modern classics, Descartes, Hegel, and the rest.

I mention all this because it shows how the reading of Maritain is a lifelong pursuit and it illustrates Simon's remark that Maritain is inexhaustible. I would like to add that even in the winter of his long span of years, Jacques Maritain has given us pages glowing with springlike freshness.

In the part of this essay devoted to Simon, I quoted him as saying in effect that he emphasized "distinguishing" while Maritain put stress on "writing" or "synthesizing." As I have already noted, the Maritain who was at his best in *synthesizing* could *distinguish* and present a closely reasoned piece of exposition.

His habit of synthesizing sometimes led to extraordinary compactness. In a paragraph-long sentence there would be included a parenthesis—a lengthy parenthesis in a sentence perhaps overlong—and yet the parenthesis was well worth the reading as it often contained an unforgettable insight!

Maritain disliked labels or labeling anyone's philosophy, including his own. Above all, he rejected the term "Neo-Thomism." He recognized that it was important for thinkers of other schools to know where you stood in philosophy, and therefore he accepted "Thomism" and "Christian philosophy" as identifying his own philosophy. He was never altogether *comfortable* with these appellations. In *The Peasant of the Garonne* he employs his coinage "ontosophy." He considers that "philosophy" and "philosopher" are somewhat ambivalent terms and takes delight in opposing "ontosophers" to "ideosophers." (There are giants in modern times whom he respects and from whom he says we can learn much and who are in his judgment not real philosophers but rather ideosophers.)

Maritain is *philosopher* in the strictest sense: he knows superlatively how to philosophize his way to definitive conclusions with rigor, clarity, and exactitude. I do believe and maintain that his philosophy comprehends a special dimensionality, expanding the frontiers of what he insisted was an autonomous discipline. How should we denominate his distinctive philosophy? Dare we label it? One of Maritain's favored disciples, Little Brother of Jesus Heinz Schmitz, called it "theo-philosophy." There is some merit in this somewhat awkward appellation. However, there is another I prefer.

Upon considering the stature, stance, and status of Jacques Maritain, and realizing the risk involved that his standing as a philosopher might be overshadowed, I have ventured to call him the *Prophet-Philosopher*. I use *prophetic* not in the full or rather specific religious sense, but as a term pertaining primarily to the temporal order, that is, to the social-economic-political-cultural *complexus*, and especially where it borders upon or is illuminated and inspired by the "religious dimension." In a word, prophecy as pertaining to the temporal, but brightened and enlightened by Revelation.

Perhaps Maritain himself would consider this treatment of his work as much too serious. In the letter he wrote to the Little Brothers of Jesus announcing his acceptance as one of them by the Congregation, he suggests half-playfully that perhaps his name should be "Don Quixoto of Saint Thomas." There is something of Leon Bloy in Maritain the elder as well as Maritain the younger. When he jokes about himself, his remarks should be taken, if not too seriously, at least as revelatory of the man's humble view of himself.

In philosophy, one is a Master when free from tutelage and free and capable of philosophizing in one's own person. Even if one is mature enough intellectually to call oneself a philosopher, or perhaps one should say "ontosopher," one can without inconsistency look upon one's teacher as the Master. Maritain, like Simon and Adler, is the philosopher's philosopher. I revere him alongside Thomas Aquinas as my Master and know I can continue to learn more and more from the inexhaustible treasure-trove of his thought.

For these reasons, I consider Jacques Maritain the Synthesizer and Prophetic Voice of our age.

The idea of attempting to encompass three thinkers of the stature of Adler, Simon, and Maritain in one presentation is something I half-regret. However, it is one thing to attempt an evaluation of their philosophy, as I have said, another to evoke recollections for the value they have in bringing out the impact concretely upon the younger generation of the 1930s to the 1950s. Along with significant differences in style, in perspective, and (from a certain point of view) even in their very conception of philosophy or, rather, in the dimensions it assumes in their intellectualizing about it, I came to recognize that there is something common in their search for reality and in their defense of the classical Tradition. Each of these philosophers has championed in his own distinctive way the Great Tradition and has sought to restore wisdom to its rightful role. In my recollection and present view, Adler is the thinker, the teacher-encyclopedist who exhorts and exhibits, particularly to those who are not specialists in scholarship, fundamental mind-saving truths. Simon is the thinker, the teacher-argumentator, whose discourse in rigorous and careful procedure leads minds to definitive conclusions about reality. Maritain is the thinker, the teacher-as-prophetic utterer, who leads persons by the hand to a realm beyond the ordinary confines of life, where dwells Wisdom interfused with Charity.

As philosophers, each of these thinkers draws near the mystery of reality and illumines it for every one of us who has a philosophical bent. Adler is the one who approaches reality through the keys of the Great Basic Books and the Great Basic Ideas they contain. Simon is the one who approaches the mystery of reality by utilizing deductive and inductive argumentation. Maritain is the person who approaches the mystery of reality by delving into its depths and scaling its heights and delivering it throbbing and existential to us.

Vivid in my recollections undimmed by time are these philosophical friends. In rather theoretical terms, I have ventured to name them as follows: Adler is the Demonstrator and Remonstrator, Simon is the Expositor and Argumentator, and Maritain is the Synthesizer and Illuminator.

Part I
Mortimer J. Adler

Mortimer J. Adler

Great Books, Democracy, And Truth*

I

Because of its title, *The Closing of the American Mind*, by Allan Bloom, sold widely, probably much more widely than it was read. Its misleading but attention-grabbing subtitle: *How Higher Education Has Failed Democracy and Impoverished the Souls of Today's Students*, lamented the failure of our colleges to serve our democratic society, but paid little attention to the dismal deficiencies of basic schooling in the United States, which are much more important as far as serving democracy is concerned.

With regard to the academic malaise that Mr. Bloom describes, but mistakenly regards as recent, his analysis of its causes is both inaccurate and inadequate. Worse, his slight effort to propose a cure falls far short of what must be done to make our schools responsive to democracy's needs and to enable our colleges to open the minds of their students to the truth.

These are serious indictments. But for me the book's most glaring defect is with regard to the undergraduate use of the great books over the last sixty years, and the more recent introduction of them to basic schooling by the Paideia program. Allan Bloom either has no knowledge of these facts or is gravely at fault for neglecting to report them. There is but one reference in *The Closing of the American Mind* to the "good old great books approach." Nevertheless, he proposes that approach as a remedy for the reform of our colleges.

*Excerpted from *Reforming Education*, by Mortimer J. Adler. Copyright © 1977 by Westview Press. New material copyright © 1988 by Mortimer J. Adler. Reprinted by arrangement with Macmillan Publishing Company.

Before Allan Bloom was born, I was a student in the first great books seminar that John Erskine taught at Columbia University in 1921. From 1923 to 1929, with Mark Van Doren, I taught great books seminars at Columbia University. At the invitation of Robert M. Hutchins, President of the University of Chicago, I brought the great books educational program to Chicago in 1930, and Hutchins and I taught the great books there long before Allan Bloom arrived on the scene. We continued teaching them while he was a young student at the University of Chicago.

Allan Bloom either is ignorant of the work that had been done at Columbia and at the University of Chicago; or worse, he intentionally ignored it in order to foster the impression that his recommendation—that the great books be read by college students—was his own educational innovation. However, this interpretation of his failure to tip his hat to his many predecessors, especially those at his own university, is partly negated by the fact that he refers to "the good *old* great books approach" (italics added). Hence, one might conclude that his recommendation of the "great books approach" is qualified by the condition that they be read and taught in the style that he, Allan Bloom, and his teacher, Leo Strauss, have read and taught them.

That is most certainly not the way that John Erskine, Mark Van Doren, Robert Hutchins, Stringfellow Barr, Scott Buchanan, Jacques Barzun, Lionel Trilling, Otto Bird (the last three of whom were students of mine), and many others taught them long before Allan Bloom arrived at the University of Chicago. When I come to the consideration of the great books in relation to philosophical truth, I will try to explain why the dialectical rather than the doctrinal style of reading and teaching the great books is much to be preferred in the education of the young.

II

Erskine's great innovation was the undergraduate seminar in which students and teacher sat around a table and engaged in critical conversation about the ideas in an assigned text. Erskine developed the first list of some sixty great books to be read by college juniors and seniors. Nothing like it ever existed before in undergraduate instruction. Seminars, in the German style, had been conducted, but they were only for Ph.D. candidates and for the consideration of their doctoral researches.

Erskine's original reading list has been considerably revised and expanded since the early 1920s—at Columbia itself, at the University of Chicago, at Saint John's College, and at other institutions (Notre Dame, Saint Mary's College) that adopted the great books seminars—but all subsequent lists of great books have retained about 85 percent of Erskine's original list.

In 1928 a grant from the Carnegie Corporation enabled Scott Buchanan (who later became Dean of Saint John's College in Annapolis) and me to organize fifteen great books seminars for adults in New York City. This, so far as I know, was the first attempt to employ the reading and discussion of great books as a major form of continued learning for adults, later to become a national program under the auspices of the Great Books Foundation. There were two leaders for each of these seminars.

Before Hutchins went to Chicago, he and I discussed the Erskine list of great books that I had been teaching at Columbia. Hutchins confessed that in his undergraduate years at Yale, he had not read more than three or four of those books. Hutchins knew that his duties as president of the University of Chicago would get in the way of his own education unless he himself taught a course in which he had to read the books he had not read in college. He asked me to come to Chicago mainly for the purpose of teaching a great books seminar for entering freshmen that he and I would conduct as Mark Van Doren and I had done at Columbia. We did so from 1930 until 1948. From that, many other achievements followed.

In 1936, Hutchins established a Committee on the Liberal Arts. He invited Stringfellow Barr and Scott Buchanan of the University of Virginia to join us in planning an ideal, completely required curriculum for a liberal arts college. The reading and seminar discussion of great books for four years were central to that curriculum. This resulted in a greatly expanded list of great books, including works in mathematics and the natural sciences that had been for the most part absent from the original Erskine list. It also resulted, in 1937, in the establishment of the completely required New Program at Saint John's College, the fiftieth anniversary of which has recently been celebrated. The renown of Saint John's College, which was generally known as "the great books college," led other institutions in the 1940s, such as Notre Dame and Saint Mary's, to adopt modified versions of the program.

There were other, even more far-reaching results of what had been started at Columbia and Chicago.

In 1940, I published *How to Read a Book*, which should have been entitled *How to Read a Great Book*. That volume contained in its appendix a list of the great books, one that enlarged Erskine's original list and the one in use at the University of Chicago and at Saint John's College. It was a best-seller in 1940 and has been in print ever since. It has been used by many high schools and colleges in English courses as an instrument for cultivating skills in reading, and was revised in 1974 by Charles Van Doren and me.

In the 1940s, Hutchins and I also established the Great Books Foundation for the purpose of promoting great books seminars for adults all across the country. In that connection, I developed the first manual of instruction for the guidance of ordinary lay persons in the conduct of great books seminars. I also trained the first generation of seminar leaders in Chicago. During that same period, Hutchins and I conducted a great books seminar for Chicago's civic leaders, many of whom were trustees of the University of Chicago. Begun in 1943, it continues to this day, although its membership has changed considerably.

There are still other significant developments of the great books movement. The University of Chicago operated extension courses for adults in University College, which was then called "the downtown college." With the enthusiastic endorsement of Dean Cyril Houle of that college, I outlined another modification of the Saint John's program. It was called "The Basic Program of Liberal Education for Adults" and began its long and successful career in the late 1940s. Allan Bloom and other students of Leo Strauss at the University of Chicago were among the young men who were enlisted to teach the great books in that program. It was his first teaching job.

In the great books seminars that Hutchins and I conducted for Chicago's civic leaders at the University Club were Walter and Elizabeth Paepeke. Their growing interest in the great books as an educational instrument for adults led in the early 1950s to the establishment of the Aspen Institute for Humanistic Studies. Starting out with just great books seminars, the Aspen seminars, especially the Executive Seminars, developed in other directions, but a handful of great books has always been at the core of the reading lists.

Another by-product of the great books seminars that Hutchins and I conducted at the University Club was the publication in 1952 by Encyclopaedia Britannica, Inc., of the Great Books of the Western World. William Benton, then a vice president of the University of Chicago, was a participant in that University Club seminar. When in 1943, he became owner and publisher of Encyclopaedia Britannica, Inc., he asked Hutchins and me to edit a set of great books for it to publish. We worked hard on that project for eight years, during which time I invented and produced the *Syntopicon* of the great ideas to accompany the set.

Then, on a grant from the Ford Foundation, the Institute for Philosophical Research was established to undertake a dialectical examination of the great ideas. Since then, it has published a series of books, beginning with a two-volume work, entitled *The Idea of Freedom*. Finally, in 1982, after three years' work with a group of eminent associates, I wrote and published *The Paideia Proposal*, an educational manifesto that called for a radical reform of basic schooling (kindergarten through twelfth grade) in the United States, and outlined a completely required curriculum that involved great books seminars in elementary and secondary schools.

I mention all this as background because *The Closing of the American Mind* and the reviews of it—both adverse and favorable—have made me realize that it is necessary to retell the story of the great books movement for the present academic generation, whose memories do not go further back than the 1960s, or at most, the end of the Second World War. It is also necessary to restate as clearly as possible the fundamental notions that underlie the selection of the great books, the proper way to discuss them in seminars, their use in a truly democratic system of education, and their relation to the pursuit of truth.

I would like, first, to discuss the ideal of a truly democratic system of education, which does not yet exist in this country and which Bloom's book nowhere considers. Second, I think it necessary to examine truth and error in the great books, and their bearing on the proper way to conduct discussions of them, which is the dialectical method, not the doctrinal style employed by Allan Bloom and his teacher, Leo Strauss. Third, I must deal with a problem that deeply concerns Allan Bloom—the prevalent skepticism about moral philosophy and the prevalence of subjectivism and relativism about values among students and professors—the causes of which Mr. Bloom inaccurately diagnoses. Finally, here and in the epilogue, I will set forth the fundamental notions and principles of the great books movement.

III

Many readers today think of democracy in twentieth-century terms as constitutional government with universal suffrage and the securing of natural, human rights. The other two quite different senses of democracy are the senses in which Plato and Aristotle in antiquity and Rousseau in the eighteenth century used the word: either for mob rule or for a constitutional government with citizenship restricted to men of property. In our terms, they used the word "democracy" to signify an oligarchy that conferred citizenship on men of small property instead of restricting it to those having large estates.[1]

Neither for them nor for Allan Bloom, who admires the political philosophy of these oligarchs, does the word "democracy" stand for the political ideal—the only perfectly just form of government. That use of the

---

[1] In Athens, at its most "democratic" extreme under Pericles, there were only 30,000 citizens in a population of 120,000. Excluded were women, slaves, and artisans.

word makes its first appearance in 1861 in John Stuart Mill's *Representative Government*. Mill was the first great political philosopher who spoke for universal suffrage, extending it to women and to the laboring classes. He thought that justice required securing political liberty and equality for all, with few exceptions. But in 1863 Mill was a reluctant democrat who feared the unenlightened self-interest of the working-class majority; and so advocated plural votes for the upper classes to help them defeat majority rule.

All of Mill's predecessors in Western political theory thought that democracy, in *their* sense of the term, was either the worst form of bad government or the least desirable of the good forms of government, and none had even the slightest conception or even conjecture of democracy, in the twentieth-century sense of the term, as a political ideal to be realized in the future.

Bloom's readers have to guess in which of these radically different senses of democracy he uses the word. On the one hand, he could not be complaining about the failure of our educational institutions to serve democracy if he did not think of it as a desirable form of government. On the other hand, can any reader of *The Closing of the American Mind* fail to detect the strong strain of elitism in Bloom's own thinking, as evidenced by his devotion to Plato, Rousseau, and Nietzsche, and by his advocacy of reading of the great books by relatively few in the student population, certainly not by all?

The recency of constitutional democracy in this country explains and may even justify our not yet having a truly democratic system of public schooling or institutions of higher learning that are concerned with making good citizens of those who attend our colleges.

In 1817, Thomas Jefferson, as much an oligarch as John Adams, James Madison, Alexander Hamilton, and all the rest of our founding fathers, called upon the Virginia legislature to give three years of common schooling to all the children of the state. After three years, he advocated dividing the children into those destined for labor and those destined for leisure and learning (and citizenship and public office), and sending only the latter to college.

In our twentieth-century understanding of the term "democracy," Jefferson's educational program was thoroughly antidemocratic, but it still exists in the United States today. Though virtually all the children in our schools are now destined to become citizens, we still divide them into the college-bound and those not going from high school to college. The quality of schooling given the non-college-bound does not prepare them for citizenship or for a life enriched by continued learning; nor, I should add, does the quality of education given the college-bound when they get to college. It is still a fundamentally antidemocratic system of schooling with a sharp differentiation between two tracks, one for those of inferior ability and one for their betters.

The first real departure from Jefferson's antidemocratic policy (dominating American education from 1817 to the present day) occurred in this century with startling pronouncements by John Dewey and Robert Hutchins. *The Paideia Proposal* in 1982 was dedicated to them because of their commitment to a democratic system of education.

In 1900, John Dewey said that the kind of schooling that the best and wisest parents would want for their children is precisely the kind of schooling that the community should want for all its children. Any other policy if acted upon, he said, would defeat democracy.

In his epoch-making book, *Democracy and Education* (1916), Dewey enunciated a position the opposite of Jefferson's. He said all the children in our nation, now that it was on its way to becoming democratic, had the same destiny—to lead lives in which they would earn a living, act as intelligent citizens of the republic, and make an effort to lead a decent and enriched human life.

Bloom's book does not manifest the slightest commitment to a program for giving *all* the children the same quality of schooling to enable them to fulfill their common destiny. Nor does it give its readers any indication that the most grievous failure of our schools and colleges to serve democracy, now that democracy has at last come into existence, lies in the early differentiation of students, with different tracks for different students. In the early 1930s President Hutchins was asked whether great books seminars, then open only to a picked handful of students, should be accessible to all the students in our colleges. His brief reply was crisp and clear. He said that the best education for the best was the best education for all. Great books seminars in our public schools and in our colleges should be available to all the students there, not only to the few who elect to take them or who are specially selected. That is not the answer to be found in Allan Bloom's book.

IV

Some basic truths are to be found in the great books, but many more errors will also be found there, because a plurality of errors is always to be found for every single truth. One way of discovering this is to detect the contradictions that can be found in the books of every great author. Being human works, they are seldom free from contradictions. Skill in reading and thinking is required to find them. But, given that skill, finding contradictions in a book puts one on the high-road in the pursuit of truth. The truth must lie on one or the other side of every contradiction. It is there for us to detect when we are able to resolve the contradiction in favor of one side or the other.

More important is the fact that the great books contradict one another on many points in the various fields of discourse in which they engage. Once again, it must be said that the relation between truth and error is a one-many relationship: if the truth on a given point is thought to be in one or several of the great books, contradictions on that same point are likely to be found in many more great books.

In any case, it is clear that, if the great books contradict one another on many points, it must follow that many errors as well as some truths are to be found there. That is why the great books are such useful instruments in the pursuit of truth. For every truth, understanding all the errors it refutes is indispensable.

What I have just said holds particularly for the philosophical and theological works that belong in any comprehensive list of great books—the writings of Plato, Aristotle, Epictetus, Marcus Aurelius, Augustine, Aquinas, Calvin, Hobbes, Descartes, Locke, Hume, Rousseau, Kant, Hegel, Nietzsche, Mill, William James. Since Bloom and his teacher, Leo Strauss, are specialists in the field of moral and political philosophy, I will draw my examples from that field of discourse.

If Aristotle's political philosophy is thought to contain a number of fundamental truths, then errors must be found in Plato, Hobbes, Locke, Rousseau, Kant, and Hegel. If J.S. Mill's political philosophy is thought to contain some truths not found elsewhere, then on these points errors must be found in Aristotle. If Aristotle's *Nicomachean Ethics* is thought to contain a number of basic truths in moral philosophy, then on these points serious errors must be found in Plato, Epictetus, Kant, Hegel, and Nietzsche.

Though the same can be said for works in other branches of philosophy—metaphysics, the philosophy of mind, and the theory of knowledge—the examples I have given from the field of moral and political philosophy will suffice to enable me to distinguish between the right and wrong way to teach the great books, if the aim in using them is to teach students how to think and how to pursue the truth. Since the kind of teaching done by Leo Strauss and by his students, among them Allan Bloom, represents in my judgment the wrong way to teach the great books in our public schools and in our undergraduate colleges, let me describe the difference between what I consider to be the right and wrong way to read the great books.

The difference between Strauss' method of reading and teaching the great books and the method that Hutchins and I had adopted (the method also used by Erskine and Van Doren at Columbia, and by Barr and Buchanan at Saint John's College) lies in the distinction between a doctrinal and a dialectical approach. The doctrinal method is an attempt to read as much truth as possible (and no errors) into the work of a particular author, usually devising a special interpretation, or by discovering that special secret of an author's intentions. This method may have some merit in the graduate school where students aim to acquire narrowly specialized scholarship about a particular author. But it is the opposite of the right method to be used in conducting great books seminars in schools and colleges where the aim is learning to think and the pursuit of truth.

When in the late 1940s Leo Strauss came to the University of Chicago and we were both on the faculty teaching great books, President Hutchins suggested that I get to know him. We met several times and discussed our reading of Plato and Aristotle. I soon learned that Strauss read these great authors as if they were devoid of any serious errors, in spite of the fact that on many points they appeared to contradict one another. I also learned that for Strauss the radical changes in our social and political institutions that have occurred since antiquity had no bearing on the likelihood that Aristotle made grave errors about natural slavery and about the natural inferiority of women. In his view, these were not errors. After a few conversations, I told Hutchins that I found talking to Strauss about philosophical books and problems thoroughly unprofitable from the point of view of leading great books seminars in the college.

The word "disciple" stresses the differences between the doctrinal and the dialectical teaching of the great books. Leo Strauss was preeminently the kind of doctrinal teacher who made disciples out of his students, disciples who followed in his footsteps and repeated again and again what they learned from him. The doctrinal teacher of disciples enables them to learn what the master thinks. The dialectical teaching of students enables them to think for themselves. I would go further and say that the doctrinal method *indoctrinates,* and only the dialectical method *teaches.*

Those of us who teach the great books dialectically exert an influence on our students, but only so far as a good use of their minds is concerned. We never make disciples of them. Strauss' use of the doctrinal method results in students learning what the master thinks about the work under consideration. I would even go so far as to say that the doctrinal method is most appropriate in reading a sacred book. It is like the orthodox Hassidic approach to reading the Talmud. But it is totally inappropriate in liberal education at the college level or in our public schools.

V

I come now to the skepticism about moral values that prevails among college students and their teachers. I will treat this matter briefly because I have written many essays that bear on the subject. One in particular was written for *Harper's Magazine* under the title "This Prewar Generation"

(1940). As the title indicates, the college students of that time generally held the view that judgments about moral values were matters of subjective opinion, different for different persons, and relative to the circumstances of time and place.

Before I go on, let me say what is meant by the distinction between subjective and objective and between relative and absolute. The subjective is that which differs for you, for me, and for other individuals. The objective is that which is the same for all of us. The relative is that which varies with the circumstances of time and place. The absolute is that which is invariant always and everywhere.

In "This Prewar Generation," I pointed out that subjectivism and relativism about value judgments on the part of students emanated from the same stance on the part of their teachers, especially their professors in philosophy and in the social sciences. At that time, the reign of philosophical positivism among Anglo-American professors gave rise to the doctrine of noncognitive ethics. This meant that moral philosophy was not knowledge, not a body of valid truths. Some went so far as to say that judgments that contained the words "ought" and "ought not" were neither true nor false. There were no prescriptive truths.

At the same time, what was known to sociologists and cultural anthropologists—that the tribal or ethnic mores differed from tribe to tribe, from culture to culture, and from time to time—led them to the dogmatic denial that there were any objectively valued moral judgments. As the positivists among the philosophers dismissed ethics as noncognitive, so the social scientists denied ethics objectivity and universality by putting the members of one tribe, culture, or ethnic group into what they called "the ethnocentric predicament," which meant they were unable to make objective judgments about values espoused in other tribes and cultures.

Is there any wonder that subjectivism and relativism should have been prevalent among college students exposed to such indoctrination by their professors in the 1930s and 1940s? That indoctrination has continued right down to the present. The moral skepticism among the students is the same as it was then and its cause is the same, though the vocabulary in which it is expressed may have changed in detail.

More recently I have returned to the defense of objective and absolute truth in moral philosophy by reviewing books by two eminent professors of philosophy—Alasdair MacIntyre's *After Virtue* and a book by Bernard Williams entitled *Ethics and the Limits of Philosophy*. Both books concede the dismal failure of philosophy since the seventeenth century to develop an ethics that can claim to have objective truth. Both books, the first more explicitly than the second, give Nietzsche credit for exposing the failures of modern thinkers to develop a sound moral philosophy. Both books concede that Aristotle's *Ethics* was sound in Greek antiquity. MacIntyre, however, called for its revision to make it acceptable to us today, and Williams rejected it as no longer tenable. The critiques I wrote of these two books argued that Aristotle's *Ethics*, without the revision proposed by MacIntyre, is just as sound in the twentieth century as it was in the fourth century B.C.

Against the background of what I have just said, I have only two points to make about the mistakes of Allan Bloom in dealing with the impoverishment of student souls in the late 1960s and continuing until the present day. If by "impoverishment" he is referring to their lack of firm dedication to objective and absolute moral truths, then that impoverishment existed as well in the 1930s, 1940s, and 1950s. He is simply wrong as a matter of historical fact.

The other mistake made by Bloom concerns the causes that generated the result he deplores and wishes he knew how to remedy. Ascribing contemporary skepticism about moral values to the influence of Nietzsche's nihilism is wide of the mark. The two causes were those already mentioned—philosophical positivism and the relativism of sociology and cultural anthropology. Nietzsche was not at all in the picture when these began to influence American thought; and if that has changed recently and his influence has become evident, it is still a minor cause as compared with the others that I mentioned.

VI

The great books, read and discussed with an eye out for the basic truths and the equally basic errors or mistakes to be found in them, should be a part of everyone's general, liberal, and humanistic education. This program should begin with what might be called "junior great books" in the early grades, continued throughout basic schooling with more and more difficult books, and be pursued on an even higher level in college. It would still be everyone's obligation to read many of these books again in the course of adult learning, for the greatest among them cannot ever be plumbed to their full depths. They are inexhaustibly rereadable for pleasure and profit.

A genuine great books program does not aim at historical knowledge of cultural antiquities or at achieving a thin veneer of cultural literacy. On the contrary, it aims only at the general enlightenment of its participants, an essential ingredient in their initial liberal education and something to be continued throughout a lifetime of learning. Its objective is to develop basic intellectual skills—the skills of critical reading, attentive listening, precise speech, and, above all, reflective thought. Through the use of these skills, the reading and seminar discussion of the great books seeks to help students pass from less to greater understanding of the basic ideas in the

Western intellectual tradition and of the controversial issues with which those great ideas abound.

Let me repeat: the controlling purpose behind this recommendation is twofold. First, only through reading and discussing books that are over one's head can the skills of critical reading and reflective thought be developed. Second, of the three educational objectives—acquisition of knowledge, development of intellectual skills, and increase of understanding of basic ideas and issues—the third is by far the most important, and cannot be achieved without seminar discussions of truly great or almost-great books.

Finally, the earlier the reading and discussions begin and the more persistently they are continued in college and in the learning of adults, involving as it must the oft-repeated reading and discussion of the same books, the more individuals will be enabled to reach their ultimate goal in the later years of life—that of becoming generally educated human beings.

No one ever becomes a generally educated person in school, college, or university, for youth itself is an insuperable obstacle to becoming generally educated. That is why the very best thing that our educational institutions can do, so far as general education is concerned (not the training of specialists), is to afford preparation for continued learning by their students after they leave these institutions behind them. That cannot be done unless the skills of learning are cultivated in school and unless, in schools and colleges, the students are initiated into the understanding of great ideas and issues and are motivated to continue to seek an ever-increasing understanding of them.

It is necessary here to distinguish, sharply and clearly, the reading and seminar discussion of great books as a lifelong educational program from the current misuse of the phrase "great books" in connection with courses in Western civilization that college students are required to take as part of a core curriculum.

Until the end of the eighteenth century, there were no great books of Western civilization that were not of European origin. Until the nineteenth century, all were written by white males. Hence if one were to read all or almost all of the great books of Western civilization, most of them would, perforce, be written by white, male Europeans.

It is certainly arguable that under the radically changed circumstances of the twentieth century, college students should be required to study global civilization, both Eastern and Western, not just Western or European. It is also arguable that many books written in this or the last century, books which are clearly not great, should be studied for their relevance to the most pressing problems of our age. But all such arguments have nothing whatsoever to do with the educational program associated with a list of great Western books, most of which were written by white European males.

The educational purpose of the great books program is not to study Western civilization. Its aim is not to acquire knowledge of historical facts. It is rather to understand the great ideas. Its objective is not to become acquainted with the variety of conflicting cultures and groups that engender the problems that confront us in the contemporary world. Its controlling purposes, as I have already pointed out, are solely to learn how to read critically and to think reflectively about basic ideas and issues, not just in school and college but throughout one's life.

For that purpose, the minimum list of great books to be read would include at least the works of 60 authors. A more intensive program would extend that number to 125. At the college level, the minimal program should include seminars once a week for two years; at the maximum, it should include two seminars a week for four years. At the level of basic schooling, it would involve seminars once a week for at least nine years—from grade three to grade twelve.

I mention these numbers lest it be thought that a required single semester or a one-year college course in the history of civilization, Western or global, with twelve or fifteen traditionally recognized Western classics in the list of required readings, is even, in small part, a great books program. Such survey courses are mainly history courses, conducted primarily by lectures. They may be supplemented by small group discussions that only faintly resemble great books seminars.

To recapitulate: A true great books program is not a course in the history of Western civilization, nor is it devoted to the scholarly study of the books read. It is concerned primarily with the discussion of the great ideas and issues to be found in those books. It may, therefore, be asked why the works read should consist entirely of works written by Westerners, both European and American, and not by authors who belong to one of the four or five major cultural traditions of the Far East.

The answer is simply that the basic ideas and issues of our *one* Western intellectual tradition are *not* the basic ideas and issues in the *four* or *five* intellectual traditions of the Far East. In the distant future there may be a single, worldwide cultural community with one set of common basic ideas and issues; but until that comes into existence, becoming a generally educated human being in the West involves understanding the basic ideas and issues that abound in the intellectual tradition to which one is heir either by the place of one's birth or by immigration to the West.

Desmond J. FitzGerald

Adler's *The Idea of Freedom*

The establishment of the Institute for Philosophical Research in San Francisco in 1952 represented for Mortimer J. Adler the achievement of a dream that went back to his Columbia University days in the late 1920s. As he has told the story so well in his *Philosopher at Large, An Intellectual Autobiography*, it was Professor John Erskine's course in the classics of Western civilization that set him in the direction of studying the Great Ideas as expressed in the Great Books. Also, as a young student of philosophy and graduate instructor in psychology, Adler's natural temperament turned him toward the ideal of a *Summa Dialectica*, a treatise matching for the twentieth century the *Summa Theologica* of Aquinas in the thirteenth century. But where Saint Thomas tried to give answers, Adler's ideal was a summa that "would rigorously abstain from making comparable judgments, contenting itself with constructing a vast but inherently uncompleteable map of the universe of discourse in which theories (which may or may not be true) are placed in revealing logical relationships to one another" (*PL* 92).

A further step towards what was to become the *The Idea of Freedom* occurred in the late 1940s when Adler undertook the production of the *Syntopicon*, the two-volume study of the Great Ideas that served as an analysis of the key concepts considered by the authors of *The Great Books of the Western World*. This project, some six years in the doing, involved the organization of team research in the humanities. While team research (that is, a number of experts working together to resolve a problem or construct a study) was sometimes done in the natural sciences (for example, the Manhattan Project to develop our atomic bomb), it was unusual in the realm of literature or the history of ideas. True, the original French Encyclopedists, or the organizers of the *Oxford English Dictionary*, were, in a sense, precursors of what Adler and his staff at Chicago did in the 1946–52 period, but what the Adler associates accomplished in researching the 102 great ideas was unmatched in American letters. It entailed great skills of organization and classification, the very qualities in which Adler excelled;

in addition, the hard work of writing the introductory essays themselves to present the thoughts of the authors in an unbiased way developed Adler's dialectical skills.

> Writing 102 essays was like writing 102 books. Each had to be adapted to the unique idea it dealt with. Each was a fresh start. In addition, I thought it imperative that ideas be written with dialectical objectivity—that they should be point-of-viewless while suggesting the diverse points of view in the great books about a given idea. It was not until I reached the ideas which began with L that I finally achieved the requisite style for writing these introductory essays, a style that involved generous quotations from the great books, so that the conflicting opinions of the authors could be expressed in their own words (*PL* 250–51).

This laborious exercise was to reap dividends later, in the dialectical construction of the arguments over the issues about the different kinds of freedom in the second volume of *The Idea of Freedom*. By this time, Adler had mastered the technique of placing the words of the philosophers together in such a way that there was created the give and take of a conversation on some particular point of dispute.

Thus, as Adler approached his fiftieth birthday, changes were in the offing. Robert Hutchins, with whom Adler had worked for some twenty-five years in partnership promoting the use of the discussion of great books in adult seminars, and who had headed the enterprise of producing *The Great Books of the Western World* set while Adler was in charge of the editorial tasks, had left the University of Chicago to become vice-president of the Ford Foundation. And it was with the support of the Ford Foundation that Adler was able to move closer to his objective of a *Summa Dialectica* through the creation of the Institute for Philosophical Research in San Francisco. It was here that the research published in the two volumes of *The Idea of Freedom* took place.

The original home of the Institute in San Francisco was a large mansion on Jackson Street in the Pacific Heights area. The building had been formerly the German Consulate and its many rooms served as offices and studies for the almost twenty Research Fellows who made up Adler's research team. Later, in an economy move, the building was sold to the California Historical Association and the Institute moved a block away to the Stern mansion, an equally stately home built by one of San Francisco's pioneer families.

The Adler group at first undertook to study the idea of man, but the many issues and complications soon made it evident that they should narrow their focus. Hence, they came to concentrate on the idea of freedom. In those first months, a great deal was accomplished, as the team studied basically the affirmation and denial of freedom of choice. By March of

1953, an impressive document was prepared for a conference at Princeton University in which the analysis of freedom was organized around the three letters: D-A-M; the D philosophers, such as Hobbes and Hume, denied free choice; the A philosophers, such as Aquinas and Descartes, affirmed it; and the M philosophers, mainly the evolutionary minded process thinkers such as Bergson, Tillich, Whitehead, and Weiss, affirmed it for the whole range of nature in some way. It was this version that was presented to representatives of local philosophy departments in 1953, and it was here that I had my first encounter with the work of the Institute on Freedom.

As Adler explained in his autobiography, he and Hutchins were hoping at this time to use the work of the Institute to promote the objective of an international academy of intellectuals, a sort of summit of great minds. The work of the Institute was to be preliminary—a kind of clearing of the way for later discussion and perhaps resolution. The technique to be used was that of the dialectical construction. Adler described early in Volume One the general character of the Institute's approach. Here are the five principles that guided the work as he listed them (*IF*, I, xix–xxi).

- It is a non-historical study of ideas.

- It is a non-philosophical approach to philosophical ideas.

- It strives to achieve a non-partisan treatment of philosophical positions or views.

- It tries to approximate comprehensiveness in scope.

- It limits itself to what can be found in the written record of philosophical thought, but it goes beyond what can be explicitly found there by trying to explicate what is there implied or only implicit. (And, as Adler adds, "In this respect the Institute's work is not mere reporting, but interpretive and constructive.")

Thus, a research fellow served Adler as a reader who specialized in certain authors, such as Hume, or a particular tradition, such as the Aristotelian tradition. As the research fellow would read, for example, Maritain's *Freedom in the Modern World*, he would note significant passages that were relevant to the issues of the debate between determinists and the defenders of free choice. These passages would be photocopied and returned to the researcher, who would underline the quotable parts and indicate on the wide margins why he believed the section was valuable. These photocopies would then go to Adler, who would arrange them in multiple files. And when Adler came to write that section he would so arrange the quotations that he would be "creating" a conversation transcending the historical context of the original passage, but being true and accurate to the original author's intent and meaning. And so a challenge to freedom of self-determination by Hobbes might be countered by a reply from Aquinas wherein Saint Thomas, analyzing the inter-causality of the intellect and will in the act of choosing, might seem to have anticipated the difficulty raised by Hobbes. This "dialectical reconstruction" was entirely the work of Adler; the associates served as his eyes, as it were, to scan the whole range of philosophical literature from the ancients to our contemporaries, for we made the attempt to study the recent periodical literature for articles that would be relevant to our study. Late in the afternoon, whatever Adler had written that day would be circulated to the research staff for their criticism and comments. It was a work of collaborative research, but Mortimer J. Adler was the sole author.

The expression "non-philosophical approach to philosophical ideas" meant that the Institute's objective was to clarify the meanings of freedom and the controversies that had developed about them, not to determine which were true and which were false. The work was regarded as a contribution to clarifying the debate, for, as it soon came to be noted, rarely did one philosopher meet the challenge of his predecessors or contemporaries. More often, a philosopher "created" the opponent he then proceeded to demolish. Thus, a determinist would insist that free choice had to be an "uncaused event" or a "chance event," and since there are no such things, there is no freedom of choice, and so on. In a paper before the American Catholic Philosophical Association in 1956,[1] Adler noted how rarely philosophers meet each other head-on in genuine disagreements; there are a few, but most of the time they hardly seem to be talking to each other. One objective, perhaps the principal objective of the Institute's work, was to prepare the way for later generations to undertake such an authentic debate.

The five categories of freedom are well known, but deserve to be reviewed again.

The first meaning of freedom recognized was named "The Circumstantial Freedom of Self-Realization"; this freedom is a freedom any being has that is not tied down or in some way restricted in its movements. (Note, it is not confined to human beings, as are the others.) Popularly, it is the freedom to do as one pleases, unhampered by one's surroundings. Obviously, a dog on a leash, or a bird in a cage, or a convicted criminal confined to a prison would lack the freedom of self-realization, abbreviated to

---

[1]Mortimer J. Adler, "Controversy in the Life and Teaching of Philosophy," *Proceedings of the American Catholic Philosophical Association*, XXX (1956): 3–22.

SR freedom in the literature. Any number of authors, ranging from Hobbes to Nowell-Smith, affirm this as the only meaning of freedom they recognize. (Note, this group often coincides with the determinists who deny freedom of choice.)

The second category of Freedom was called "The Acquired Freedom of Self-Perfection." This understanding of freedom has a long history, ranging from Plato to Gabriel Marcel; it was featured by the Stoics, such as Epictetus and Seneca, and generally affirmed by the great teachers of the Christian tradition, such as Augustine, Anselm, Aquinas, Luther, Calvin, Barth, and Tillich. Not everyone enjoys this freedom, for it is the freedom of the virtuous person, whose higher self dominates his passions or lower self; it is acquired by the hard work of developing good habits, and one of the controversies of the second volume relating to this freedom was whether or not it could be acquired independently of the help of divine grace.

When most people think of the question whether or not they are free, they are raising the third category, which was called "The Natural Freedom of Self-Determination." This is basically the ability, everything about you being the same, to have made a different choice; it is the power to do otherwise. It is called freedom of choice,[2] *liberum arbitrium*, since, at the crucial moment of choosing, a person makes a judgment insofar as his will as an efficient cause either determines itself to a particular good or directs the intellect as formal/final cause to continue deliberating, examining other particular goods as alternatives. It is this freedom that strikes determinists as impossible, for it seems to involve an uncaused event, the self-movement of the will on the created plane for which Adler coined the insightful phrase, *causal initiative*: the ability to be a cause without having been an effect. It was this notion that seemed such a scandal to the determinists, who judged it contradicted the premise that any state of affairs was the effect of the immediately preceding state of affairs, and from one set of causes, one and only one effect can follow.

The fourth freedom, Political Liberty, is simply a variation of self-realization; however, Adler and his associates, noting that it had received such attention in political literature since the end of the Middle Ages, judged it should be recognized with a category of its own. Political writings speak of the full freedom of citizenship, the right to vote, to be a can-

---

[2]It is called free *choice*, rather than free *will* since, in the Scholastic tradition, the will is determined to seek Absolute Goodness, or the Good as such.

didate or to rally support for the candidate of one's choice, as well as the freedom Americans associate with their First Amendment.

The final freedom, "Collective Freedom," is the most recent to appear in the literature, dating back only to the middle of the last century. This is freedom promoted by such philosophers of history as Auguste Comte, Mikhail Bakunin, Karl Marx, and Friedrich Engels, who argued mankind is, in a way, enslaved or at least not yet emancipated. Men in general are leading lives burdened by the forces of nature or oppressed by the consequences of the private ownership of the means of production. Some time in the future, when living men gain control of their lives, through science or a political revolution, they will come into their own and enjoy a collective freedom. This is the time hailed in Marxist rhetoric when political oppression will cease and the state will wither away. Interestingly, these authors identified with collective freedom are not classed as affirming the other categories of freedom that were distinguished. Thus, there is no philosopher the Adler associates studied who affirmed all five categories of freedom. However, a small number are listed as affirming the first four: SR, SP, SD, and Political Liberty. These philosophers are Aquinas, Locke, Maritain, Montesquieu, and Yves R. Simon.

Again, it is of special interest to the American Maritain Association members to note that three of the five are closely allied to each other and to us. Jacques Maritain was a consultant to the Institute and, while not directly active in the work, was kept in touch with the work in progress. Some years earlier, at a banquet in New York heralding the publication of *The Great Books of the Western World* with its *Syntopicon*, Maritain had supported the project of a *Summa Dialectica* and praised Adler's work. Maritain said:

> At the core of the work undertaken in publishing *Great Books of the Western World*, there is abiding faith in the dignity of the human mind and the virtue of knowledge. Such a work is inspired by what might be called humanist generosity (*PL* 257).

Nor was Yves R. Simon's work neglected. His various writings relating to freedom were regularly quoted, especially the *Traité du libre arbitre* and *The Community of the Free*. In fact, it was out of this work of the Institute that Adler's assistant—Peter Wolff—and I worked together to prepare for publication the translation Simon had made of his own work, but had left unfinished with his untimely death in 1961.

In concluding volume one of *The Idea of Freedom*, Adler proposed a general understanding of freedom that sought to clarify the common denominator of the different meanings. He took a number of pages to develop his analysis, which reads:

A man is free who has in himself the ability or power whereby he can make what he does his own action and what he achieves his own property (*IF*, I, 614).

While distinguishing the different meanings of freedom was a formidable task for Adler and his associates, the publication in 1958 of Volume One was in a way only the start of the dialectical preparation for the debate over freedom. Each meaning had not only supporters and opponents; even those who agreed on a type of freedom disagreed in turn over a number of issues within a certain category. There is not time to go into these issues here, but, in *The Great Ideas Today*, volumes for 1972 and 1973, Charles Van Doren has a long, masterly essay that distills the essence of this work. Van Doren's analysis is not a mere digest or abridgement of the Adler volumes but a re-statement that represents the study according to his own structure.[3]

The reception of the two volumes was disappointing. That should be qualified. Those who read the volumes were practically unanimous in their praise. A reviewer such as James Collins could write of the second volume:

Knowing the existence of this massive report on the status of the question of freedom we would be well advised to consult it before launching out on the next phase of thought on what makes men free, if they are free.[4]

But there was a significant gap between those assigned to read the book as reviewers for different journals and the general audience of those teaching philosophy in the different departments of our colleges and universities. My impression is that the book did not come into their hands or, if it did, it was too much for them to sit down and read. I cannot document this guess, but I can give a couple of further instances that support my conjecture.

In the mid 1960s, two important encyclopedias in English were in production: *The New Catholic Encyclopedia* and *The Encyclopedia of Philosophy*. The article on "freedom" in the latter by Professor H. Partridge mentions the Adler set in its bibliography, but the content of the article does not reflect any use of the Adler categories. The article on "determinism" in the same set by Richard Taylor gives a classic account of the

---

[3]Charles Van Doren, "The Idea of Freedom—Part One" in *The Great Ideas Today*, 1972; Part Two, *The Great Ideas Today*, 1973.

[4]James Collins, *America*, Jan. 13, 1962.

variations of determinism, but, again, reflects no acquaintance with the Adler analysis nor any mention of the work in his bibliography. Of two articles by Paul Nolan in *The New Catholic Encyclopedia* relating to free choice and psychological determinism, one mentions Adler in its bibliography while the other does not, but in neither article was use made of the substance of the Adler study (although interestingly, reference was made to the essay on the idea of "liberty" in the *Syntopicon*). Jacques de Finance de Clairbois, a professor at the Gregorian University, wrote the "freedom" article and he mentioned both the *Syntopicon* and *The Idea of Freedom* in his bibliography. Granted, this sampling of encyclopedias is small, but, to repeat, they were both published in 1967 and so it is fair to assume the articles had been assigned and were being written a few years after the Adler Volumes appeared. Even stranger to me was the fifteenth edition of the *Encyclopaedia Britannica*, whose editor was Mortimer J. Adler. Checking the articles on "free will" and "determinism" in the Micropaedia, only a couple of paragraphs were given on each topic and there was no bibliography.

Vernon J. Bourke's *Will in Western Thought; An Historico-Critical Survey*[5] did better by Adler, since he refers to Adler's analysis a number of times and in a footnote presents a summary of the five distinct meanings. Bourke's book developed out of a seminar he conducted at Saint Louis University in the early 1960s. In similar fashion, Professors Robert E. Dewey and James A. Gould, in their textbook on *Freedom: Its History, Nature, and Varieties*,[6] included a selection of some eight pages summarizing the varieties of freedom. This was not entirely surprising, since Robert Dewey was one of the original research fellows recruited to work at the Institute when it began in 1952. But this analysis is all too spotty, being limited to a few books that happen to have been on the shelves of my office when I came to sum up.

More important than this is to reflect on *The Idea of Freedom* as a stage or marker in Adler's intellectual career.

It is now some thirty years beyond the publication of Volume One, and just short of thirty years since the production of Volume Two, which constructed the controversies about the different freedoms. Adler was in his late fifties when this was done, at a time when most intellectuals are at the

---

[5]Vernon J. Bourke, *Will in Western Thought; An Historico-Critical Survey* (New York: Sheed and Ward, 1964).

[6]Robert E. Dewey and James A. Gould, *Freedom: Its History, Nature, and Varieties* (New York: Macmillan, 1970).

peak of their productive years. These later chapters took enormous concentration and energy as he created the exchanges over causal initiative, predictability, responsibility, and the theological issues. As we associates would leave the Institute at five p.m., we would hear the click clack of the typewriter as Mortimer worked on, and in the morning he would be in before others as if he had been working all night.

However, this was only a stage in a most productive and still productive career. As the work on *Freedom* came to a close, the dialectical examination of the meaning of other ideas was under way. After the move was made for Adler to return to Chicago, volumes studying other ideas came out on love, justice, progress, written by Adler associates with his guidance and support.

Then, in his own mid-sixties, when other academics are moving towards retirement, Adler launched into a new phase of amazing creativity.[7] Year by year one important book followed another: *The Conditions of Philosophy* (1965); *The Difference of Man and the Difference it Makes* (1967); *The Time of Our Lives* (1970); *The Common Sense of Politics* (1971); *Some Questions about Language* (1976); *How to Think about God* (1980); *Six Great Ideas* (1981); *The Angels and Us* (1982); *How to Speak, How to Listen* (1983); *Aristotle for Everybody* (1983); *Ten Philosophical Mistakes* (1985); *We Hold These Truths* (1987), and, along with these, the extraordinarily interesting autobiography, *Philosopher at Large* (1977). Further, all along went the editorial work on the fifteenth edition of the *Encyclopaedia Britannica*, the annual yearbooks to the Great Books set, *The Great Ideas Today*, and now, in the 1980s, the enormous work devoted to the reform of our education system with the series of writings relating to *The Paedeia Proposal*.

Further, as Adler indicated in talk last evening, still forthcoming are his works on *Reforming Education* and *Intellect: Mind over Matter*, in about 1990. What a truly remarkable career as a philosopher and teacher!

At this meeting devoted to the associates of Jacques Maritain, I offer this paper on *The Idea of Freedom* in recollection of my association with Adler some thirty years ago.

---

[7]In the discussion following the paper, Adler volunteered that it was Jacques Maritain who insisted at this time that he had devoted enough effort to the dialectical process, and that it was now time to write as a philosopher presenting his own position.

Otto Bird

A Dialectical Version of Philosophical Discussion

Adler's work on freedom has been of two distinct and different kinds: one has been philosophical, in which he has developed and expressed his deepest and best thought about the nature of freedom, work accomplished in his most recent books. The other has been dialectical, in the work he has done with a large staff in analyzing the idea of freedom and the controversies concerning it that have run through the entire history of philosophy.

Adler has long been deeply concerned with controversy in philosophy. It wasn't so much that, like Kant, he deplored the existence and extent of disagreement in philosophy, as that the disagreement was not sharp and clear enough, being more often merely non-agreement of minds not even meeting and hence not capable of genuine disagreement such as to establish a valid controversy. Hence, from the time of his first book in 1927, he has called for the construction of a *Summa Dialectica* to analyze, map, and clarify the controversy regarding basic philosophical ideas. For that purpose, the Institute for Philosophical Research was established in 1952, and the method of analysis perfected and put to work that resulted in the two-volume *The Idea of Freedom*. It is about that method that I wish to talk to you for the next few minutes.

However, I must say and warn you at once that I shall not talk about that method as applied to and displayed in the analysis of freedom. For my purposes, it is better to take not freedom but the idea of justice. I have two reasons for this choice. In the first place, I served only as a consultant for the work on freedom, whereas I was responsible for the Institute's book on the idea of justice.[1] Secondly, there is another and weightier reason. As

---

[1]Cf. Otto Bird, "The Idea of Justice," *The Great Ideas Today*, 1974 (Chicago: Encyclopedia Britannica, 1974), 167–209.

Adler wrote in the foreword to that book:

> The work that the Institute has done on the ideas of freedom, progress, happiness, and love . . . has not eventuated in the formulation of a controversy that is nearly as well structured as . . . in the case of justice (xi).

Hence, the idea of justice offers a simpler and clearer instance of that method than freedom does. In expounding that method, let me say at once that my understanding and practice of it has come from a long association with Mortimer Adler. With this as introduction, we can begin to consider a simplified version of how a genuine controversy can be constructed.

If disagreement is to be real and not merely apparent, so as to give rise to a genuine controversy, there are certain basic conditions that have to be met. The first of these conditions is that the participants must be talking about the same thing and not just about the same word, if that word is used to mean different things. Nor need the word for that thing be the same in every case. It is possible for one person to speak of "freedom," whereas another uses "liberty," and yet both be talking of the same subject. This much, of course, is obvious especially in the case of writers who use different languages. In other words, there must be an identifiable subject of discussion that is addressed by all who enter into that discussion, whatever the word.

This first requirement must be understood in a minimal sense. It is not necessary that all talking about justice should mean the same thing by it in every respect. It is sufficient that there is some one respect in which all agree.

The second requirement is that this one identifiable subject be such that questions can be raised about it that elicit different answers and so establish different positions with regard to the issues posited by those questions. In short, there can be no disagreement if there is not first some one subject about which questions can be raised and to which different answers can be given.

Thirdly, for the answers and positions to be such as to generate any considerable controversy, they must have some relation to one another and be coordinated into a theory that claims to explain and make understandable the subject and the issues about it.

There are three remarks to be made about these three preliminary conditions for controversy. The first is that for disagreement, real not apparent disagreement, to exist there must be initial agreement upon at least the three points that are involved here: (1) agreement upon the subject under discussion; (2) agreement upon the questions that can be asked about it; and (3) agreement upon what constitutes an answer to those questions.

The second remark is that in the actual historical analysis and treatment of a basic idea it is rare indeed to find any of these agreements made explicit and commented upon. Even Aristotle, who began a dialectical analysis of the thought of his predecessors, did so for his own doctrinal purposes, to distinguish the true from the false in their accounts and adopt the true for the development of his own doctrines. Hence, for the most part, in order to analyze and clarify, it is necessary to construct the controversy by establishing its basic subject and issues so as to identify the positions genuinely opposed.

Thus, in investigating the idea of justice, the first task consists in examining the major theories dealing with justice. Thus, one has to spend considerable time and effort studying those theories with a view to determining which of them fulfill the basic conditions. Such a work calls for the writing of many reports analyzing writings about justice, from Plato and Aristotle down to the present, all looked at from our particular point of view. As the result of such studies, it finally becomes possible to identify a common subject that would obtain the agreement of many authors as a subject they would recognize as justice. The subject is identified by the notes or the characteristics that it is judged to have, and these notes can be gathered from a consideration of the kinds of things that the theories would agree upon in calling "just." In the case of justice, this consideration yielded three notes for the idea: justice is a social norm; it is approbative; it is obligatory.

To say that justice in our minimal sense is a social norm is to claim that it is a relational concept in that it involves many terms; that it is social in that it applies to persons in association with one another; and that it serves as a norm for directing persons in their dealings with one another.

But more than this one note is needed, since society has more norms than justice alone. There are norms of manners and decency, of taste, of grammar and of logic, and none of these are matters of justice except in an extended sense. Justice is more closely associated than these with law and morality. However, neither law nor morality can supply a further note for justice as a common subject of dispute, since there is disagreement precisely about the relation of justice to both law and morality. Yet there is agreement in the theories that justice is an approbative concept. For when a writer, in expounding his theory of justice, claims that x is just, he is evaluating that x is good and is something that he would approve of. It is an expression of a *pro*-attitude towards x. Thus, it involves also the emotional side of man and enters into the world of value.

The third and final note that determines justice as a common subject of discussion is that it is obligatory. It establishes an *ought*: the just thing to do is something that ought to be done; the unjust thing, something that ought not to be done. The foundation of this *ought* is an issue in dispute, e.g., whether it is moral and objective, for instance.

These three notes that determine the idea of justice, whether or not they are always explicit, have been found in the literature about justice. It is in this sense a dialectical discovery, since it concerns how men have thought and written about justice. Such a discovery may be of help to a person endeavoring to work out a true understanding of what justice is. However, that is not the purpose that we have for these notes. We have located and identified them as a means of obtaining better understanding of the dispute and controversy about justice. These notes, in establishing a common subject, provide the evidence needed to show that participants in the dispute are indeed talking about the same thing.

The next step in constructing the controversy consists in identifying questions regarding the common notes that all writers on the subject can be seen to answer and even to answer differently. Not all questions are equally useful. Some theories of justice may emphasize special concerns, as Hegel does about freedom or Del Vecchio about spirit, which others do not consider at all. Such concerns may illuminate the nature of justice. But they do not illuminate the controversy, since they are not of common concern and hence not fundamental to it, in our sense.

The questions fundamental to the controversy as a whole are those that formulate issues regarding the common notes; issues on which differing and opposed positions may be taken; answers which, taken together, constitute a theory that claims to explain those notes. For the idea of justice, six questions are sufficient to distinguish and identify the major different theories. They are as follows:

- Is justice the same as legality?

- Is justice a criterion of law?

- Is justice based on natural law?

- Is justice, in any other sense than that of legality, an objective norm of human action?

- Is justice obligatory on its own, apart from legal or social sanctions?

- Is justice a distinct virtue?

In most cases, the wording of the issue shows its relation to the common notes. Thus, law establishes a norm that is in some sense both obligatory and approbative. Hence the first four questions deal with justice as a norm: whether or not it is based on natural right.

Each of the questions is such as to elicit a "yes" or "no" answer and thus provides a dichotomous criterion of classification. Some of them are so related that the answer to one question entails an answer to another. For example, to say that justice is the same as positive legality is also to deny that it is a criterion of law and that it is based on natural rights. As a result, it is possible to obtain different combinations of affirmative and negative answers to the questions; and these answers put together are such as to identify the basic theories of justice, and so map the controversy as a whole. On seeking answers to these questions in the literature on justice, we find only three theories of justice that are basic or paradigmatic to the whole controversy.

One theory answers the first question in the affirmative—justice is identical with positive law—and all the remaining questions in the negative. Hence, it can be called the Positive Law theory of justice. Of this theory, Hobbes and the contemporary Scandinavian Alf Ross are good representatives.

At the other extreme from this is the Natural Right theory of justice. This answers the first question in the negative, denying that justice is identical with legality, and then answers all the remaining five questions in the affirmative. Aristotle and Adler himself are holders of this position.

The third paradigm, the Social Good theory of justice, falls in between these two. It answers the first and third questions in the negative, by denying that justice is identical with positive law or founded on natural right. And it replies in the affirmative to questions 2, 4, and 5, by claiming that justice is a criterion of law, that it is an objective norm, and that it is obligatory apart from legal sanctions. It qualifies its affirmative answer to the sixth by assimilating justice to the virtue of benevolence. Hume and John Stuart Mill are typical representatives of the Social Good theory of justice.

These three paradigmatic theories are basic to the controversy concerning justice in that they identify the positions from which the entire controversy can be viewed and analyzed, by providing the types according to which any theory can be measured and located. Of course, combinations of any of these three may also occur. In fact, many of the recent theories, and especially those put forward by Anglo-American thinkers, can be understood as efforts to combine the Social Good and the Natural Right theories, notably the highly touted theory advanced by John Rawls.

The main purpose of making such a construction, for construction it is, lies in its effort to make sense of the frequently confusing discussion of philosophers. It does so by attempting to find the issues on which there is real, not merely apparent, agreement and disagreement and to state those issues in a language that is both clear and neutral with respect to any of the theories it analyses. Some philosophers, notably Descartes, Kant, and Wittgenstein, have attributed philosophical confusion to the lack of proper method for solving philosophical problems. Adler's contention, in the respect with which we are here concerned, is that it has not been a good controversy in that the issues of agreement and disagreement have not been clearly stated. The result: not disagreement, but non-agreement—trains passing in the night.

The method of reading philosophical literature that we have analyzed and identified is one way of making sense of that literature. Its matter is provided by the literature produced during the long history of philosophy. Yet the method and its results are neither philosophical nor historical, neither a philosophical nor an historical account of thinking about justice, but rather the theories and literature about that idea. Philosophical it may be, in that it reads the writings of philosophers; historical, in that they occurred in an historical context. Yet the result of the method is neither philosophical nor historical, but dialectical.

However, to identify the method as dialectical is not immediately illuminating, since dialectic has meant many things in philosophical discussion. Adler, while he was at work perfecting this method and putting it to work in the analysis of the idea of freedom, had occasion to write an essay on the subject of the dialectic. In this essay, he distinguished this dialectical method from two other kinds of dialectic.[2]

One theory of dialectic is that which identifies it with the method of philosophy and the knowledge it achieves. It is Noetic dialectic, of which the foremost representative is Plato.

Another kind of dialectic may be called Regulative, in that it is taken as the fundamental law underlying the development of both reality and history. This dialectic we know best from the work of Hegel and Marx.

The third basic dialectic is identified neither with philosophy nor with ontological and historical development. It is taken as an auxiliary to philosophy, not philosophy itself. Hence, it may be called the Reflexive theory of dialectic. Here, Aristotle is the earliest and foremost example.

The method that has been analyzed and exemplified here is obviously closer to the Reflexive kind than to either the Noetic or the Regulative. Yet is differs sharply from Aristotle's use of it. He made a dialectical examination of the work of his predecessors, but he did so with a doctrinal, not a dialectical, purpose in view. He used their work as a means of advancing his own examination of things. His writings reveal his use of that method for the further purpose of discovering the truth about reality.

---

[2]Mortimer J. Adler, "The Idea of Dialectic," *The Great Ideas Today*, 1986 (Chicago: Encyclopedia Britannica, 1986).

The dialectical method of our concern here does not reach so far. The truth at which it aims is truth about philosophical discussion and literature, such as that devoted to freedom and justice. Its hope, of course, is that it may offer help to further the philosophical search for the truth about the ideas with which it deals. But by itself it does not claim to do so much.

Ralph McInerny

Adler on Freedom

When I was asked to prepare this paper I saw it as an opportunity to pay tribute to a man whose philosophical work over the years, while it has had a tremendous effect, has not yet had anything like the effect it deserves. There are various reasons for this, some quite incidental, but one at least is a trifle unsavory. You know the story of Thales who, in order to show that the philosopher could be an entrepreneur if he chose, cornered all the olive presses and made a killing at harvest time. We easily imagine the reaction of the olive growers. But ask yourself what Thales' fellow philosophers would have thought.

Mortimer has borne with Stoic dignity the burden of being the most highly paid philosopher in the United States. Thales would have been proud of him. But perhaps academic philosophers, nursing economic and other grievances, have been less receptive to what Mortimer Adler had to say. For the best of reasons and highest of motives of course. Then, too, *Time* long ago branded Adler a Peeping Thomist. In short, the entrepreneurial Adler and crafty Thales have been in the same boat, doubtless comforting themselves with Thales' lost work on celestial navigation.

Perhaps you will recognize the allusion to Chesterton's reply when asked the famous question: "If you were stranded on a desert island and could have only one book what title would you choose?" GKC did not hesitate. He would like a book entitled *How to Build a Boat*. That has an Adlerian ring to it, not simply because Chesterton would of course have needed one other volume, namely, *How to Read a Book*, but also because the reply has that down to earth, feet on the ground, let's get on with it tone that one associates with the philosophical production of Mortimer Adler.

When I accepted this assignment, I imagined myself writing the paper in the warm confines of the Maritain Center on the seventh floor of the Hesburgh Library, to which we shall all repair after this session. There the *opera omnia* of Adler would be at my elbow as well as those of Jacques Maritain and Yves R. Simon. As one does when such projects are but a twinkle in the mind's eye, I imagined coming before you on this occasion with a comprehensive overview of Adler's discussions through the years on the concept of freedom. To do this well, it would be necessary to take up allied topics and I would be able to show and not simply assert that some of his books that seem to have been mere by-blows of a collective effort are all but definitive treatises. I remember thinking, when *Some Questions About Language* came out in 1976, that here was a book which, better than any other in that seemingly overworked field, laid out the issues, indicated solutions, and would define subsequent discussion. (The book was dedicated to Jacques Maritain.) Similar praise can be heaped on other works of Mortimer Adler, and I hoped to use this occasion to do some heaping.

This is not the paper I had hoped to deliver. When I sat down to write, I found myself, not on this campus and in the Maritain Center, but high above Cayuga's waters warming the Kaneb Chair in Catholic Studies. Cornell has an excellent library, but nothing like the Maritain Collection here, with its repository of Adleriana gathered in grand indifference to the Library of Congress, to say nothing of the Dewey Decimal system. I do not mean to suggest, of course, that if I had stayed home I would have written the paper I hoped to write, one that would be worthy of Adler's work. But perhaps the distance between cup and lip would have been somewhat less.

I. The Adlerian Voice

To pick up any work of Mortimer Adler, early, middle, or late, is to be called to order. One imagines him looking at his watch, waiting for us to settle down, and then, when he has our complete attention, beginning. He is a schoolmaster, a *scholasticus*. There is work to be done and we are here to do it.

Consider the 1965 volume *The Conditions of Philosophy* with its subtitle: "Its Checkered Past, Its Present Disorder, and Its Future Promise." At the very outset, Adler acknowledges that he seems embarked on a tiresome, even trite, exercise. How many dozens of attempts have been made over recent centuries to overcome the so-called "scandal of philosophy"? That is, the undeniable fact that the history of philosophy presents us with a cacophony of voices, endless disputes, seemingly no generally accepted solutions.

This situation leads some to take on the burden of remedying the problem by constructing out of whole cloth, as it seems, a worldview. Others become disciples of these sturdy souls so that we have not simply Descartes, Locke, Leibniz, Hume, Kant, and Hegel, but Cartesians, Lockians (Turnkeys), Leibnitzeans, Humeans, Kantians, and Hegelians.

I think it fair to say that Adler from the very outset of his studies at

Columbia was struck by this scandal. And, going by the excerpts from his youthful writings he gives us in *Philosopher at Large*, he meant to do something about it. The confidence he showed not only in his own reason, but in human reason itself, to move through and beyond this dissonance and uncommunicating diversity fairly lifts from the page. The issues philosophy addresses are simply too important to be left in this parlous condition. This state of affairs cannot be allowed to continue. But how to remedy it?

Mortimer Adler seems never to have been tempted by the prospect of inventing an Adlerian worldview. Nothing could be farther from his outlook than the Cartesian willingness to wipe the slate clean, to pick the lint from his own navel, and, madly to mix more metaphors, forge in the smithy of his soul the uncreated conscience of his race. What Adler did, instinctively at first and then with growing awareness of the method, was to look for clues within the diversity of philosophical positions as to how the situation could be bettered.

In short, he became a dialectician in the Aristotelian sense. Like Aristotle, he refused to think that intelligent human beings were simply in disagreement with one another on basic issues. Like Aristotle at the outset of most of the treatises, e.g., the *Physics*, the *De anima*, the *Metaphysics*, Adler wants us first to acquaint ourselves with what has been said. He has an Aristotelian confidence that beneath the surface disagreements will be found at least tacitly held common ground. But if this approach has Aristotelian origins, the task in the mid-twentieth century was enormously different from what it was in the mid-fourth century B.C.

II. The Idea of Freedom

The task as it thus appeared to Adler was vast and it could not be accomplished by a single person. A collective effort was required. It was this recognition that led to the formation of the Institute for Philosophical Research and his formal departure from the Academy. I say formal because some of his most important books are the result of the Britannica Lectures delivered at the University of Chicago. The first result of the formation of his *equipe* was *The Idea of Freedom*, the two-volume work Adler wrote against the background of the Institute's research, and which appeared in 1958 and 1961. (Adler has observed in his autobiography that the interval between the appearance of the two volumes prevented the work from having maximum impact.)

Book One of Volume One of *The Idea of Freedom* is a masterful statement of the method Adler hit upon. His Institute's approach to the study of any controverted issue, in this case of freedom, is characterized as follows:

- it is a non-historical study of ideas;

- it is a non-philosophical approach to philosophical ideas;
- it strives to achieve a non-partisan treatment of philosophical positions or views;
- it tries to approximate comprehensiveness in scope;
- it limits itself to what is explicit or implicit in written works.

Adler and his team would dare to ask precisely what disagreement and controversy are and what sort of agreement he envisaged.

It is the distinction between dialectical and doctrinal agreement that will surely catch the eye. What Adler hopes to achieve is agreement that the issue has been fairly and accurately stated, and this provides the context within which future discussion can take place. He cites this comment of Jacques Maritain on the neutrality of the language of dialectical formulation. In order to be neutral, Maritain wrote, it must be

> "echoless," i.e. strictly limited to what is barely stated and deprived of any further doctrinal overtones or connotations. Just because such assertions or formulas, having no actual philosophic life of their own, are, so to speak, only in potency in regard to some philosophical wholeness or totality, every philosopher in the group concerned can subscribe to them; but in doing so each will infuse into them the connotations or overtones peculiar to his own entire doctrine, and foreign to the doctrine of his colleagues (*IF*, I, 68).

Taken just as such, this would not seem to be worth it. Indeed, it echoes with some of Maritain's hopes for the Universal Declaration of Human Rights. In that case, he might seem to be saying that an agreement can be had on statements even though there is radical disagreement as to the meanings of the terms in the statements. Of course, he did not mean anything so vacuous, and we can be sure that Adler does not either. What Maritain meant and what Adler went on to say he meant was that it is "only through the medium of constructed formulations which are neutral in language and intent that philosophers can be brought to the recognition of their dialectical agreements as well as of their doctrinal agreements and disagreements. Without this medium as a *tertium quid*, each philosopher tends to remain in the world of his own thought and is conversant there with other philosophers only in the guise which he gives them when he imports them into his own world" (*IF*, I, 68).

What is the most indeterminate and neutral statement of the idea of freedom?

> A man is free who has in himself the ability or power to make what he does his own action and what he achieves his own property (*IF*, II, 16).

The development of the controversies is in terms of freedom as self-realization, freedom as self-perfection, political liberty, and collective freedom.

Obviously, the only way to profit from this massive effort is to read the book according to the method of the master's *How to Read a Book.*

What continues to dazzle in this effort is the steady determination to discover in twenty-five hundred years of discussion the precise nature of the controversies and conflicts. That a man and his cohorts should have devoted long years of their lives to this self-effacing effort to overcome the scandal of philosophy is heroic. We should expect that discussions of freedom since 1961 would be appreciably different from before, that discussants would avail themselves of the vast groundclearing dialectical achievement of *The Idea of Freedom* and get on with it. I do not think one can say this has happened. The freedom not to read a book may have been overlooked. Has Adler's career been a quixotic one; must we see him as one who sought to present a great gift to the philosophical community only to be spurned or, worse, ignored?

III. The Results

I don't think we should pass quickly over this point. The success of Adler's effort cannot be likened to, say, a poet who works in obscurity producing his oeuvre, which is then effectively ignored by mankind. Reception apart, the poetry either is or is not good. And, should this ultimately be recognized, say on the order of the discovery of Catullus or the belated reputation of Hopkins, they are welcomed into a tradition of poetic work.

But Adler did not seek simply to make his own contribution to the ongoing tradition of philosophy. His was the far more ambitious task of introducing order into the philosophical community so that its future might be different from its past. There is a thematically practical aim underlying his effort. His success will be measured in terms of how much or how little he has effected what he sought to effect. And I suggest that, to date, the results are not favorable.

One of the greatest obstacles has been the obscurantist disinterest among professional philosophers. I recall reading a review of Walker Percy's collection of essays on language in which a professional philosopher condescendingly offered to provide Percy with a reading list if he wished seriously to get into the problem of language. Adler, of course, has all the appropriate academic credentials, he has been on the faculty of two of the best universities in this country, but some professional philosophers regard him as something of an interloper. This is unfortunate and one can only hope that the work of the Institute for Philosophical Research will find a warmer welcome in academe than has been the case till now.

Fortunately, if the jury is still out on the success of the Institute's effort to restructure the way philosophical controversy is conducted, there is another side of Adler's effort that can be pronounced successful here and now.

Adler's sustained dedication to the dialectical efforts of the Institute never diverted him from the ultimate aim, which was to achieve substantive agreement on philosophical matters. The dialectic was meant to overcome the scandal of philosophy by providing philosophers with a neutral statement of the *status quaestionis*, which would then influence their future substantive work. It can be said that one undeniable beneficiary of the efforts to Adler the dialectician is Adler the philosopher.

IV. The Britannica Lectures

The original sin of Adler's academic career was that he wrote a best-seller, *How to Read a Book*. This made him as welcome among philosophers as Barbara Tuchman is among academic historians. I once heard a young historian say of Philip Hughes, the great church historian, that he wasn't a real historian. It wasn't simply that Hughes was readable; he didn't have a pedantic bone in his body. Adler gets a firm grip on his reader's lapels from the first sentence, but from that point on it is the flow of the narrative that holds the reader. Mortimer Adler has the great knack of communicating difficult ideas in a jargonless language understandable by any intelligent reader. This is unforgiveable.

Not only that, what he communicates is both his own confidence in reason and arguments that enable the reader to share that confidence. For contrast, look at Thomas Nagel's *What Does It All Mean?* Here we have a professional philosopher of great talent writing a book for the masses on the main issues of philosophy. Of Nagel it can be said, he's no Mortimer Adler. I don't mean that he gives us philosophical jargon; the problem is the same as that of Bertrand Russell in his popular efforts. The answer Nagel gives to his question is: probably nothing but it doesn't really matter. The jaded skepticism of academic philosophy makes even thinner gruel when it is freed from the protective garb of jargon.

Brand Blanshard was among those who praised *The Idea of Freedom* for its fairness and objectivity. Adler the dialectician does not load the case. But when Adler does philosophy he profits from that vast dialectical working up of 2,500 years of philosophy—he may be more knowledgeable than any other living philosopher about philosophy's past—and he provides his reader with the elements of a substantive answer to the great questions.

Just consider the titles of his non-dialectical work: *The Difference of Man and the Difference it Makes; The Time of Our Lives; The Common Sense of Politics; How to Think About God; The Angels and Us.* This is a partial list. All of these are extremely good; some, like *The Time of Our Lives,* are, I will not say Great Books because there are only a hundred of those, but better than anything else done on the subject in our day.

V. One Popular Statement

Let me conclude, then, with a discussion of freedom to be found in one of Adler's recent books addressed to a wide audience, *Ten Philosophical Mistakes.* (If Adler has a gift for titles, he is delightful in his subtitles too: "Basic Errors in Modern Thought—How They Came About, Their Consequences, and How to Avoid Them.") This was a Book of the Month Club alternate, which indicates that, whatever our judgment on the success of Adler's effort to alter philosophical discourse generally, he is hugely successful in the works that profit from his own advice.

Chapter 7 is concerned with Freedom of Choice and anyone who has read the two volumes of *The Idea of Freedom* will notice how it provides the background for the discussion. Adler begins by alluding to the unquestionableness of freedom as a fact: people think of freedom as something that cannot be denied. We are able to do as we please, but of course unless you are a multimillionaire you cannot avail yourself of freedom of the press on the level of the Ochs or Hearst families. But even a slave is free in some ways. This freedom, like political freedom, is affected by circumstances, as freedom to will as one ought and freedom of choice are not. It is the last which is most controversial. "Freedom of choice consists in always being able to choose otherwise" (*TP* 147).

The claim to have a right to freedom seems to refer only to what Adler calls circumstantial freedoms, not to moral liberty or freedom of choice. But the claim to have a right to other freedoms makes little sense if we do not have freedom of choice. "If we do not have freedom of choice, what reason can be given for our right to do as we please or to exercise a voice in our own government?" (*TP* 147). With that connection, Adler can stress that the controversy over free choice has far-reaching consequences.

Is the denial of free choice a philosophical error that can simply be pointed out and corrected? No. "I cannot show that the exponents of free choice are right and the determinists who oppose free choice are wrong. The philosophical defect here is not so much a demonstrable philosophical error as a manifest misunderstanding of the issue itself" (*TP* 148).

What is the misunderstanding? Those who question free will on the basis of physical determinism fail to understand "that the exponents of free choice place the action of will outside the domain of physical phenomena studied by science" (*TP* 149). If free choice were a physical event and if all physical events are causally determined, then the proponents of free choice would be in trouble. If mind and will are not physical, it is another matter. Nonetheless, some acts of mind and some acts of will are necessitated. Mind cannot withhold assent to self-evident truth; the will cannot not will the good, the *totum bonum*. With respect to all goods other than the comprehensive good, with regard to partial goods, the will is not necessitated. This indeterminacy of will with respect to partial goods is not physical indeterminacy. This is what Adler means by saying that the denial of free choice is based on a misunderstanding of what its proponents claim. Adler concludes that the defense of free choice is sounder than its denial. If there were a sound argument on behalf of determinism, the mind's necessary acceptance of it would differ from causal determinacy.

The discussion is of course schematic, but it enables us to see how dialectic operates within the effort to achieve a doctrinal truth. Alternatives are carefully designated and the pros and cons of each developed. One alternative is judged sounder because of what is offered on its behalf and the discussion ends with a kind of reductio of the naysayer's position.

Adler's reader comes away with some sense of how a rational defense of what he holds in practice can be formulated. The suggestion of the complexity with which the issue could be developed is not accompanied with any skepticism as to the outcome. Adler does not endeavor to replace the beliefs of the plain man, to make his mind a blank slate and confer on his reader his first true judgment. Like the Aristotelian he basically is, Adler assumes that everybody already knows certain things and that philosophy provides clarification and defense of these truths. He is not shy to say that modern philosophy has generated many mistakes about basic matters.

VI. An American Philosopher

Let me conclude with the remark that there is something quintessentially American about Adler's work. His *Paideia* program aims at enabling his fellow citizens to fulfill their tasks as members of a free society. The sturdy confidence that led him through the thickets of philosophical controversies over 2,500 years toward a clarification of the points at issue was meant to lead on to the resolution of the major differences. The practical importance of this is that a society such as ours cannot function as it should if there is fundamental confusion about the concepts and truths on which it is founded. So it is that Mortimer Adler became a public philosopher, an intellectual who dared to engage in the great conversation all his fellow citizens, in the conviction that common sense is indeed common. That it is uncommon for a philosopher to say such things nowadays is a sign of how grateful we should be for Mortimer Adler.

John Van Doren

Mr. Adler and Matthew Arnold

I hope it will not seem frivolous if, in casting about for some way to respond to the invitation of the American Maritain Association on this occasion, I venture to say something about the connection, as it seems to me to be, or at least the parallel, between Mr. Adler and Matthew Arnold. It should at any rate not seem far-fetched. Nothing is better known about Arnold than his decision, made after the publication of two books of poems, to devote himself thereafter to criticism, on the ground that poetry could not again be the great thing it had been until criticism had provided it with a "current of fresh and new ideas" on which to draw. Nothing has been more important in Mr. Adler's intellectual development than his belief, arrived at early on from his reading of Lovejoy and Husserl, that philosophy cannot again be the great thing it has been until someone has clarified the ideas on which it can stake its claims—an undertaking he calls dialectical, and to which he has devoted the greater part of his career. And this is but the most obvious point of comparison between two men who in other ways also have made it their business to describe "things as they really are," in Arnold's famous phrase, correcting what they conceived to be errors, challenging the assumptions of modernity as they went along, and signing even with the same initials.

Of course it does not prove, just because propaedeutic efforts—the one to poetry, the other to philosophy—were made in each case, that there is any similarity to the efforts as such. They may have been undertakings quite different in substance—as different, perhaps, as the difference between poetry and philosophy—and, if so, we would not expect to learn anything we do not already know from measuring them against one another. But in fact it is rather less simple than that. For one of the subjects to which both Arnold's criticism and Mr. Adler's dialectic are directed is poetry itself, in which Mr. Adler has taken what may be called a philosophical interest, and on which he and Arnold have reached different conclusions. They have reached different conclusions as well about a second subject, which is education, and which belongs to neither of them

73

entirely. Thus the difference between them seems to be something more than the ancient quarrel, as Plato said it was, between poetry and philosophy. It is a difference rather in the assumptions with which the two men began, and in the larger intention of their lives, notwithstanding that both of them have in a sense had the same mission, or thought so.

How Arnold began, or at least came to his decision, is well known. As stated in the Preface to the reissue of his poems (1853), he had come to think that the longest one of these was lacking in the qualities a poem should have, which were such, he said, as would constitute a "criticism of life." The poem in question, "Empedocles on Etna," in his judgment had failed of that purpose, and so he had not reprinted it. This failure he thought not personal to himself, however, but a consequence rather of the modern spirit, as he believed it was, in which he perceived a "bewildering confusion" that made it incapable of accomplishing what he thought poetry should accomplish, which was to render what is "great and passionate."

What he meant by this he explained in "The Modern Element in Literature," his inaugural lecture as the Professor of Poetry at Oxford. There, he said that the modern defect in poetry was a failure of what he called ideas, without which "facts" could not be regarded in the critical spirit that was required if a literature "adequate" to them were to develop. What he thought adequate to the ideas of its time was the literature of ancient Greece. What he thought inadequate was, for example, the poetry of his own age—the poetry of Byron and Shelley and "even Wordsworth"—that, greatly felt as it was, "did not know enough," by which he meant that those poets did not know "the best and most permanent ideas" by which men live, and for the reason they had not read enough in the writers who understood such ideas.

In "The Function of Criticism at the Present Time," having gone on to define criticism as "a disinterested endeavor to learn and propagate the best that is known and thought in the world," Arnold explained why this now needed to be done, and why he had decided to be one of those who tried to do it. The critical power, he said, was not the same as the creative power, which he conceded was the greater thing. Yet the lesser thing in this case was prior, he said, to the greater. As he put it, the critical power "tends . . . to make an intellectual situation of which the creative power can ultimately avail itself . . . to establish an order of ideas if not absolutely true, yet true by comparison with that which it displaces; to make the best ideas prevail." Criticism could supply that order, he thought, and must in times like those in which he found himself—times unlike the epoch of Aeschylus and Sophocles, when ideas had been made easily available. "In an epoch like that is, no doubt, the true life of literature," he said of this; "there is the promised land, towards which criticism can only beckon"; to which he added, with the Virgilian melancholy he recognized in himself and sought earnestly to escape, that it was a promised land which he and his contemporaries would not enter; that they must die in the wilderness, content with having desired to enter that land, "to have saluted it from afar."

We cannot help being reminded, I think, reading these familiar essays, of the dialectical function that Mr. Adler has undertaken to perform over the course of his long career in the service not of poetry but of philosophy. Arnold's sense of the historical moment is more acute than that of Mr. Adler, who does not have his quasi-religious fervor; and Arnold's use of terms, as with the word "ideas," is doubtless very imprecise as compared with what Mr. Adler would require. But the conviction in both is that a lack of power in their respective disciplines has developed, and that it cannot be overcome without a preparatory effort on someone's part. Absent this, both disciplines are seen as ineffectual—which is to say, as incapable of realizing their proper ends.

Mr. Adler's interest in dialectic shows up very early, in the book he published with that title—a book that should have been his dissertation—when he was only twenty-five. Here already, having in mind what Scott Buchanan had called "the great conversation" in the Western tradition of thought, Mr. Adler conceived the grand outline of a *Summa Dialectica* that would transcend both doctrine and dogma in organizing the field of philosophical discourse. He was diverted for a time from this ambitious scheme by other projects, such as the work on evidence he wrote with Jerome Michael and his remove from Columbia to the University of Chicago, where he was caught up in the battle of what he hoped would be an academic revolution. But the project he envisioned was soon enough begun, after a fashion, and on a smaller scale. Indeed, it is fair to say that a dialectical purpose has never been far from his thought, having appeared explicitly or implicitly in nearly every book that he has written and every sizable project—such as the *Syntopicon* to *Great Books of the Western World* and the schematically reformed *Encyclopaedia Britannica*—he has directed.

A couple of illustrations only will suffice for this discussion. Thus, in *A Dialectic of Morals* (1941), Mr. Adler defined what he called "the dialectical task" as being one that did for the modern age what the Greeks had done for themselves. What the Greeks had done for themselves was to sift through the opinions of men with the aim of determining what knowledge they could be said to contain. This, Mr. Adler said, was and is the necessary condition—in the sense of providing the necessary material—for philosophy to maintain that the one position or another, on any subject, is true. The focus was on morals, and the cultural moment was one, Mr. Adler felt, in which skepticism denied all truth to moral propositions, because it denied any possibility of what it thought of as objective knowledge to those propositions. In this predicament the only recourse for the philosopher was, Mr. Adler said, to do what philosophy had done when it was dialectical—that is, at the time of Plato and Aristotle—and prepare the ground by challenging opinion once again to discover what it might be said to know. He recognized the social implications of this venture. "I have chosen the topic of moral knowledge—the objectivity and universality of moral standards—because it is so relevant to this critical moment in our culture," he said:

> It will not be necessary to engage in distinct dialectical enterprises for the separate fields of ethics and politics. If skepticism about moral truths can be overcome at all, if any judgments about good and bad can be shown to have the status of knowledge, then a foothold is won for political as well as moral standards.

Without such a foothold, he maintained, no philosopher who argued for this position or that as true in ethics would be taken seriously. To which he added: "I am assuming, of course, that a philosopher who is alive today should try to talk to his contemporaries, and by this I mean an audience much wider than the inner circle of his like-minded fellows in the philosophical enterprise." We all know, I think, how seriously Mr. Adler has come to take that obligation.

Later, when he had set up the Institute for Philosophical Research and commenced the project we now know of as *The Idea of Freedom* (1958–61), he described this task in still more general terms—or perhaps I should say, he advance still farther toward the *Summa Dialectica* he had once imagined. The two large volumes devoted to Freedom were a very ambitious undertaking—the work of many hands and the distillation of much study—in which every serious treatment of the subject was considered. Yet the limits of even so vast an effort were acknowledged in the report of its success. "The dialectician's contribution to the pursuit of philosophical truth," Mr. Adler wrote,

> lies solely in the clarification of a field of thought for the sake of progress in that field. The progress itself must be made by the philosopher, not merely by the creative effort which adds new theories or insights but also by the equally creative efforts to supply the arguments and counter-arguments that are called for by the issues which exist and either have not been disputed at all or have been inadequately debated.

And, despite this claim for creativity in dialectic, which Arnold never made for criticism, Mr. Adler subsequently, recalling the very words here quoted, characterized what the Institute had done (by that time, with Love, Progress, Happiness, and Justice, in addition to Freedom) as "second-order work in philosophy . . . of the dialectical type represented by the Institute's efforts to clarify philosophical opinion. . . ." At the same time, he expressed the hope that, if the work of the Institute is ever carried out, "there need be no division of labor between the dialectician working at second-order tasks and philosophers trying to answer first-order questions"; that philosophy "might finally become the collective and cooperative pursuit that it should be." One may recall here Arnold's praise of Goethe as one who, more than any other modern, combined the virtues of the poet and the critic.

The issue between Arnold and Mr. Adler in the matter of art or at least poetry, to which I have referred, is a real one, notwithstanding this similarity in their aims—and its reality is a function, as I have suggested, not so much of the real difference between poetry and philosophy (assuming one knows what the real difference is) as of what seems a different bent of mind in each case. We note the tone of high moral seriousness in Arnold, the "spiritual perfection" he expected not only of criticism but, ultimately, of poetry itself. It is true, the way to this perfection seems in his view to have been psychological, or perhaps the perfection itself was that, at least to start with. His notion, at the time of his preface to *Poems*, was that poetry should have a therapeutic effect, raising the spirit of the reader about the tendency to inertia and mental distress that the age seemed to him to foster. He wanted, as Lionel Trilling has written, "the stability or poise of the faculties which follows upon the *catharsis* Aristotle had described, the quieting of the mind in equilibrium, not the bald presentation of confusion itself." But, for all the Aristotle there is in this—and there is certainly some—Arnold clearly has in mind the reader, not the thing read, as the end, and the poem itself as a means. "His theory of poetry," Trilling acknowledged, "is a theory for mental health." Or in Mr. Adler's terms, what for Aristotle is merely a property of poetry—its moral and psychological effect upon the audience—is for Arnold the essence of the thing. He is thus at bottom a Platonist, not an Aristotelian, in the way he thinks about poetry, like his spiritual descendant in criticism, T.S. Eliot. Of course we find Mr. Adler objecting to any such notion—that is, to the idea that there is a correlation between the goodness of the work of art and the goodness of the man to whom it is directed, on whom it is conceived to have a salutary or an injurious effect. Not "the good man in every sense," but only the man who is "good intellectually, whose aesthetic sensibility is technically trained," is Aristotle's concern in the *Poetics*, Mr. Adler writes—and while I am not sure how complete the correlation between art and virtue really is for Arnold, it is sufficient, I think, to be defining.

The same can be said with respect to education as between Arnold, the reluctant inspector of schools, and Mr. Adler, the critic of them and, in recent years, the proponent of a scheme for their reform. Arnold's belief that the State was the medium through which education could come, and must, is once again Platonic, while it is not surprising to find Mr. Adler recalling that in the *Laws* Plato advocates a Minister of Education who would also be a censor—something Arnold would perhaps not have opposed, were the censor's efforts aimed in the right direction. The "culture" of which he spoke in *Culture and Anarchy* had as its object "to make reason and the Will of God prevail," and Arnold does not let us doubt the moral and ultimately even the religious sense of this—a sense, to be sure, that was not explicitly doctrinal, but which as we consider it has very much the flavor of Christian piety.

We would not expect such a man to trust, as Mr. Adler does trust, the myriad outcomes of classes in locally regulated schools to bring about a social change that is, all the same, hardly less complete, as envisioned, than what Arnold called for. Mr. Adler seems to believe in the capacity of all human beings everywhere to teach themselves what they need to know. Perhaps he would allow that Arnold was right, as far as then could be seen, to lack faith in what struck him as a rabble in the populace, for, when he wrote, the democratic age had hardly begun in the Western world. But it is an interesting contrast, all the same, this trust of Mr. Adler's as compared with the whip that Arnold thought would be needed before "reason and the Will of God" prevailed—interesting because Mr. Adler is so much more severe as a critic than Arnold was, even when taking on poor Bishop Colenso, or the otherwise forgotten Francis Newman, and because severity and trust do not seem temperamentally to go together. It is more than interesting, it is strange to find such trust in reason on the part of a man who finds so little of it going on about him—almost as strange as that a man who believes so strongly in good will, as Arnold did, should have said it must be coerced. But these are perhaps only minor paradoxes in the different philosophical positions, as I think they are, that have been noted here.

George Anastaplo

Democracy and Philosophy: On Yves R. Simon and Mortimer J. Adler

"Then, as the saying goes, 'let a man stand by his brother.' "

—Socrates

I

It is only natural to praise Mortimer J. Adler and Yves R. Simon for that lifelong dedication to truth and the common good evident in their work.

Anyone privileged to work personally with them, and to learn from them, could not help but notice close at hand the traits that help account for the quality of their work. One could see native intelligence, a determination to learn and to teach, and intellectual integrity, all of a high order.

I consider myself fortunate to have been able to study with Mr. Simon, as a graduate student in the Committee on Social Thought at the University of Chicago, and with Mr. Adler, as an associate in the ambitious Paideia program he has developed for secondary education in this country.

II

It is reassuring that these two admirable men should have been able, during their long association, to acknowledge each other's merits.

Whatever differences they had as students of philosophy, the things they agreed upon separated them widely from most of their contemporaries in departments of philosophy and political science in this country and abroad.

Both Mr. Simon and Mr. Adler, in their political works, celebrate the democratic faith. They are very much moderns in this as in other respects. In speaking about them together on this occasion, I may not always speak precisely about either of them. Those who know their work will know as

79

well what needs to be said to modify, in applying to each of them, the things I say further on in these remarks about the type of contemporary theorist of democratic thought that each of them somewhat represents.

III

Both Mr. Simon and Mr. Adler are Thomists. As such, they are respectful of Aristotle. Also, both go beyond Thomism when they praise democracy as the best form of government, at least for the modern world.

We need do little more than mention on this occasion certain critical differences between these two men, on the one hand, and most of their contemporaries, on the other—contemporaries who confidently proclaim that we now know that there are no absolutes and contemporaries who consider it fashionable to insist that one man's vulgarity may be another man's lyric. The most popular alternative approaches, at least in academic circles, to the Adler-Simon approach seem now to be intellectually bankrupt: positivism, relativism, perhaps also historicism. Most participants in this Symposium are apt to regard the Adler-Simon natural-right or natural-law approach as more attractive than the more popular approaches of our day.

An intriguing feature, at least for me, of the Adler-Simon approach, which is so respectful of both Thomas and the ancients, is the massive difference developed by this approach from the greatest of the ancients with respect to political things, a difference which Mr. Simon and Mr. Adler recognize. I presume to suggest that this difference, to which I will turn directly, may depend upon the modern failure to appreciate the depth and subtlety of the ancients. In particular, there may be a failure today to recognize that the ancients did see for what it was worth the good to be found in democracy. Thus, the refusal of the ancients to regard democracy as the very best form of government may not be due, as the contemporary democrat tends to believe, to the limited and limiting circumstances of the ancients. History may be far less important here than the contemporary democrat believes it to be.

IV

A critical problem is implicit in what has already been noticed about the obvious dedication of Mr. Adler and Mr. Simon to both truth and the common good. We can put aside as not decisive here the Scriptural assurance that "you shall know the truth and the truth shall set you free." How that assurance is to be taken depends on what kind of truth is referred to and on what being set free means.

Of course, truth and the common good do go together, but not all the time or all the way. One must wonder whether the contemporary democratic theorist is equipped, intellectually and, even more, temperamentally, to deal with the significant divergences sometimes encountered between truth and the common good. On the other hand, another modern, Thomas Hobbes, recognized that even true philosophy, which he himself espoused, can pose a threat to the common good, and when it does its public expression may properly be curtailed by the ruler who knows what he is doing.

A reminder of the occasional divergence possible between truth and the common good calls to mind the Platonic recourse to the noble lie. Democrats, however, are reluctant to think through the implications of the philosopher's rhetoric, such rhetoric as is obviously employed by Socrates, Plato, and Xenophon, less obviously but nevertheless employed also by Aristotle and Cicero. This reluctance can leave decent democrats prey to those among us who manipulate "communications"—to those, that is, who take readily to deception and hence are not adverse to using ignoble lies.

Among the things that the ancient philosophers believed to be true was the proposition that the many are "constitutionally" unable to grasp all truths that the thoughtful can. That inability contributes to the hostility that the many can be expected to show from time to time toward those who dare to speak certain truths. That inability also contributes to the ability of the unscrupulous to exploit the innocent and to destroy the good. (All this, I should at once add, is aside from, although not unrelated to, the problems derived from the tension between reason and revelation.)

The most thoughtful minds—that is, the true philosophers—depend upon a firm and reliable grasp of nature. It is in large part because of natural differences among men, the ancients argued, that not all can profit in the same way from the truth.

Nature is much more complicated here than the modern democrat believes. For one thing, nature points to a critical difference between superior and inferior. One implication of that difference is the possibility of the existence of the natural slave, an implication which can so arouse the hostility of moderns that they are tempted to repudiate the very recognition of natural differences that that possibility reflects.

Of course, a recognition of natural slavery does not legitimate—indeed, it can even undermine the case for—conventional slavery, which is what almost all slavery has always been. But the proper abhorrence of conventional, or institutionalized, slavery helps turn democrats away from anything that acknowledges natural differences among human beings. The intelligent democrat must concede that some differences may become significant, but they are explained away as due to nurture, not nature. It should be appreciated that although nurture may well account for many differences among people over the centuries, that may not be the whole story.

V

I return now more specifically to Mr. Adler and Mr. Simon in my effort to consider further the modern democrat.

A key element in Mr. Simon's account of politics is *conscience*; a key element for Mr. Adler is the *common sense* of politics. I have the impression that they are looking at the same "phenomena" or are depending upon the same premises in their respective invocations of conscience and common sense. Although Mr. Adler rarely uses the term "conscience," he does work with "common sense" somewhat the way Mr. Simon does with "conscience" in making judgments about the good life and the good society.

It is instructive to notice that one does not find in Aristotle's *Nicomachean Ethics* any term that should properly be translated as *conscience*. Perhaps *thumos* had in it some of the compulsion that we associate with *conscience*. But that which we call conscience seems to have waited upon the emergence of Christianity for its decisive manifestation. In Aristotle's *Politics* that which we call *common sense* is somewhat limited, influenced as it is by the not altogether reliable opinions of the people at large. Political philosophy, as a reasoned account of the nature of political things and the right social order, goes beyond what common sense offers. It seems to be more, or at least something other, than the refinement of common sense that Mr. Adler speaks of. He observes that "everybody through common sense is knowledgeable about what good all men should pursue." But what is the status for common sense of that radical pursuit of truth for its own sake that philosophy, and hence political philosophy, depends upon?

Whatever the difference in terms used by Mr. Adler and Mr. Simon, they seem to agree that the more decent moderns have an improved awareness of what justice calls for in social relations. But, it can be wondered, is the general awareness itself improved or is it merely that conditions are now better for applying standards of justice that thoughtful men have always been aware of?

Mr. Adler and Mr. Simon seem also to agree that it can be useful to refine the natural openness of the human being to justice. Instruction is called for and it is that which they have supplied again and again in an effort to help democrats secure more thoroughly that which they really want.

The differences in the terms used by Mr. Simon and Mr. Adler reflect their distinctive points of departure. One, firmly grounded in his religious heritage, makes much of *conscience*; the other, moved by intense intellectual interests since his youth, makes much of *common sense*. Both are persuaded that moderns are more sensitive to certain moral and social issues, and particularly that the moderns can appreciate, to an extent or in a way that the ancients could not, the natural equality of all men.

One consequence of this heightened respect for the equality of all men is to undermine the legitimacy of measuring one person by another—and this in turn leads to making much of, or at least putting up more with, what each person happens to be. That is, individuality becomes critical, something evident in the list of things that Mr. Simon extols in the closing lines of his *Philosophy of Democratic Government*: "communion with universal nature, the conquest of time through everlasting faithfulness, temperance, dignity in poverty, holy leisure, contemplation." It is the individual who is very much in view at the end of this treatise on politics, not the citizen. Similarly, Mr. Adler concludes his treatise, *The Common Sense of Politics*, by holding out hope of "progress toward fulfilling the capacities for understanding and wisdom, for friendship and love, that are the distinctive powers of the human mind and spirit."

Aristotle's *Politics*, on the other hand, concludes with an extended discussion of the music appropriate in the training of citizens. Thus, the perspective of the political is retained to the end, whatever the moral purposes (as indicated at the end of the *Ethics*) for turning to the *Politics* in the first place. Modernity is characterized, in part, by the tendency to assign to the public life of a community the finest expectations of private life. This is in large part what the Enlightenment means.

VI

Is the ascendancy of the Enlightenment related to the decline of philosophy? The Enlightenment does seem to have contributed to the depreciation of the significance of natural differences among human beings—and hence to the depreciation of that very *nature* upon which philosophy depends.

A vigorous, even ruthless, exploitation of nature may be seen in modern technology, with its conquest of nature. It may be hard to take seriously as a guide that which is to be systematically conquered and exploited. Besides, technology has served to conceal significant natural differences among human beings, making much more instead of the many things that all human beings do have in common. One recalls the frontier pistol known as "the Old Equalizer."

The democratization of philosophy, which the Enlightenment depends upon and encourages, may be seen in the titles of the two books I have drawn upon from Mr. Adler and Mr. Simon. To emphasize, as Mr. Adler does, the common sense of politics, however much that common sense may be occasionally and temporarily refined by philosophy, is to take a democratic approach. It may be usefully compared to such observations as that by Socrates in the *Crito* where he assumes that the opinions of the many are as apt to be wrong as right. Even so, does not common sense instinctively respect the difference between the natural rulers and the natural ruled, however mistaken people may be at any particular time in identifying one or the other? This is not to deny that the fashionable doctrines of a regime can subvert this instinctive respect for the superior.

The democratization of philosophy is even more dramatic in the title of Mr. Simon's book. No one in antiquity, I dare say, would have spoken of any "philosophy of democratic government." Aristotle in his *Politics* spells out the opinions that democrats hold, opinions which seem to be as much in need of correction as those held by oligarchs. Neither set of opinions is considered by him to be philosophical.

The Adler-Simon approach reflects, then, a democratization of the very study of politics—a democratization, perhaps, of political philosophy itself. Such democratization can keep scholars not as gifted as Mr. Simon and Mr. Adler from becoming aware of how perceptive true philosophy can be and how rare the true philosopher is. And this, I have suggested, contributes to the contemporary failure to recognize how much the ancients anticipated the implications of democratic theory, not needing to see them spelled out in action as conditions changed.

VII

Various questions raised by our inquiry remain for further consideration, including whether both the Enlightenment and technology can be safely exploited in the decades ahead. It may be that both have to be risked, considering the size and the complexity we have permitted modern societies to assume. But does not this also mean that the Enlightenment and Technology make truly independent communities on a human scale virtually impossible in the modern world? If so, have we not had to settle for inferior forms of government? Unfortunately, the modern democrat is not likely to be equipped, either by training or by temperament, to take this question and its implications seriously.

The steadily increasing recourse to individuality and privacy in this century may be an instinctive, however self-defeating, response to the growing awareness that the modern form of social organization is not well suited to the natural capacities of human beings. I say "self-defeating" because intermittent despotisms, benevolent or otherwise, lie along the path upon which we are stumbling. Only if we are properly aware of our limitations can we hope to make the best of our situation.

Be all this as it may, we can see in the humane careers of Yves R. Simon and Mortimer Adler the blessings that modernity, with its democratization of everyday life, *can* offer. That is, we see what can happen in those times and places that permit natural talents, no matter how modest their social origins, to develop and flourish. We are all beneficiaries of this development, especially those of us privileged to take advantage of the conscientious work of these two scholars.

Part II
Yves R. Simon

Catherine Green

Freedom and Determination: An Examination of Yves R. Simon's Ontology of Freedom

S imon reacts sharply against the popular conception of freedom as in-determinacy. Such a notion suggests that true freedom must be outside the realm of causal influences, undetermined by any material or accidental cause. Freedom of this nature would be characterized by an absolute unpredictability, similar to the atomic swerve of Epicurus. This understanding of freedom received support when Heisenberg's principle of the indeterminacy of atomic particles became widely known (*FC* 13–15).[1] In the absence of complete determination of ultimate particles, a theory of personal freedom based on radical indeterminacy seemed more plausible. For Simon, freedom of choice is not simply the ability to choose between right and wrong, but is more a perfection which frees us from the ignorance and vice that restrict our ability to choose.

In his discussion of freedom, Simon often uses the notion of the atomic swerve of Epicurus as a foil, because it represents the antithesis of his own understanding of freedom, which is in fact superdetermination within the realm of final causality (*FC* 11, n. 10). As Simon notes, so long as one's understanding of freedom is in terms of material causality and at the level of ultimate particles, the notions of indeterminacy, formlessness, irrationality, etc. are a necessary consequence (*FC* 14–15). Only by looking for causes within the realm of final causality and in relation to fully organized beings can one understand freedom in a way that is consistent with our rational experience of it.

---

[1]Here, Simon notes that the search for freedom was largely centered around the question of freedom of ultimate particles, rather than questioning the possibility of freedom as a function of an organizing unit.

The problem, then, is to understand the difference between the determination that the materialists want to avoid and the determination that Simon wants to acknowledge. For Simon, the matter rests with the kind of causality operating here. Simply put, the nature of the end that is pursued by all creatures is such that, in those creatures where rationality is present, the infinity of the end points up the necessary finitude of any particular object that an agent could desire. The agent, insofar as he is acting rationally, must choose to act in a way that pursues one or another imperfect object.

Any particular object desired is incapable of satisfying the desire for good in terms of either its extent of goodness, or in terms of its duration. This insatiability of desire results from the nature of the final object desired, and forces choices about the relative merit of any particular good pursued. It is this superdetermination by the good that we all desire, and which no particular act can come close to satisfying, that provides the ground for freedom of choice. We will examine here the nature of free choice in relation to the good which is its end. In order to do this, we must look first at the nature of habit. Habit is a necessary basis for freedom and may also be a deterrent to free choice. Understanding the causal nature of habits will help us understand the difference between the two kinds of determinacy that interests us here. Next we will look at the nature of the final cause, that is, the comprehensive good, and the problem of indifference that is necessary to freedom of choice. Finally, we will examine the characteristics of free choice in order to show more clearly how determinacy and freedom inhere in the same act.

I

The issue of habit provides a good example of the problem of formal and material causality in freedom of choice. It is particularly interesting because for Simon, as for Aristotle and Thomas, *habitus* provides a necessary ground for virtue; it is the genus for virtue.

Simon clarifies a distinction between habit, which by its nature does not allow free choice, and *habitus*, which Simon suggests is what Aristotle and Thomas have in mind when speaking of habit as the genus for moral virtue. Simon suggests that the Latin term *habitus* and the Greek term *hexis* have no adequate corrolary in English. To translate *habitus* into "habit" as was frequently the case prior to the 1950s, is to imply an automaticity and a lack of rationality that are not strictly true of either Aristotle's or Thomas' understanding of the issue. It seems clear that, in the case of true habit, there is an absolute determination of the act such that choice is precluded. The cigarette smoker who lights a cigarette only to notice that there is one already burning in the ashtray provides an excellent example of the automaticity of habit. In fact, in virtue, this is precisely why habit is helpful. Habit allows us to act immediately, even unconsciously, to do what we know ahead of time we would choose to do in a given situation.

While habits may support freedom, acts that result from pure habit are not themselves free. In order to make this more clear, we will look at the characteristics of habits in relation to *habitus*. The most important difference is that of voluntariness. Acts grounded in *habitus* are voluntary and therefore conducive to creative or vital thinking, whereas habits lead to acts that are involuntary and even "thoughtless." Voluntary acts are characterized by, first, a knowledge of the particular circumstances, next, a relation to an end, and finally, freedom from constraint (*FC* 19–23).[2] For Simon, the most important issue here is that voluntary acts are directed toward an end. This end is objective, it is conducive to human happiness, and it constitutes the terminus toward which all actions serve as means. The agent must be aware of the specific circumstances of the act *as relative to this final end*. The agent must be cognizant of the specifics of the particular situation and that this act is a means to a greater good. This relation to a determining end provides the crux of human freedom. Freedom from constraint, while important, is less of an issue. Like Aristotle, Simon recognizes that even in cases where constraints are in effect, for example in threats of violence, the agent nevertheless often makes a choice, which, with knowledge of the circumstances, gives the choice some character of the free.

Habits may be developed with an end in mind, as would be the case with defensive driving skills, and to the extent that these habits are truly automatic, they better support the virtue that is their cause. Nevertheless, they are not themselves essentially relative to this end, but rather provide the disposition to act in specific circumstances to carry out the means to the end. Thus, habits are primarily relative to the means rather than to the end. For example, a nurse who gives medications to patients has in mind the end of providing safe, accurate care. The nurse develops the habits of meticulously checking labels and dosages, calling the patient by name and explaining the name and effect of the medicine to the patient prior to administering a drug. Further, the nurse develops the habit of stopping to investigate anything that seems out of the ordinary. The end is safe, accurate care. Habit provides the disposition to carry out consistently a multiplicity

---

[2]Here, Simon uses an example of two drivers, who both end up in the hospital after turning their cars into a ravine to avoid hitting an object in the road, to draw out the essential characteristics of voluntariness.

of specific actions conducive to that end, but it does not bring that end into focus.

Habitus, on the other hand, is precisely that way of being related to the end such that the end is always kept in mind. The nurse, even when very busy with critical patients, remains alert to the final end, rather than becoming lost in the proximate ends that may not be conducive to safe, accurate care. *Habitus* keeps one's mind on the final goal in the midst of difficult and often conflicting particular circumstances. Simon suggests that it is this relationship of habits and *habitus* that allows the creativity and plenitude of virtue. It is the positive relation to the end that induces one to develop good habits. After developing these habits, one has more time and energy to concentrate on the end itself and to be alert to other creative ways to achieve it.

Finally, the necessity of habit is subjective rather than objective. This is best understood in terms of the character of human acts. The nature of human action is such that every act carried out changes the subjective nature of the agent. The character of the will and the intellect and their relation to each other and to their final end are altered with each human act. It is beyond the scope of this paper to discuss at length Simon's understanding of the nature of practical wisdom.[3]

The necessity of *habitus*, on the other hand, is objective. In *habitus*, the agent consciously pursues a particular objective or end, which then deter-

---

[3]Simon's ontology of practical wisdom was examined by this author in a Master's thesis entitled "The Nature of Moral Action: An Examination of Yves Simon's Metaphysics of Morals" (Catholic University of America, 1987). But it is important to note that, in human action, the intellect with its judgment provides the formal determination that this act is good for me. The will, as the efficient cause, first moves the intellect to search more or less vigorously for truth, then moves the particular judgment into action. The nature of both the will and the intellect are changed toward or away from the good by the acts that they specify and enact. They become the matter in a matter-form relation with the good. It is important to recall that Simon insists that will and intellect are active together in the one agent who acts, whose character is changed. This ontological change in the agent is the basis for habit. Each act thus disposes us to act again similarly.

mines specific acts that can truly achieve that end. As one becomes more clear about the true nature of the end desired, one also becomes more clear about what particular acts are truly conducive to that end. Habits determine our actions, then, in the mode of formal and material causality. In the mode of formal causality, they dispose or form the will to act in accordance with their determining factor, i.e., picking up a cigarette. In the mode of material causation, actions carried out in accord with habit change the nature or the matter of the agent such that the form of future actions is limited by this changed nature. The essential characteristics of habit, then, include involuntariness, subjectivity, relation to means rather than ends, and determination in the realm of formal and material causality. *Habitus*, on the other hand, is supremely voluntary, is relative to the objective end, and determines action in the order of final causality. Acts resulting from *habitus* are explicitly rational and thoughtful, since they are explicitly related to the end they support. Simon suggests that, in human action, habits are something akin to a mathematical limit: approachable yet never completely realizable.[4] I would suggest that *habitus* provides a similar limit on the opposite pole. Actions resulting purely from habit would be unconscious; those resulting from *habitus* would be completely conscious of both the nature of the end and the means it determines.

II

Having distinguished the essential differences between habit and *habitus*, we now turn our attention to the final end itself. Simon grounds the understanding of free choice in the nature of the comprehensive good and the relationship between the comprehensive good and the human agent. The comprehensive good determines all actions of man in the manner of a final cause.[5] All creatures act for an end, an end that perfects their nature and that completely determines their acts. For non-rational beings, the relationship to the end is expressed spontaneously through their physical nature. In animals, this determination by the end is known as instinct; in elements, it is known as chemistry. For rational beings, this

---

[4]Simon does not think that in human action pure habits account for very much of the causal relation: "I think that even in actions which we perform out of habit, there is always something else, distinct from, irreducible to and perhaps even opposed in character to what we call habit. Thus purely mechanical habit is a kind of 'limit,' something that can be approached without any definite restrictions, but which can never be attained" (*MV* 48).

[5]Yves R. Simon, "To Be and To Know," in *Chicago Review* 14 (Spring, 1961): 89.

relationship to the end is also expressed spontaneously through all the actions of the will. But this relationship has the further possibility of being expressed voluntarily when the agent is aware of the fact that particular acts are conducive to his happiness. Finally, this relationship can be expressly chosen when the agent chooses to pursue the good not simply as good for him, but as good in itself. The good that determines human action must be understood in terms of its possible relations to man. The comprehensive good is such that it can be realized in all the possible goods any agent might desire. Every act an agent carries out is a means to this end, but, because of the finite nature of human acts, each act fails to realize the infinity of the end. The comprehensive good itself is neither finite, as are particular human goods, nor infinite, as is the infinite good. But the comprehensive good is infinite in its capacity to include the infinity of possible goods in which it can be realized. The comprehensive good might best be understood as the totality of all goods possible to the entire community of man: all human perfection for all time. Each individual person, then, strives for the perfection of his unique character within the context of this possible perfection for all of mankind.

No matter how good any particular action is, if it is pursued to the exclusion of all other particular goods, it necessarily destroys the agent. We are reminded of the allegory of the cave in Plato's *Republic*, where, after going out of the cave, the philosopher finally is able to see the sun, the highest good. But he cannot simply stay in the world of mathematical objects and ideal forms to contemplate the good. Still a mortal, he must attend to the activities of daily life as well. The nature of his finite relation to the infinite good forces him to choose between the lesser of two evils, death by starvation, or return to the cave and the land of the *polis*. The comprehensive good, though, is not Plato's ideal form of the good. What we find here is that, rather than choosing between two evils, the truly free agent chooses among a variety of goods.

When we recognize that any particular act, while satisfying some aspect of our desire, is nevertheless unable to satisfy us completely, we are forced to choose whether we wish to act on it or perhaps to pursue some other good that is more complete. This choice is the necessary condition for freedom. But how can a choice be both determined and free? To make a choice is to decide in favor of one thing rather than another. If the choice is free, what determines that one pole of the choice be excluded and one accepted? Simon suggests that this issue often confuses the problem of freedom (FC 120–21). The agent is determined by the comprehensive good to act in ways that pursue some aspect of the good. Using his intellect to evaluate the truth of the good he desires, the agent recognizes the necessary partiality of each particular good. He is not determined to pursue this or that particular good, but he is determined to act in some fashion that has an aspect of the good. This provides an indifference of the judgment: he recognizes that either act has aspects of good and limitations.

Simon suggests that passive indifference, of the sort, "I don't know quite what I want," is commonly confused with freedom. He correlates this with the doubt found in theoretical judgments. The person recognizes that he lacks important data, and is unsure of the correct solution. This indifference results from a lack of knowledge and determination, a lack of perfection, and leads to relative inaction. The more severe the indetermination, the more difficult it becomes to act. This passive indifference is contrasted with active indifference, in which the agent recognizes that, while both actions are lacking in perfection, one may have more of the character of the good and thus be more worthy, or perhaps that both are equally good and limited. In either case, his determination by the good provides enough surplus actuality to endow one pole of the choice with enough good to move it into action. The nature of the comprehensive good is such that, by desiring it, the agent is endowed with actuality, with a real ability to act. The agent is able to say of any object desired that this object is one that is good for him and he will now move to achieve it.[6]

This determination to act in accordance with goods desired provides the agent with both the ability and the necessity of making choices. In practical judgments, the intellect evaluates the aspects of goodness of any object desired and presents a suggested action to the will.[7] The suggested

---

[6]"In stopping the deliberation, in bringing it about that such a judgment is last, the will acts according to the actuality which its adherence to the universal essence of the good confers upon it. . . . Because of its natural determination it possesses enough actuality to add to the least of particular goods all the surplus of goodness which it needs in order to be found constituted of absolutely desirable good" (FC 150).

[7]It is important to note that in order to understand Simon's conception of practical judgments, it is necessary always to keep in mind that the distinction between will and intellect is a purely formal one. In all cases, it is a unified agent who acts. The rational agent is a complex but nevertheless unified being. To become too enamored of the will or intellect as separate entities is to miss the most important aspect of the practical judgment, that is, the necessary interrelation of the faculties to make a whole.

action takes into account the necessary limitations of the good it can achieve. The will, depending on its objective relation to the good as true, is more or less disposed to act immediately in accordance with the judgment presented by the intellect.[8] The will, then, is determined by the good in two ways. In all rational beings, the comprehensive good determines the agent to act in accordance with some form of the good. In persons who have more often exercised their rationality in choosing one good over another, the good as true or that which is good in itself will be more apparent, and they will be more disposed to act in accord with it.

Here, it might be worthwhile to look at the determination of habit versus that of the good. As we saw earlier, habit disposes us to act in a specific way, automatically, and without much rational consideration, perhaps with none at all. Habits can be developed to dispose us to act in accordance with the good as true, or they may develop in such a way that they dispose us to act in accordance with our appetites. The good determines us to act first of all in accord with it, regardless of what form that might take. The good further determines us to acknowledge that there exists a discrepancy between the relative plenitude of the particular good we desire and the comprehensive good as such. It determines us to make a choice between this good and another, both bearing some aspect of good and some greater aspect of privation. Habit determines us to act in a specific way; the good determines us to choose between particular acts.

III

We have seen the nature of man's finite relation to the comprehensive good and the indifferent judgment that necessarily results from that radically unequal relationship. We are now ready to turn to the problem of freedom itself. Both voluntariness and choice are necessary for freedom of choice. As we saw earlier, voluntary actions are identified by their relation to a specific end, their lack of constraint, and their being enacted with knowledge of the particular circumstances that prevail. Choice, while found in the realm of voluntary acts, is not necessarily coextensive with that realm (*FC* 28). Choice is of a means rather than an end and regards an act that is within the capabilities of the agent, an act that is really possible. As we saw earlier, voluntary acts are toward an end rather than a means.

---

[8] It must be remembered here that the objective relation of the will to the intellect is the initial determining factor that inclines the intellect to search more or less vigorously for truth. Thus, the subjective character of the will, of the agent really, is the most important issue in practical wisdom.

Choices require rationality, while voluntary acts require at least recognition of the particular circumstances and that they are conducive to some other good.

The relationship between the agent and the comprehensive good, then, is that the agent wills the end and chooses specific means toward this end. Earlier, we saw that for Simon the end determines all acts of rational and nonrational agents. How, then, can we say that we will the end? This can be understood in two ways. First, there are proximate ends that are not specifically determined by the final end as comprehensive. These proximate ends have the character of means to the final end, in which sense they may be chosen, and also have the character of being ends in themselves, in which sense they may be voluntary or willed. The other way we can understand the voluntariness of our actions toward the comprehensive good is in willing it as true, as good in itself. The particular acts in which the comprehensive good is realized are not necessarily moral or good as such, but may be simply good for the agent at the time. The consciously rational agent recognizes that there exists a correlation between actions that are good in themselves and the extent and duration of the enjoyment he experiences as a result. The agent, then, is inclined to choose acts that have more of the character of the good as such. Thus, the end determines us to pursue good, but our specific relationship to this end is both willed and chosen by us. It is chosen in the sense that specific acts we choose change our attitude toward the end. If we choose actions that are directed toward the good as true, our position *vis á vis* the good is altered and becomes more accurate. Pursuit of the good is voluntary in the sense that we then will the end as true. It is important to remember that this change in the agent that results from actions is a metaphysical rather than a psychological change. Thus, while the good as comprehensive may not itself have moral specification, all actions change the relation of the agent to the good as true and in fact do change the moral character of the agent in question. Thus, no actions seem to be morally neutral.

Simon discusses two different levels of freedom. Initial freedom is that found in all rational creatures and results from the very fact that they are rational and are determined by the comprehensive good. They are thus forced to make choices about the means for reaching this end. Freedom, then, is intrinsic, resulting from our rational and appetitive nature, and in a sense cannot be destroyed by extrinsic forces. Those who choose to exercise their rationality more fully in pursuit of truth and wisdom become free in a higher sense. Simon speaks often of the plenitude found in true freedom. This plenitude results from the nature of the good for which we strive. For the person who is free in the immature sense, the choice is often between exercising rationality in evaluating this good or simply following sensuous desire. The choice, then, is necessarily limited. For those who choose to exercise their rationality to the greatest extent possible, the number of real options becomes almost infinite, because the comprehensive good is such that it can be truly realized in infinitely many particular acts. The rational agent thus can choose among a variety of acts, all of which are truly good. Real freedom, then, is directly proportional to the exercise of rationality. The difference between this and Plato's ideal good is that, for Plato, the exercise of rationality occurs most perfectly only in the realm of theoretical contemplation, not in the practical realm. Thus, to be forced to make practical choices has a necessary aspect of evil: one is forced to turn away from the good. For Plato, the ideal good demands spontaneous theoretical assent. Such assent is necessary as soon as one sees the good; it is not voluntary, it is not chosen, and it is not free. We see here, however, that the exercise of free choice is necessarily experienced only in the practical realm. To exercise one's freedom is to make choices that lead toward the good, not away from it. For us, the comprehensive good demands practical choices, freedom.

The terminus of freedom for Simon is found in the agent who is both free and autonomous, that is, in the agent who has made the good internal. He has consistently pursued truth and acted in accord with it to the extent that his nature has taken on the character of the good as true. Terminal freedom ends up bearing a striking resemblance to what Simon speaks of as the good intuitively and intelligently grasped: "Adherence to the comprehensive good intuitively and intelligently grasped is the most voluntary, the least constrained, the least coerced, the most spontaneous of all actions. Yet this supremely voluntary action involves no choice and accordingly no freedom" (FC 27).

In examining the issue of the comprehensive good intuitively and intelligently grasped, Simon is trying to make clear that there exists at least one possible instance in which voluntary action is not at the same time free. In this case, the action of willing the end meets all the criteria of voluntariness, i.e., relation to the end, lack of constraint, and intellectual understanding of the specific circumstances prevailing. It is also completely spontaneous in the sense that this adherence to the true good follows naturally from the intuitive grasp of it. The comprehensive good determines all action toward it. The intuitive, intelligent grasp of the good would be a case in which theoretical and practical knowledge coalesce, such that, when the truth of the good is grasped, the act of willing it is then determined by the nature of the comprehensive good. Voluntariness results from the good willed as true; complete determination results from the nature of the good willed as comprehensive.

The question then is whether this can be called freedom. Here, there is no longer any choice. The agent is fully determined by the nature of the object and by his recognition of it as true. As we saw earlier, choices are strictly relative to means rather than ends. Insofar as the agent is capable of acting or of making choices, he would be free in the highest sense. He would only be choosing among specific means that truly characterize the good. He would not be free to will another end. Recall that it is strictly proper to speak of freedom only in terms of the means to the final end, and not in relation to the end itself. Given the necessarily finite nature of human creatures, it seems unlikely that terminal freedom as such could be found among men. Nevertheless, the continuum between initial freedom and terminal freedom constitutes an endless range of human possibilities as regards the perfection of this uniquely human capacity.

Freedom of choice, then, is a function of rationality and is perfected in correlation with the perfection of practical wisdom. Freedom cannot be separated from virtue. Virtue is the *habitus* necessary for true freedom. Freedom is a necessarily intrinsic quality and, as such, cannot be destroyed by incarceration or other external elements. While habits support the development of freedom, they do not allow for freedom, to the extent that they are strictly automatic. Thus, the determination by habits is of the sort that denies free choice. On the other hand, determination by the comprehensive good, in relation to man's rational being, is the necessary and sufficient ground for freedom.

S. Iniobong Udoidem

Metaphysical Foundations of Freedom In the Social and Political Thought Of Yves R. Simon

What is freedom? This is a perennial question in the history of philosophical thought. Any attempt to give it a clear-cut answer always results in the kind of perplexity that St. Augustine discovered when asked, "What is time?"[1] We often use the word "freedom" in our daily discourse and endeavors, yet when asked what we mean by it, we find it hard to explain. Common usage of the notion of freedom shows this ambiguity. For example, nations have gone to war claiming to defend freedom, and what to others appears as aggression has been justified as support for "freedom fighters." Children have absconded from families in search of freedom, and marriages have broken up on account of denials of or demands for freedom. The feminist movement has been described as a phenomenon reflecting a search for freedom by women. People have served time in prison for defending freedom. In the face of these confusing attitudes regarding freedom, one is lead to wonder not only what is "freedom," but also whether freedom is possible at all, and what the conditions are of its possibility.

In response to these metaphysically grounded questions, scholars in the behavioral sciences (like Herbert Spencer, Sigmund Freud, and B.F. Skinner), who, in the wake of the modern reaction against metaphysical

---

[1]St. Augustine, *The Confessions of Saint Augustine*, trans. and ed. John K. Ryan, 2 vols. (New York: Doubleday, 1960), 2: 287.

and non-empirical knowledge, attempted to apply the strict deterministic laws of the physical sciences to human studies, have argued that there is no such thing as freedom, since all human actions must necessarily have causes. For them, talking about freedom is talking about an illusion. But, as Antonio Moreno points out, even their theory, i.e., interpretation of physical realities, is nothing but an exercise in freedom of choice among several possible hypotheses.[2] Einstein, too, admitted that the fundamental principles of physics "cannot be extracted from experience but must be freely invented."[3] These assertions by physical scientists point to the fact that even with scientific determinism there is still a way of acting that supports our sense of freedom.

Among those who defend the reality of freedom in human society, we find thinkers like P.J. Proudhon, J. Rousseau, K. Marx, R.P. Wolf, and others, who, because they want absolute freedom for the individual, call for a society without political authority. But others, like Jacques Maritain, Yves R. Simon, Mortimer Adler, Robert Neville, and R.T. DeGeorge, take a more moderate view of the relation between the individual and society and defend freedom within social bounds.[4]

Yves R. Simon's special contribution consists in his formulation of the basic metaphysical assumptions in which the notion of freedom is grounded. As he sees it, freedom is not opposed to authority and determination, for these actually provide the framework for its authentication. In this paper, I propose to examine Simon's explanation of this complex relationship between freedom and authority. My approach will be more of an interpretive exercise than a critical review.

Yves R. Simon first made public his ideas about freedom in his Aquinas lecture at Marquette University in 1940, in which he argued emphatically that "social happiness depends on the felicitous combination of authority and freedom" (NF 1). In all his works after then, he consistently maintained that freedom is an essential element in human sociability and that, far from opposing each other, in their essential relation authority and freedom are complementary.

---

[2]Antonio Moreno, "The Heisenberg Uncertainty Principle and Free Will," *Proceedings of the American Catholic Philosophical Association* 1 (1976): 14.

[3]Albert Einstein, *Essays in Science*, trans. A. Harris (New York: Philosophical Library, 1934), 17.

[4]For philosophical discussions on the nature, structure, and scope of freedom in this tradition, see George McLean, ed., *Freedom: Proceedings of the American Catholic Philosophical Association* (1976).

In the 1940 Aquinas lecture, Simon defined freedom as the power to choose among the means to a proper end. He argued that freedom takes place in deliberate actions rather than by chance, that freedom is experienced when we feel we dominate a situation. Thus, for Simon, freedom is mastery—the mastery that is attained when the will is infallibly directed toward man's ultimate end. Contained in this notion of mastery are the intrinsic elements of freedom that Simon describes as *superdetermination, autonomy, and free choice* (FC 158).

I. Superdetermination

Freedom as superdetermination is characterized by a unidirectional choice. To understand what this means, we must take note of the two types of freedom that Simon distinguishes, namely, initial freedom and terminal freedom. Initial freedom is the capacity of choosing either the good or the bad, while terminal freedom is the disposition that enables one to choose the good only. This means that while initial freedom, which is sometimes called free choice, contains the possibility of error, terminal freedom, which is the true *freedom of choice*, excludes the possibility of error. It is this terminal freedom that Simon says is metaphysically inseparable from autonomy. Commenting on Simon's notion of terminal freedom, Clarke Cochran notes that for Simon freedom consists in the superdetermination that enables man to choose the proper means to his end from the variety available to him. It depends on the possession of virtue and strength of character, which allow him to keep what is good and good for him clearly in view.[5]

As a supreme example of a superdetermined freedom, Simon points to the absolute freedom of God, which proceeds from the absolute necessity of the divine perfection, the absolute necessary achievement of the divine Being. Something like this is also true of human endeavors, for every accomplished virtue guarantees its own performance. For example, to have prudence means not only to know what is right, but actually doing the right thing. In other words, chosen and guided by prudence, our actions are superdetermined. The freedom of choosing is not taken away. On the contrary, when there is no longer any possibility of making a wrong choice, freedom is exalted.

The crucial point to bear in mind here is that the end as such is not the object of choice. Choice, *electio*, is concerned with means. Since freedom is

---

[5]Clarke E. Cochran, "Authority and Freedom: The Democratic Philosophy of Yves R. Simon," *Interpretation* 6:2 (1977): 111.

manifested in the power of choosing the means within the limits defined by the end, any condition that puts the end itself at risk is profoundly in conflict with the very essence of freedom and being. This is why Simon says that "the most serious imperfection of human freedom lies in its ability to choose evil" (*FAC* 41). Anything, therefore, that removes the possibility of a wrong choice and enhances firm adherence to the end—*bonum in communi*—represents an unqualified improvement of the will and the freedom of the individual. For example, in submitting to legitimate authority, the predominant inclination of the will no longer conflicts but spontaneously agrees with the precepts of law, and the law becomes interior to the will. In such a case, as Maritain has argued, terminal freedom becomes both freedom of choice and autonomy (*FMW* chap. 1).

Simon holds that freedom is promoted by any social environment that gives the individual "more firmness, more cool-headedness, more self-control, more clear-sightedness, a more lucid insight into his own aspirations and the end he has to pursue" (*FAC* 41). And just as the personal freedom of choice is exalted by the removal of the indifference of potentiality, so the freedom of the group is exalted by the suppression of the disorderly forces that tend to impair a resolute course in common action. Thus, the interiorization of the law is as valuable to the social body as it is to the individual. Simon writes:

> Just as an individual person, through virtue, protects himself against the risk of making wrong choices, so a group, a society or a political body may effectively strengthen its loyalty to the common good by incorporating into its legal structure, its customs, uses, and collective beliefs, tendencies spontaneously agreeing with the common good (*FAC* 46).

In other words, the common good as the end of common action and of law becomes the superdetermined source of freedom for the community as well as the individual.

The questions that are likely to be raised here are, "But does not such superdetermination represent actually an infringement on freedom? How can internal direction of an autonomous person be compatible with direction by an external authority?" Simon solves this dilemma by arguing that an autonomous person, because he accepts the precedence of the common good over his particular good, interiorizes both the law and the authority that aim at the common good. Thus, the traffic regulations or tax laws, rather than being external commands or sanctions, represent for such a person but the normal embodiments of a moral obligation to support the common good. In the case of a political society, it is this commitment to the common good that makes the citizens freely accept the authority of the government at the same time as that government safeguards the autonomy and freedom of the citizens. For it is only when the citizens are free that they can become creative, innovative, and better disposed to serve the community effectively. An ultimate commitment to the common good and the human end is thus revealed as a superdetermined source of human freedom, and we come to understand that without a fundamental commitment to the common good and human vocation, there is no true freedom.

II. Autonomy

In the context of our discussion, autonomy may be defined as the climax of a process of interiorization of the law of being (*FAC* 15; *CF* 30). While similar to the Kantian notion,[6] this understanding of autonomy is by no means the same as Kant's. The big difference is that in Kant the autonomous law is of the self exclusively, whereas Simon allows for the possibility of an external law being recognized and interiorized by the self. This interiorization takes place when a human being, in the exercise of his rationality, wills and chooses the proper means that lead to his or her rational end as a human being. When this happens, the person is said to be self-governed or exercising autonomy.

Metaphysically speaking, a person is radically composed of two elements, namely, the subsistent individual and his or her rational soul. These two elements have led to two interpretations of autonomy. One is characterized by an emphasis on the individuality of the person and inevitably leads to the spirit of arbitrariness. The other is characterized by an emphasis on the rationality of human nature and leads firmly to the appreciation of its laws. For example, what is called natural law is divine law as revealed by reason, and man-made laws, if they are to be just, must reflect that natural law. A person, then, is said to exercise autonomy in his or her free choice of a proper means to a rational end. In a further explanation, Simon distinguishes between absolute autonomy and relative autonomy. An absolute autonomy is attained when an agent is said to be identical with its law. This is the kind of autonomy that Kant advocates. But this, Simon says, applies only to God. In the case of relative autonomy, which is proper to human persons, an agent is autonomous when its law, without being identical with its being, dwells in it and governs it from within, so that the spontaneous inclinations of the agent coincide with the exigencies of the law (*FAC* 18). This is the kind of autonomy attainable by created ra-

---

[6]Immanuel Kant, *Foundations of the Metaphysics of Morals*, trans. Lewis W. Beck (Indianapolis: Bobbs-Merrill, 1980), 30.

tional beings. It has the character of a vocation, a conquest, or a terminal accomplishment. In other words, when a person has, through rational endeavors, achieved a state of choosing only means that would lead to true human good, he is said to be self-dependent, self-governed, and autonomous. When the choice is made in accordance with human vocation, autonomy is perfected.

III. Freedom of Choice

The expression "freedom of choice" has at least two meanings. In one sense, it implies that the choice is free from impediments or coercion and is made between alternatives. But, for Simon, this type of choice has only the character of an initial and rather illusory freedom. For this sense of freedom of choice contains the possibility of making a wrong as well as a right choice with regard to the means to our desired end. Simon writes:

> Freedom is the power to make a choice between the means offered to our activity. Now, there are authentic means, those which lead to the end, and illusory means, those which lead us away from our end. Freedom to choose illusory means is itself only an illusion of freedom, for a means which does not lead to the end is not a means (FAC 4).

A bad means leads us away from our supreme end and is thus not a means in the true sense of the word, since it does not lead to the proper end. To remove the possibility of a bad choice, therefore, is, for Simon, "to liberate free will from a deceitful appearance and to restore to it its genuine object—the veritable means, the means which leads to the end" (FC 106). The possibility of a choice that excludes the choice of a wrong means is thus the second and more profound meaning of freedom of choice.

This second sense of freedom of choice, which precludes the possibility of error or falsehood, Simon calls "terminal freedom." It is a free choice properly so called, because the volition of the end contains the choice of the means. Here, the predominant inclinations of the will no longer conflict, but spontaneously agree with the precepts of the law that has become interior to the will. The choice in this instance, Simon says,

> proceeds not from any weakness, any imperfection, any feature of potentiality on the part of the agent but, on the contrary, from a plenitude of being and an abundance of determination, from an ability to achieve mastery over diverse possibilities and from a strength of constitution which makes it possible to attain one's end in a variety of ways (FC 153).

For Simon, then, it is the adherence to the true means that perfects freedom of choice precisely as free choice. This is the point that he insists must be understood, if we are to understand the metaphysics of his theory of freedom. Thus based on the distinction between illusory freedom and authentic freedom, false means and true means, initial freedom and ter-minal freedom, his ontological framework persuasively accommodates in-dividual autonomy with political authority in the service of the community.

Within this structure, authority is seen both as an independent act and as a means to freedom, while freedom is understood as necessarily calling for the exercise of authority. And what may have at first appeared as enig-matic assertions now make perfect sense: "The more definitely a com-munity is directed toward its common good and protected from disunity in its common action, the more perfect and the more free it is" (*PDG* 141). And so Simon is able to conclude that "what we find at the core of the most essential function of authority is that autonomy renders authority neces-sary and authority renders autonomy possible" (*PDG* 71). In other words, authority and freedom, rather than being opposed to each other, are con-nected by complementary and constitutive relations. At the ontological level, there is no question of the priority of one over the other, because they are mutually constitutive. This constitutive character is found already in individual autonomy. For only an autonomous and free person is capable of exercising authority. If there is no freedom, there can be no authority; and if there were no authority, freedom would not be known to exist.

This interpretation cannot but have a salutary effect in the modern world, where the notion of freedom has been for the most part grossly mis-construed. Our freedom and autonomy are grounded ontologically in our individuality. But Simon correctly reminds us that our freedom and autonomy as rational persons are authenticated and perfected only through interiorization of just laws: divine, natural, or human. This is the kind of understanding that should make everyone realize the value of being free citizens. For it is only the truly free individual who can be both creative and law abiding. Thus, constitutional governments that guarantee freedom for their citizens will not only be respected; they will also prosper. Moreover, freedom and authority so understood will reveal forms of governments and institutions as instruments and mediating structures for self-government, freedom, and autonomy for lesser communities as well as individuals. And such enhanced shared responsibility and respect-ability among citizens belonging to different groups could even spill over into relations among nations. And then the whole world would come to understand that freedom as well as authority is a necessary condition of human development and progress.

Robert J. Mulvaney

Freedom and Practical Rationality in The Thought of Yves R. Simon

Yves R. Simon (1903–1961) was one of the greatest modern students of the ancient virtue of practical wisdom, called *phronesis* by Aristotle, and *prudentia* by Aristotle's great Christian commentators in the Middle Ages, such as Saint Thomas Aquinas. Simon's interest in this issue was both theoretical and practical. He was concerned with the role of practical wisdom in resolving major modern moral problems, particularly in social and political philosophy, such as the problem of freedom and authority in a democracy. But he was also concerned with the profound foundational problems underlying the virtue of practical wisdom, particularly those in moral epistemology. In addition, he was uncommonly aware of the specific historical vicissitudes that led to the decline of practical wisdom as a central feature of modern moral philosophy. The revolution in epistemology we associate with figures like Descartes had momentous repercussions, not only in the foundations of mathematics and natural science and in basic metaphysical issues, but also in moral and political philosophy, and in the psychology of the human act. Modern ideals of a unified science, the triumph of the deductive method, and the mechanical interpretation of nature were involved in this revolution. They constitute some of the elements in a rich concept of "modernity." At least one utterly new chapter came to be written in the history of Western civilization, entitled "The Social Sciences."

Two texts, largely unknown these days, show some of these developments. Both date from the mid-seventeenth century. Both support the generalization that the Age of Descartes is a critical one in the history of practical wisdom. In 1653,[1] a book appeared by the Spanish Jesuit Baldesar Gracian that was soon to become something of a minor classic. It was entitled *Oraculo Manual y Arte de Prudencia*. Literally rendered, the title is *The Oracle, Handbook and Art of Prudence*. The book went into innumerable editions and translations, some of which are instructive. One of the first English translations remains quite close to the original title: *The Art of Prudence; or a Companion for a Man of Sense* (1702). The first Latin translation goes in part: . . . *De prudentia civili et maxime aulica* (1731). Schopenhauer's translation was (again in part) . . . *Kunst der Weltklugheit* (1861). The modern English version (1892) is close to Schopenhauer: "The Art of Worldly Wisdom."

No book about prudence so vividly exemplifies its crisis as this one. Part of the tradition of courtly literature stretching into the Renaissance, it is clearly a proto-Dale Carnegie manual, designed to assist the early modern yuppie in the techniques needed to get on at the court. It is egoistic, amoral, and this-worldly. Perhaps most importantly, it is a book of maxims, easily remembered techniques for survival in a world of political intrigue and ambition. And, of course, it is at the antipodes of the concept of practical wisdom championed by Aristotle and Aquinas. For them, practical wisdom is sharply distinguished from all forms of technique. For them, although there is a monastic form of such wisdom, it is primarily social and political in nature, having the common good for its end and not primarily the private good. A title such as *The Art of Prudence* would seem almost a contradiction in terms.

An equally fascinating text survives from no less a figure than the illustrious Gottfried Wilhelm Leibniz. Not usually taken as a moral philosopher, Leibniz in fact considered himself chiefly a moralist and wrote much on ethics throughout his life. Some scholars have taken the *Monadology* as a kind of foundation for an aristocratic ethics. In a relatively obscure text early in his career, Leibniz has an interesting analysis of Aristotle's theory of intellectual virtue. When he comes to the doctrine of practical wisdom, he finds Aristotle troubling. How can there be a virtue that is both moral and intellectual, both perfective of the understanding in its practical employment and of the concrete actions performed by flesh

---

[1]For these bibliographical details, see the appendix to Joseph Jacob's introduction to his translation, *The Art of Worldly Wisdom* (New York: Macmillan, 1943), l–liv.

and blood people acting in the world? The Cartesian revolution of mind and matter is powerfully operative in Leibniz's notes. I quote a brief excerpt: "Prudence is nothing other than the habit of seeing in each case what is useful. Art indeed [is the habit of] doing [in each case what is useful]: the former is an impression in the cognitive parts; the latter an habituation in the active [parts]. The former is found in knowledge of precepts, the latter is the exercise itself. . ."[2] In other words, practical wisdom is a kind of science, and art the habit of acting in accordance with that science. A wisdom that is neither science on the one hand, nor art on the other, seems to elude the Sage of Hannover.

It did not elude Yves R. Simon, and part of my motivation in introducing my paper with these two somewhat antiquated texts is to show that Simon's recovery of practical wisdom is a profound challenge to some key elements in modern ethical theory. Practical wisdom is not science, it is not art, it is not self-centered. All three of these elements enter into the modern concept of "prudence." Practical wisdom, then, is not "prudence," and its intelligibility offers special problems to modern consciousness. Simon saw these problems more clearly, I think, than any recent commentator.

It will be impossible to do justice in a short paper to the manifold dimensions of the topic I have chosen. What I can begin to accomplish here is an account of the way in which Simon integrates the practical understanding and the will into the final moral action, subsequent on all deliberation and internal choice. This in itself is a vast task, and I shall limit myself to two texts, the recently reprinted *Freedom of Choice* and the unpublished *Practical Knowledge* recently edited by me, after an important start by Ralph Nelson and Ernest Briones.[3] My paper, then, will be a kind of preview of some of the last things Simon wrote about practical wisdom and its relationship to other moral psychological issues, especially those connected with the will.

The first chapter of the unpublished *Practical Knowledge* consists of the famous article Simon published in 1961 in *The New Scholasticism*, entitled "Introduction to the Study of Practical Wisdom."[4] This article was intended by Simon himself to be the first chapter of his projected book on

---

[2]Gottfried Wilhelm Leibniz, "Notae ad Jacobum Thomasium," *Sämtliche Schriften und Briefe*, Academy Edition, VI, 1, 60.

[3]*Practical Knowledge*, unpublished at the time of this paper, has been accepted for publication by Fordham University Press.

[4]Yves R. Simon, "Introduction to the Study of Practical Wisdom," *The New Scholasticism* XXXV (1961): 1–40 (hereafter referred to as "Introduction").

practical knowledge. It is a masterful study of one of the most difficult aspects of the classic virtue of practical wisdom, the element of "command," "imperium." No feature of the Thomistic or Aristotelian theory of practical wisdom is as difficult to accommodate to modern dualistic theories of thought and action as this one, in spite of its clear conformity with common sense. As Alasdair MacIntyre has observed, the "following" in "following orders" should be no more mysterious than the "following" in "following premises." If in the one case an action "follows," and in the other a propositional conclusion "follows," the relationship can still be described in quasi-inferential terms.[5] Simon saw this as clearly as anyone in our time, and pursued its depths more thoroughly.

I do not mean to deny that the theory has difficulties. It is one thing to say that an action "follows" upon deliberation and that a "command" follows upon an exhaustive analysis of the rules and circumstances of a specific moral action. But the concept of command involves a metaphysical dimension that is still challenging and paradoxical. Command, we are told, is the "form" of action; that is to say, it is the specific ideal component of it. It is "as practical as action itself."[6] This formal identity of a command and the action directed by it holds great problems for Cartesian and post-Cartesian metaphysics. Again, if indeed we are to avail ourselves of Aristotelian terminology at all, the temptation is to claim that command may be the form of some internal choice, but surely not of the external action performed. In this case, it seems that we ought to employ some theory of technique or of art as the specifying formality of action. This is how I take the reasoning of Leibniz in the text cited earlier, articulated under the enormous weight of Descartes' new philosophy.

One way to overcome this difficulty is to use the analogy of analyzing one and the same action teleologically as well as efficiently. If I open the door to let the cat out, I can explain the sequence of events both mechanically and intentionally. If both explanations are true and complementary, then why may I not understand each moment of that decision as involving complementary specifying forms? The door remains a door, turning on its hinges, in conformity with relevant laws of nature. But it is equally an instrument of my choice, conforming to analogous laws in the domain of choice and decision. Overlapping explanations may offend some principle

---

[5]See Alasdair MacIntyre, *After Virtue*, 2nd edition (Notre Dame: University of Notre Dame Press, 1984), 161–62; also, MacIntyre's *Whose Justice? Which Rationality?* (Notre Dame: University of Notre Dame Press, 1988), 138–40.

[6]Simon, "Introduction," 4.

of parsimony, but they are not incompatible.

The concept of command invites us to analyze a given human action in terms of all four causes. Command provides the formal and final dimensions of this etiology. Although we primarily associate the concept of form with non-ethical explanation, no definitional necessity requires this custom. Formal explanation is also appropriate in the realm of practice, not merely at a remove from action, but at the moment of action itself, as Simon says: "... when the distance between thought and action is nil, when thought has come down into the complex of human action to constitute its form, it is described as practical in an absolutely appropriate sense."[7] The conclusion of the practical syllogism, then, the action itself, is a conclusion of a deliberative process in which the primary element, the command, is not anterior to the action performed, but an integral metaphysical component, on the model of form in a natural or artificial object.

Having said all this, we ought still to be somewhat troubled. There is a persistent tendency to telescope the quasi-syllogistic account of action found in Aristotle into the inferential structure of the theoretical syllogism. This is one way of defining "intellectualism." But the scientific and moral syllogisms are throughout radically different. Aristotle's sharp distinction between *sophia* and *phronesis* is his challenge to this intellectualism. Unlike the theoretical syllogism, the practical syllogism is marked by change and contingency. The rule might be otherwise, the means to the end might be otherwise, and the action performed might be otherwise. Human action is necessarily conditioned by the particularities of time and space, embedded in the situational circumstances of human life, in the "mystery" of matter, one might say. There are huge constraints upon the intelligibility of moral decision and of moral action. The ever-present necessity to act can obscure these constraints. Deliberation of itself can proceed ad infinitum, since the conditions in which action takes place are necessarily infinitely complex. This aspect of deliberation can produce in the agent an anxiety that can frustrate resolve and block action altogether. One might argue that only the external and non-rational circumstances of time and place can terminate deliberation, a dimension of situationalism that lends that theory peculiar force. Thomas Aquinas himself seems unusually sensitive to the temporal dimension of practical wisdom and stresses the knowledge of things past, present, and future as properly involved in the virtue of

---

[7]*Ibid.*, 5.

prudence.[8]

Neither Thomas Aquinas nor Yves R. Simon takes the situationalist route, of course. Simon, to return to him, instead invokes the second great challenge to intellectualism, after Aristotle's distinction between wisdom and prudence. He takes a step outside the realm of cognition, and into the realm of will. However much we may wish to argue that there is a doctrine of will in ancient Western philosophy, it is clear that the major impetus for such a theory comes from another tradition entirely, that of Jewish and Christian myth. The stories of fall and redemption, of divine law, of personal responsibility and choice, all determined a different mode of moral psychological explanation in Western philosophy. Augustine is of course the great figure in this account. But the full range of Augustine's theory of will winds up in Aquinas too. In fact, if we can make anything of statistics, it looks as though will for Aquinas is at least as important as understanding, possibly twice so. In his taxonomy of the human act there is at least one act of will for every act of understanding, and perhaps two.[9]

Yves R. Simon is as much heir to the Augustinian and medieval theory of will as he is to Aristotle's theory of practical cognition. Both his *Freedom of Choice* (rather obviously) and *Practical Knowledge* contain a number of passages relevant to the role of will in action. Again, we concentrate on the role of will in its relation to the element of command, focusing therefore on the moment of action itself, rather than on the deliberative antecedents. Commenting on the natural tendency to dichotomize will and understanding, Simon, in *Freedom of Choice*, lays stress upon their intimate union. "The practical judgment," he writes, "causes the act of the will not only by proposing an end for it but also by constituting its form" (*FC* 98). It is an act of knowledge that makes a given choice a choice of such and such a kind. It *specifies* it. Nowhere is this relationship more significant than in the act of command, since it is command that provides the formal principles in the ultimate act of choice, the actual deed performed.

At the same time, one must not grant efficacy to acts of knowledge as such, except in some derivative way. The formal cause moves nothing, although it renders what is moved intelligible. It is the will that finally moves toward some good. The will "brings it about that a certain practical judgment terminates the deliberation and constitutes the decision" (*FC* 148). Simon's answer, then, to what ultimately determines the natural anarchy (if that is not too strong a word) of the deliberative process, is that

---

[8]Thomas Aquinas, *Summa Theologiae*, II–II, 47, 1.

[9]*Ibid.*, I–II, 8–17.

the will terminates it.

This is hardly a transparently clear thesis. Part of it can be elucidated by reference to the concept of "use." The differences between art and practical wisdom are many. One of them lies in the fact that the artisan, craftsman, or technician can turn his art to any use he pleases, for good or for ill. But practical judgment is so bound up with action itself that, where the judgment is sound, the use must be humanly good. A practically wise person cannot make poor use of wisdom, and the action conformable to practically wise deliberation must itself be of good use. In scholastic language, "use," an act of will in the conclusion of the practical syllogism, must be good when the ultimate practical judgment is made truly.[10]

Another way of elucidating the relation of will to understanding is by reference to the nature of practical truth itself. The problem of truth claims in matters of practical reason is a highly controverted one. There is first the sifting of factual claims from evaluative ones. Conformity with states of affairs can suffice in determining factual claims, even in practical deliberation. This is a relatively straightforward view, and perhaps involves the concept of truth in a primary and unqualified way. But there is another kind of truth, "practical truth," the truth ". . . of direction, of a truth which does not consist in conformity to a real state of affairs but in conformity to the demands of an honest will, in conformity to the inclination of a right desire."[11] This "truth of direction" supplies certainty in practical decisions. It makes a "command" "true."

This notion of "practical truth," a truth neither deductive nor statistical, but dependent upon the condition of the appetite itself, brings us to a third, and I think conclusive, elucidation of the relation between will and understanding. The appetites (including the will) are perfected by moral virtue. The person of virtue, then, can safely and surely terminate the deliberative process, simply by the habitual exercise of moral virtue itself. Deliberation establishes only probabilities in conduct. There is no possibility of reaching a deliberative conclusion with the apodictic necessity of a deductive argument. And yet there is the need to act under this degree of uncertainty. But the presence of virtue in the will can provide this degree of "affective knowledge" or "knowledge by inclination," by which a real and trustworthy (a "certain") conclusion may be made in practical reasoning.[12] It is because the agent is a person of good will that the natural

---

[10]Simon, "Introduction," 10ff.

[11]*Ibid.*, 15.

[12]*Ibid.*, 20ff.

vicissitudes of practical reason are of no ultimate destructiveness in practical life. Simon develops this point interestingly. So, for instance, the limits on intelligibility in moral action are no scandal, since the important thing is to act well, whatever degree of understanding we may have for acting well. What counts is the fulfillment of our moral obligations, not necessarily their intelligibility. I take it that this position has particular relevance to a theory of political wisdom. This is not to say that blind obedience is preferable to explanation. The explanatory dimension is uniquely human, "animated by an aspiration towards the most rational modalities of fulfillment."[13]

But the need for the moral virtues is established nonetheless, not in some artificially compartmentalized account of a "bag of virtues," but in a densely intricate theory of their interconnection. It is the person of moral virtue whose practical judgments we can trust, because such a person knows when, where, and how to act. This concatenation of virtues, by the way, includes theological as well as natural virtues. Simon has some excellent pages on the virtue of poverty, discussion of which must be deferred.[14]

In summary, Yves Simon's analysis of modernity rests upon his perception of the role of practical wisdom in the catalogue of virtues. Practical wisdom simply cannot be rendered by the term "prudence" in modern languages, given the reducibility of knowledge to a single methodology, and given the self-interest occasioned, if not engendered, by the powerful individualism of Descartes. There is a new intellectualism in early modern thought, a new identification of knowledge and virtue, such that science can be employed in the resolution of all human problems, societal as well as individual. Simon, by a thorough reconsideration of Aristotle and of Thomas Aquinas, brings us once again the two major elements of a critique of this new intellectualism. First, he recovers the essential irreducibility of practical knowledge to theory and art, especially at the moment of action. And, secondly, he insists that moral virtue, and therefore the will, are internally necessary to the deliberative process. Without the habitual excellence of a person of good will, deliberation will never terminate successfully. The conclusion of deliberation lies in command, but command is found in action itself, and action is good only if the will chooses well. The conclusion of deliberation, then, lies in an inseparable unity of moral and intellectual virtue.

---

[13]*Ibid.*, 40.

[14]Yves R. Simon, "Christian Humanism: A Way to World Order," in *From Disorder to World Order* (Milwaukee: Marquette University Press, 1956), 208.

Marianne Mahoney

Prudence as the Cornerstone of The Contemporary Thomistic Philosophy of Freedom

The objective of this essay is to show that a full elaboration of "prudence" must be the cornerstone of any distinctively Thomistic public philosophy. In contemporary philosophy, Yves R. Simon makes the most comprehensive contribution to the work of elaborating a prudence-centered public philosophy.

Prudence reigned as one of the four cardinal virtues of Plato, Aristotle, Cicero, and Aquinas. In modern ethical and political philosophy, however, prudence has taken on a narrower and more self-interested persona. Aristotelian-Thomistic prudence integrates human cognitive and moral faculties and opens the person to the whole range of the comprehensive good; Hobbesian and Kantian[1] prudence defines and promotes the well-being of one individual only. Contemporary moral and political philosophers as well as the assumptions of everyday speech favor and employ the narrower, more self-focused views of prudence, to the point that one cannot assume that a prudential motive is a moral motive.

The first section of this essay will contrast the fuller and self-focused views of prudence, showing how the differences over the scope of prudence reflect basic axiological cleavages within contemporary political philosophy. The first section will conclude by suggesting that the justice-dominant axiologies cannot serve as adequate bases for the range of moral issues any public philosophy ought to address. The second section of the essay provides an overview of the public philosophy of prudence,

---

[1]Immanuel Kant, *Groundwork of the Metaphysics of Morals,* trans. H.J. Patton (New York: Harper & Row, 1964) 83–84. Alan Gewirth, *Reason and Morality* (Chicago: University of Chicago Press, 1978), 71.

primarily as Yves R. Simon elaborates it. The third and final section of the essay deals with the distinction between the common and particular good. The interest of prudence in political life involves promoting the common good and doing justice to the autonomy of human persons who legitimately pursue the particular good. In this section, the issue will arise whether members of a political community must have some degree of agreement on the nature of the common good, the virtues of citizens, and the particular good.

I. Prudence and the Axiological Patterns Of Contemporary Democratic Theory

Axiological patterns refer to any aspects of an ethical theory that single out some dimension of the human good as central or primary, along with any explicit or implicit ranking rules for ordering different aspects of the human good. Metaethical distinctions such as "consequentialist" and "deontological" have an axiological import, because they identify maximizing consequences or observing side-constraints in action as central concerns.

Differences in axiological patterns make themselves felt in the two major issue cleavages of contemporary democratic theory: principles for determining whether the enforcement of morals is a legitimate activity of the democratic state, and principles governing distribution of advantages and burdens among members of a society. Axiological patterns in political economy separate contemporary democratic theorists readily along redistributionist versus minimal-state lines. John Rawls' *A Theory of Justice*[2] elaborates a theory of moral knowledge that justifies the principles of the modern welfare state, namely, equal liberty and a distribution of benefits and burdens with the perspective of the least advantaged man as a point of reference. In *Reason and Morality*,[3] Alan Gewirth envisions an even more aggressively redistributionist political order. From his central thesis that all human agents must recognize the rights of freedom and well-being in themselves and others, Gewirth derives further arguments supporting redistribution of resources and affirmative action. Such redistribution empowers persons by eliminating obstacles to their efficacy as agents. While the principles of Simon's political economy derive from teleological and axiological premises entirely different from the principles of Rawls and Gewirth, Simon would probably have found the institutional framework

---

[2]John Rawls, *A Theory of Justice* (Cambridge: Harvard University Press, 1972).
[3]Gewirth, *Reason*, 312–27.

of Rawlsian political economy congenial. Simon believed that workers require unions to empower them to seek commutative justice in social exchange and to articulate their resistance to laws that favor the richer classes (*PDG* 97, 98). Simon also believed that while private property could serve autonomy of the person and the family, an egalitarian dynamism within democratic societies might erode it.

By contrast, such theorists as Robert Nozick,[4] Frederich von Hayek, and Milton Friedman try to show that we cannot justify redistributionist schemes or political structures more extensive than the minimal state. Like Rawls and Gewirth, these theorists focus on the rationality and autonomy of human agents, but their view of rationality and autonomy takes shape around the entitlement to enjoy the proceeds of one's own labor, ingenuity, and property.

The issue that creates a special opportunity for the public philosophy of prudence arises out of an issue nexus that Sir Patrick Devlin called "the enforcement of morals."[5] Despite major disagreements on the redistribution issue, Rawls, Gewirth, and Nozick all clearly share a justice or rights-dominant approach when delineating the legitimate scope of government authority. Welfare state democratic theorists and libertarians alike share a distaste for any ethical structure that would take government beyond the concern with equal liberty and economic rights, however differently these theorists interpret economic rights. Rawls elaborates a "thin theory of the good" that names basic "goods" such as income and wealth, opportunity, and self-esteem. But his general reflections on axiology indicate that he would like to derive a full theory of the good from a theory of right, making all ethical claims a matter of either rights or duties. Thus the deontological political theorists share the common belief that while rights-discourse is meaningful, claims about the goodness of human pursuits (pursuits that are consistent with justice) cannot bind the conscience of the public. As a consequence, rights claims about economic goods and lifestyles legitimately enlist the coercive measures of the law, while goodness claims cannot.

Simon's philosophy of prudence regards justice as a cardinal virtue of persons as well as a feature of institutions, yet regards justice as only one aspect of the larger comprehensive good. Simon's respect for the moral autonomy of persons and small communities in the principle of autonomy

---

[4] Robert Nozick, *Anarchy, State, and Utopia* (New York: The Free Press, 1974).

[5] Sir Patrick Devlin, *The Enforcement of Morals* (London: Oxford University Press, 1965).

means that the public philosophy of prudence would not contemplate enforcing every requirement of the human good. But the public philosophy of prudence gives the good and not just one aspect of it a presence in every dimension of political life. In the philosophy of prudence, no one dimension of the comprehensive good enjoys a status of independent intelligibility or self-subsisting dominance. The Thomistic theory of prudence maintains that all moral goods, including those pursued in public policies, are relative to the comprehensive good. The balance of this essay shows why Simon's theory of prudence holds more promise as a public philosophy than does the justice-dominant approach.

II. Dimensions of the Good in the Public Philosophy of Prudence

The human capacity for prudence affects both the justification and the legitimate scope of political authority. The public philosophy of prudence orients itself to the good in the dispositions of persons, to the particular good of persons and smaller sub-regime communities, to the common good of the society both formally and materially considered, and to the comprehensive good, which is the ultimate object of all goal-directed action.

According to a method Simon elaborates in *Critique de la connaissance morale*,[6] one can consider the comprehensive good either speculatively or practically. The comprehensive good is the primary operative moral entity in moral knowing, esteeming, and doing. Human wills and intellects approach the comprehensive good through the virtues, through every goal-directed human act, and through the intellect's love of the good and the desire to become one in nature with it (affective connaturality). The comprehensive good can coincide with pure act or the infinite good (God), according to Simon, but the good of human experience does not achieve this coincidence. That is why Simon describes the comprehensive good as transcending every good action or good thing we experience without being vitiated by any conceivable limitation of the good (*FC* 25).

The speculative and practical intellect both reach out for the comprehensive good. In its speculative activities, the intellect seeks to grasp an undiminished good that it cannot change, a good that cannot fail in the

---

[6]Yves R. Simon, *Critique de la connaissance morale* (Paris: Desclée de Brouwer et Cie, 1934), chapter 7, especially 103–04. In 1980, Professor Ralph McInerny kindly duplicated and sent me a copy of a translation he made of *Critique*.

face of deficient or partial human efforts to understand it or achieve it. The good has a metaphysical nature, and, *qua* being, it is approachable through intellect; but the comprehensive good is also an entity that causes desire.[7] In its practical activities, the rational will reaches out for the comprehensive good as it forms the goal of each proposed action. The comprehensive good accounts for the human desire to do good and avoid evil, or the general will-guiding principle that Thomas Aquinas called synderesis. The comprehensive good operates as a final cause in the life of every rational agent, but the *bonum in communi* does not depend on the agent's express awareness of it. The degree of virtue operative in the agent's will determines how open he is to the comprehensive good. Rational agency is the formal cause of the human agent, and this formal cause refers to the agent's governance of himself or herself in making moral choices.

But the human will must be trained in openness to the comprehensive good. This openness of the will to the whole range of the good derives from the "existential readiness" (*MV* 115) of the agent. The human person can attune his or her personality to the whole range of the good through learning the dispositions to act which are called virtues. Beyond acquiring the virtues through action, the person must learn an attitude of active impartiality (indifference) toward the good. The degree to which the comprehensive good operates in a person's life varies with the degree to which she voluntarily displays an openness toward it in framing her particular purposes and in choosing the means or ways in which she pursues her goals. Connaturality of the virtuous and impartial will with the comprehensive good is not so much an intellectual act as a commitment to the good as the thing loved and an openness to something outside the will.

The unity of the good can be seen in the way in which all the cardinal virtues work together to produce moral choices. One reason for the coherence and unity of the human good in the system of cardinal virtues is that the tendencies to evil, or to moral compromise or backsliding, are also multiple and reinforcing. Justice alone cannot provide an adequate "zone defense" against vices which would defuse a person's determination to act well. Each virtue shields the will from a specific failing in human use. Prudence, by insisting that the judgment take the requirements of justice, moderation, and courage simultaneously into account, prevents the progressive weakening of execution that can occur when one virtue alone is relied upon to keep the appeal of moral compromise at bay. Prudence

---

[7]Yves R. Simon, "Introduction to the Study of Practical Wisdom," *The New Scholasticism* 35:1 (January, 1961): 9.

shows the appeal of partial goods for what they truly are. Moderation and courage govern the physical passions of the human person, especially those having to do with the desire for pleasure and the fear of death. Governing passions that may determine the will without any reference to the requirements of the good, moderation and courage free the person to act justly toward others when it is unpleasant or dangerous.

A public philosophy concerned above all with justice, even if justice is understood strictly as distributive justice, cannot be indifferent to the other virtues. Greed begets welfare fraud, which in turn begets both resentment and proposals to end income transfer programs that the disadvantaged really need. The justice of Rawls and Gewirth also holds equality of opportunity for women to be a requirement of justice, yet the decision of whether to look at pornography in which women are portrayed as nonautonomous objects is held to be a matter of private unaccountable choice. Redistribution and equal dignity are tenuous because moderation is optional, private.

The need for properly oriented inclinations derives from the practical nature of moral judgment.[8] Interestingly enough, many of the sources of the need for virtuous and impartial inclination in situations of practical choice coincide with causes of contingency that create the need for authority.

Aristotelian science concerns itself with the unchanging and the necessary. The unchanging and the necessary are eminently knowable. But human moral action occurs in an environment of constant change and uncertain outcomes. The contingent circumstances of human moral choice have many causes: the availability of multiple means; the unforseeability of other persons' actions; the partiality of our information about the goals of an action when someone proposes that we join them in a common venture; the lack of foresight into the consequences of our own choices, such as the unknown effects of a relatively new technology; and the contingent quality of some natural phenomenon, such as a hurricane (*PDG* 27, 278; *FC* 20; *MV* 110–111).[9] A lack of virtue is not an essential cause of the need for

---

[8]These comments on how contingency creates a special role for prudential judgment have many sources. See Simon, *Critique,* especially chapters 1 and 2; *Moral Virtue* chapters 4 and 5; *Philosophy* 19–35; *Freedom of Choice* 99–102; and "Introduction to the Study of Practical Wisdom": 15. See also *Summa Theologiae,* II-II, 47, 2 and 3.

[9]The example of the natural phenomenon not amenable to scientific knowledge (in the Aristotelian sense) is my own.

practical wisdom in its guidance of the will's choices; rather, the activity of virtuous inclinations creates even more choices for the will to make. Likewise, the lack of virtue among members of society is not among the essential reasons for authority, although the common contingency of deficient virtue does account for many of the activities of authority.

When the philosophy of prudence takes the comprehensive good as its object, several important implications follow for contemporary thought. First, acknowledging the practical and contingent nature of moral judgment need not lead us to embrace moral subjectivity in the ordinary sense. Simon grounds the subjectivity of the human agent in ontology, in the ample being known as the comprehensive good. Inclination must be attuned to that comprehensive good; inclinations opposed to the interest of the *bonum in communi* are wrong inclinations. Second, Simon's philosophy of prudence offers an opportunity to question the self-evidence and utility of the sharp distinction liberal democracy draws between the public and private realms of life, especially with respect to what ethical judgments society may desire that its good citizens share. Simon does not explicitly undermine the public-private distinction, but his political thought does point out a way to respect the particular good of individuals and simultaneously insist on the critical nature of the interest the common good can take in virtue of individual persons. All dimensions of the good impinge on the choices of persons in their individual capacities and as members of various communities. The philosophy of prudence recognizes the particular good of sub-regime communities and of individual persons, but the comprehensive character of human desire would not support a public-private distinction that would sanction two separate realms of moral judgment. In other words, the spirit of the philosophy of prudence recognizes the special character of the particular good and its service to autonomy without condoning a wholly private sphere of judgments concerning good and evil. The comprehensive good ranges over the desires of persons pursuing particular goods and over the aspirations of communities. No dimension of the human good is inherently private or in principle shielded from public view, however prudent and good it may be to commit many matters to the autonomous pursuits of persons.

III. The Common Good, the Particular Good, And the Activities of Authority

Human action, however inarticulately, yearns for the comprehensive good. In the concrete circumstances of a political community, however, the quest for the human good plays out its course in the relations between the common good and the particular good. The entire community seeks its common good in united action. A community's very interpretation of the human good constitutes an important aspect of its common good, as Aristotle points out in Book I of his *Politics*. Functional concerns with the ongoing business of a social order make up separate activities of the common good: defense, justice, transportation, agriculture, education, housing, etc. Another dimension of the common good inheres in the "communion causing" communications of the society. These communications call attention to the common life and common good of the community, building and strengthening the community simultaneously (*PDG* 58, 66–67). Another constituting aspect of the common good is the community's use of authority to command the means to realize united actions needed by the society.

While the common good belongs to the entire community, the particular good belongs to smaller communities or to autonomous persons. Consistent with the prudential nature of political judgment, Simon does not list rules about what particular goods of persons cannot be violated in the interest of the common good. Yet the way Simon distinguishes despotic and political regimes suggests a strong institutional framework of protection for the particular good of persons. Whether democratic or not, political regimes feature institutional means for persons and organizations to resist the government, or to pursue autonomous goods (even goods having apolitical or non-political purposes). Despotic regimes do not permit such institutionalized resistance to government action, and consequently place the population in a status resembling that of a slave (*PDG* 74–75). Following Aristotle, Simon's despotic regimes do not even sacrifice the particular good of persons to the common good. Instead, they sacrifice both particular good and common good to the private good of the despot or the despotic group.

A society that does not recognize a common good, as well as a society that would relativize the particular good of persons to the point that the particular good has no definite content, may have great despotic or exploitative potential. The role of the common and particular good in securing the good of the community and the good of persons against depredations suggests that institutions alone cannot guarantee the dignity and autonomy democratic theorists desire. For the common good tells us what may never be appropriated for our private use; the particular good tells us what pursuits we must attempt in all good faith to leave to the autonomous pursuits of persons and of smaller communities. Some public understanding or political culture of the common good and of the particular good of autonomous persons may be required to secure the institutional framework of liberty and autonomy so central to the democratic theorists of the 1970s and 1980s.

The particular good of autonomous persons comes to view when one considers which means virtuous persons must commit to realize the common good. Virtuous persons, as long as they formally will the realization of the common good, can prefer, and prefer intensely, to withhold materially what the common good may require in a particular instance. Simon's example involves a woman whose husband has been convicted of a crime and now faces imminent execution. The woman formally wills the common good and generally wills that justice be done; she does not offer illegal, violent resistance to the execution decree. How is the woman's wish that the execution decree not be carried out consistent with the requirements of justice? Simon's justice requires that all persons formally will the common good. But the automatic goodness of the particular good means that people can cherish and prefer not to alienate that which belongs to one's particular good.

One can imagine supporting military service generally and wishing that one's nation could win a just war. Also wishing that one's only son, or some special son, not be required to risk his life would be to embrace a particular good. How far one could go in this different example becomes a delicate matter. The military manpower example operates in zero-sum fashion for two young men and for two families. If my son obtains an occupational or medical exemption, the draft board will find someone else to go to war in his place. By preserving my particular good in this case, I will the consequences that you must yield what is probably just as precious. Eventually, the exemptions will be used up, and some families will give up their sons for those who were able to use the laws to their advantage. In the draft example, the only general actions consistent with justice would generally be to work for peace, as a matter of principle. A generalized desire that one's son never be called could also be just. But if the call comes, the lad's parents cannot preserve their particular good without raiding the particular good of another family. Under the superintendence of prudence, distributive justice requires that persons not transgress against another's particular good.

Critiques of Plato's *Republic* from Aristotle to Simon and Alan Bloom point up the absurdity of social arrangements that abolish the distinction between the common good materially and formally willed. In the *Republic*, the guardian class has mass weddings and the whole ensuing generation of babies will grow to adulthood calling the men and women married at the time of their birth mother and father. The adults in turn will call all children their sons and daughters. Plato realized that the preference for one's own, one's adherence to one's particular good in one's biological offspring, detracts from the intensity of one's commitment to the common good and what it requires. This theme is also strong in Homer's *Iliad* and in Aristophanes' and Euripides' "women and war" plays. The abolition of the family and private property and the repression of eros in Plato's *Republic* represent violations of human autonomy through the abolition of the particular good. Simon believes that the common good is best served when autonomous persons and smaller communities have charge of pursuing and protecting the particular good. A particular good that is appropriated commonly ceases to motivate the person. A child who belongs to a whole generation, as Aristotle points out, is really no one's child. His common status makes him an orphan.[10]

Simon's insistence on the "automatic goodness of the particular good" has very definite consequences for the way a political order is constituted. The material willing and realization of the common good requires that specific means be chosen to further some requirement of the common good. These means lie in specific policy choices, choices that command resources, distribute benefits and burdens, permit and proscribe categories of activities, and compel united action. The moderate representative regime that emerges from *Philosophy of Democratic Government* features a distinct governing personnel. This distinct governing personnel materially realizes the common good and cannot consider the impact of any salutary policy measure on its particular good. Simon believes the common good is best served if the regime empowers autonomous persons and organizations to seek justice in exchange (labor unions) and to form parties that can

---

[10]Simon's critique of Plato's *Republic* occurs in *Philosophy* 52–57. See also Aristotle, *Politics*, 1260b 27–1264b 25; the status of children who are held to be common offspring is discussed at 1261b 31. Alan Bloom's interpretive essay following his outstanding translation of Plato's *Republic* is not so much a critique as an argument that Plato was attempting to show the difficulties in abolishing all particular claims on a person in favor of the common good. For Bloom, Plato's purpose was to show the abolition of the common good, especially as it inheres in human gender differences and attachments to one's own children, to be ridiculous. Plato, *Republic*, trans. Alan Bloom (New York: Basic Books, 1968). The interpretive essay begins on p. 307. Aristophanes depicts the hostility of women, as such, to war efforts in *Lysistrata*. In *The Congresswomen*, ruling women abolish the options of males to choose their sexual partners, subordinating the particular good of eros to a comically conceived distributive justice. In a more tragic vein, many of the Trojan War plays of Euripides show the particular good of family and of femininity in a defeated political order to be destroyed utterly by war. *Hecuba*, *The Trojan Women*, and *Iphigenia* are a few examples.

help the deliberative-consultative assembly of the civil multitude to define a political agenda. The man-wife community serves an irreducible and irreplaceable function in taking particular care that their own union and the welfare of their children be advanced. Likewise, the family farm and rural democracy become special autonomous preserves of the particular good. Only a prudential judgment that some serious deficiency requires the exercise of paternalistic interference can justify temporary rule of the autonomous particular realm by the common good. When the essential conditions of authority are in place, the particular good must be pursued autonomously.

Respecting the demands of the common and particular good demands that the impartiality or indifference of the will be in act. In fostering impartiality, or an openness to the vastness of the comprehensive good, prudence seems to require that persons take a certain attitude toward the good that cannot be realized by any finitely good action. Here the work of Germain Grisez[11] offers a way of amplifying Simon's treatment of indifference or impartiality. To respect the comprehensive good, a good action that is finite—as are all political policies and social means—(1) must never act directly against another requirement of the good, and (2) must openly acknowledge the good that cannot be done by the finite action. These requirements point up that the human good is indivisible, a quality deeply resonant with its comprehensiveness; they also point up that the good is heterogeneous within its unity, because one aspect of the good is not substitutable for another. This amplification of Simon shows that the philosophy of prudence offers side-constraints that prevent us from contemplating the violation of the particular good in favor of some other good.

The next proposed extension of Simon's philosophy of prudence argues that a public teaching about the content of the particular good is necessary. In chapter 4 of *Philosophy*, Simon speaks of the "problem of recognition." The "problem of recognition" as Simon employs it there refers to problems the democratic electorate has in recognizing the qualifications of prudence in those who would be governing personnel. The recognition problem comes in when Simon acknowledges that these evidences of active prudence are difficult to recognize in human persons. The act of recognition and intelligent voting itself therefore requires much

---

[11]Germain Grisez, *Abortion: The Myths, the Realities, and the Arguments* (New York and Cleveland: Corpus Books, 1970) and *Life and Death with Liberty and Justice* (Notre Dame: University of Notre Dame Press, 1979).

prudence.

In the current environment of advanced relativism, an analogous recognition problem makes itself felt when one considers the content of the particular good. The particular good is critical in public philosophy because the common good prudently directed must make every presumption in favor of its autonomous promotion by persons and independent organizations. If public consensus about what the particular good is deteriorates too much, both the common good and the good properly committed to autonomous promotion become vulnerable to violation. It is one thing to say that the particular good should be left to autonomous promotion in every possible instance, but it is entirely another thing to say that what the particular good includes must be left to individual interpretation. The principle of autonomy sanctions independent promotion of a particular good that has a fairly definite content. If people cease to cherish or desire an aspect of the particular good, this abandonment of the particular good in one or more aspects constitutes a deficiency in recognition, as well as a failure of inclination. Society cannot effectively employ its authority to protect the autonomous particular good of persons if persons do not agree on what this good of persons is.

Rawls deals with this problem of recognition effectively within the limited axiological scope of his theory. Rawls realizes that a theory of distributive justice has, as a requirement, a theory about what may be distributed justly or unjustly. The "thin theory of the good" in Rawls identifies basic goods such as liberty, opportunity, income and wealth, and self-esteem as states of persons or of their possessions that are desirable, whatever else one seeks and considers good. Rawls believes that all rational persons would want to see these primary goods justly distributed.

The feeble moral discourse our society is still capable of wants to allow each person to draw up his or her own list of particular goods while simultaneously professing bafflement about drug use and the lack of affect behind violence and one-parent families in our underclass. Autonomy has been stretched to mean that one has the right to define what one's particular good is, but society also wants to encourage us not to destroy certain aspects of this same menu of optional particular goods. An anti-drug commercial shows eggs being dropped to fry in an oiled skillet. A voice-over declares: "The eggs are your brain. This is what drugs do to your brain. Any questions?" If legitimate authority in a democratic order cannot tell persons what to cherish, authority cannot be sure it will engage the conscience of the public when the neglect of an "optional" particular good threatens public health. What if a healthy brain, or a healthy baby, or a maximally supportive nuclear family simply fail to make people's menus? If we join Rawls in pointing out that self-esteem is a minimal basic good that persons require in order to accord justice to others, the relativist will reply that everyone should have self-esteem, but that what self-esteem means to the person whose actions make him vulnerable to AIDS or to the woman who knowingly uses crack while pregnant is not the same as what self-esteem means to a more fortunate individual. Tolerance yields to condescension. Relativism with respect to the content of the particular good undermines public philosophies based on justice-dominant concerns almost as much as it undermines the belief and inclination conditions that would favor the public philosophy of prudence. The quest for consensus about the human good in general and in particular constitutes the heart of rational discourse and affective communion. This quest for consensus and the inevitable affirmations of the good in the public realm is itself an aspect of the common good.

David T. Koyzis

Yves R. Simon's Contribution to A Structural Political Pluralism

This essay presupposes an acquaintance with Yves R. Simon's political theory and, more particularly, with his general theory of authority as set forth in *Nature and Functions of Authority*, *Philosophy of Democratic Government*, *A General Theory of Authority* and *Freedom and Community*. I shall here argue that within this theory is to be found the basis for what might be termed a *structural political pluralism*. A structural political pluralism differs fundamentally from the two dominant western political theories of individualism and collectivism. While individualism reduces society to an aggregate of constituent individuals and collectivism views individuals and smaller communities as components of an all-embracing human community, a structural political pluralism recognizes the distinct ontological status of a plurality of human communities and sees a place for them apart from the arbitrary will of individuals or the dictates of the state.

Historically, this pluralism is associated with the principle of subsidiarity, articulated in the works of Leo XIII,[1] Maritain,[2] and Simon.[3]

---

[1] See his encyclicals *Immortale Dei* (1885), *Rerum Novarum* (1891), and *Graves de Communi* (1901).

[2] For example, see his *Scholasticism and Politics*, *Integral Humanism*, and *The Person and the Common Good* (Notre Dame: University of Notre Dame Press, 1968).

[3] A similar tradition of pluralism is to be found within the Calvinist tradition as it has developed particularly in the Netherlands during the last two centuries. Known in these circles as "sovereignty in its own sphere" (*souvereiniteit in eigen kring*), this pluralism has been developed in the writings of G. Groen van Prinsterer (*Unbelief and Revolution*, 1847), Abraham Kuyper (*Souvereiniteit in eigen kring*, 1880), and Herman Dooyeweerd (*A New Critique of Theoretical Thought* [Presbyterian and Reformed, 1953–58]).

Simon perhaps develops this principle most systematically. He provides a theoretical foundation for subsidiarity (1) by distinguishing among the different functions (and implicitly, the different types) of authority, (2) by distinguishing between the two varieties of particularity in relation to the common good, (3) by differentiating between political and democratic regimes, and (4) by developing the two principles of authority and autonomy. In so doing, Simon has affirmed the legitimate status of both private (or particular) goods and the common good.

I. Pluralism and the Functions of Authority

In establishing that authority has different functions, Simon shows that the need for authority in human society rests on the positive aspects of human nature and not entirely on human deficiency. To counter the familiar argument that authority would not be needed in a society of perfectly good human beings, Simon distinguishes between *substitutional* and *essential* functions of authority. So-called deficiency theorists believe that all authority *substitutes* for a deficiency on the part of the ruled. If the ruled were able entirely to conquer this deficiency, then authority itself would disappear. But, according to Simon, those who argue in this way have failed to distinguish between those functions of authority that are essential (i.e., are required by the *esse* of human nature) and those that can indeed be dispensed with in the society free from human deficiency.

The major distinction within Simon's theory of authority is between those functions that are substitutional and those that are essential. A third major category is the *perfective* function, which betters those who are already good.[4] Within these major categories, Simon further develops six specific functions of authority, four of which he articulates in some detail in *Democratic Government* and the remaining two in *General Theory*. I shall not list all of these functions here and refer the interested reader to the complete list in the long footnote on page 61 of *Democratic Government*. For now, it is only necessary to point out that the greater perfection of a community causes authority's substitutional functions to diminish, while the essential functions remain and even increase authority's role in society.

For example, paternal (or perhaps *parental*, to be more inclusive) authority is necessitated by a deficiency on the part of the subject, namely, immaturity. But, as the subject gradually grows to maturity and is able to take charge of his own affairs, the need for parental authority diminishes

---

[4]Simon discusses the perfective function in chapter 4 of *General Theory* (133–56).

(or at least ought to) accordingly. If, however, there is a variety of means to a given end; if all of the means are equally good; and if the entire society must settle upon only one means; then authority must determine which means will be taken. This is true even in the society of perfectly good persons, since there is no foundation for spontaneous unanimity among such persons. In this case, authority's function is essential. Insofar as authority determines the common good in any sense more than a formal one, its function is *most essential* and will not diminish as the community achieves greater perfection. To the contrary, as a society becomes larger and more complex and the range of alternative goods expands, authority becomes even more necessary than it was in the smaller and more primitive society.

Simon's theory of authority's functions is primarily intended to combat deficiency theories of authority. But there is a secondary significance to his theory as well, which is more immediately relevant to the argument of this essay. In discerning among these functions, Simon has also laid the groundwork for a pluralistic view of society that recognizes different *kinds* of authority and a variety of authoritative persons and institutions. For example, theoretical authority, or what he has labelled "authority in the realm of theoretical truth" (*GT* 81ff.), is only indirectly the concern of the state. For the most part, this type of authority is exercised by educational institutions and by ordinary persons in the course of their daily activities. Parental authority, whose function is substitutional, is frequently exercised by the state in a variety of situations (e.g., by a federal government over sparsely settled territories or by penitentiaries over prisoners), yet it is most appropriately exercised by parents over their children within the context of the family. The most essential function of authority in determining the substantive requirements of the common good is best exercised by the state, which is uniquely responsible for the care of the body politic.

The fact that there are different kinds of authority and different institutions exercising authority militates against a potentially totalitarian conception that sees all authority as derivative from a single source in society. In the truly pluralistic society, there are multiple sources of authority, each of which checks the "imperialistic tendency" of centralized authority.

II. Particularity and the Common Good

According to Simon, there is a legitimate diversity of goods pursued within human society. In setting forth a most essential function of authority, Simon has attempted to establish the goodness of ends that are not directly pursued by the community as a whole. In so doing, he is by no means legitimizing self-seeking in an egoistic sense. Rather, he is affirming the Aristotelian dictum that everything aims at a good which constitutes the end of that thing. Although the common good is indeed the most comprehensive good, the goodness of those ends that are less comprehensive is not thereby diminished.

For example, by demonstrating the legitimate status of the marriage and family communities, Simon undoubtedly wishes to prevent the charge of egoism from being levelled against those seeking goods narrower than the common good. No one, after all, would fault a woman for loving her husband, even if he is a criminal who has violated the common good. Nor is a man considered selfish whose principal concern is with the care of his own children. These are areas in which a person is expected to focus more narrowly. To attempt to care for all children equally means that one's own children will suffer from neglect.[5] This would hardly serve the common good. In Simon's words, "That particular goods be properly defended by particular persons matters greatly for the common good itself" (*PDG* 41).

Having established that particularity is not incompatible with the common good, Simon's analysis identifies two ways wherein something can be particular. On the one hand, there is the *particularity of function* and, on the other, there is what Simon has referred to as both *particularity of subject* (*GT* 60ff) and *particularity of the homestead* (*PDG* 56).

Particularity of function rests on the notion of specialization within the pursuit of the common good. In seeking the common good, a community requires certain institutions that specialize in a *part* of the common good. These are directly subordinate to the community and possess no initiative of their own. They relate directly to the common good, both formally and materially, but only to a small aspect thereof. The diversity of these institutions is merely a functional diversity and is rooted in the need for a division of labor and not in a diversity of autonomous goods that they might seek. The relationship between the larger community and these institutions can be understood almost entirely in terms of a whole and its parts (*GT* 60ff). The military, for example, is directly accountable to the political authority of a civilian government and does not pursue a private good materially distinct from the common good of the state as a whole. Rather, it pursues a specialized task within the common good.

Particularity of subject, on the other hand, involves a genuine autonomy of self-ruling agents each of whom pursues a private good. A multiplicity of private goods is compatible with the common good, yet they are not directly related to the latter. In *Democratic Government*, Simon refers to this type of particularity as that of the homestead. This illustrates

---

[5]See Aristotle, *Politics* II, 1262a.

the fact that it is rooted in a genuine ontological private good rather than in a mere specialization within the overall pursuit of the common good. Particularity of subject calls for an initiative that mere specialization does not permit. Particularity of function "removes confusion" (GT 62) in that it clearly delineates areas of responsibility of which the various subunits of the body politic are in charge. Particularity of subject may also remove confusion, but this is not the principal reason for its existence. Particularity of subject has its own status, which is rooted in human freedom and cannot be reduced to the need for specialization.

Simon takes note of a continuing tradition in political theory, whose origin he traces to Plato's *Republic*, which attempts to account for all particularity in a society in terms of specialization. In more recent times, various forms of rationalism have tried to suppress the particularity of subject and exalt in its place "the clarity of function" (GT 65). Since function has the advantage of appearing more neat and systematic, it is far more congenial to the rational mind than the seemingly chaotic plurality of autonomous subjects.

But Simon sees such a functional ordering of society as flat and lifeless. The heirs of Plato have not understood that particularity of subject is itself good and contributes significantly to the common good, even though its relation to the latter is indirect. It is quite in accordance with virtue and the common good that persons should seek goods which are narrower than that of the community as a whole and, furthermore, which are materially different from the latter. It is right and proper that families seek the good of families, marriages that of marriages, and the larger community that of the larger community. It is not desirable that private goods be absorbed into the common good, nor is the opposite to be desired.

The fact that common and private goods are ontologically distinct and may come into conflict materially even within the virtuous society demonstrates for Simon the need for authority in its most essential function. This authority is most essential in that it meets the need for an agent to will and intend the common good both formally and materially. The legitimate plurality of goods in a society precludes the eventual disappearance of authority in its most essential function. For present purposes, the significance of Simon's argument relates not so much to the need for an overall authority per se, but to his recognition that a society can and ought to be organized in such a way as to protect the legitimate pursuit of a variety of goods by both individuals and smaller communities.

III. The Distinction Between Political and Democratic Regimes

In addition to distinguishing among the functions of authority and between common and particular goods, Simon also provides a foundation for pluralism by distinguishing between the political and the democratic regimes. The term "political" is one used by Simon in a special sense to describe a regime that may or may not be democratic. Though the two concepts may be said to overlap, they may be better described as different measuring standards that run perpendicular to each other. Both of these criteria Simon adapts from Aristotle.

The word "political" ought properly to be contrasted to "despotic," and each term can be applied to differing regimes or types of rule. In Aristotle's usage, the rule of freemen in a city is different from that of a master over slaves. The former involves a genuine common good, whereas the latter involves rule primarily for the benefit of the master.[6] A city governed despotically, i.e., in the fashion of a master over slaves, is not a genuine state or city. But citizens are "free" and autonomous, and this is what constitutes the political character of the regime. In Simon's words, a political system is that "which gives the governed a legal power of resistance" (*PDG* 74). In this respect, a political regime may be said to be necessarily pluralistic, insofar as it calls for some authority to be retained by the people and for a certain autonomous sphere to be held onto against what Simon refers to as the "imperialistic tendency of authority" (*FAC* 86).

A political regime is one wherein it is recognized that the state is not absolute and that other institutions possess legitimate authority of their own. Such authority can even be used against the state, should the latter overstep its proper limits. But this in no way implies that democracy is present. As Simon emphasizes, "a political regime may be thoroughly non-democratic" (*PDG* 75). To demonstrate this he points to the structure of premodern feudal regimes, wherein "aristocracies possessed such powers of resistance that the authority of the king often became merely nominal" (*PDG* 75). In such regimes, the monarch was to a great extent dependent on the nobility, which possessed a real power that served to check the potentially expansive ambitions of the monarch. The feudal regime was political without being democratic.

However, the political regime does contain within itself at least the potential for democracy. The direct power to elect and turn out office-bearers can be a potent means of limiting the abusive power of government and may be said to grow out of the logic of the political regime. Yet democracy itself may turn the tables and spawn a non-political despotic regime. Although Simon is certainly a partisan of democracy, he neverthe-

---

[6]See Aristotle's *Politics* III, 6, 1278 b30 ff; cf. III, 1, 1275a, and also Simon, *Freedom and Community*, 52.

less recognizes that democratic checks do not in themselves protect non-state communities and individual persons from the expansive power of the state, which explains why the written constitutions of most democracies include a charter of rights. Moreover, some modern ideologies even demand, in the name of democracy, the expansion of the state at the expense of non-state institutions. The freedoms of the church and press are often the first to suffer from this variety of democracy, according to Simon (*PDG* 137). Since neither the church nor the press, it is argued, is directly accountable to the people, the progress of democracy (and thus of its agent, the state) means that the former must be eliminated or at least subordinated to the democratic will of the people. In this way, democracy and the political regime can come to oppose each other.

This type of democracy is the heritage of the Jacobin tradition, of which Rousseau, the French Revolution, and ultimately Marx are representative (*PDG* 127–43; *FAC* 60–62). This tradition has no fear of overgovernment, in contrast, for example, to the Lockean tradition. Within the former, lie the seeds of modern totalitarianism. Given Simon's French birth and upbringing, it is perhaps not surprising that he should react so strongly to this Jacobin notion of democracy. Because of the abuses historically associated with manifestations of this notion (e.g., the Reign of Terror, suppression of the church and of religious orders), Simon is at pains to emphasize the value of nondemocratic elements within a constitution. Such institutions as an hereditary or appointive head of state (i.e., monarch or state president) and/or upper house (e.g., the British House of Lords or the Canadian Senate), act at once to check and preserve democracy.

> Any regime, in order to work well or merely to survive, needs or may need the operation of principles distinct from, and opposed to, its own idea (*PDG* 106).

This is the insight embodied in the classical "mixed" regime of Aristotle, Thomas Aquinas, and many others, who have sought to bring together in a single polity monarchical, aristocratic, and democratic elements in the service of the common good.

Institutional checks on democracy from within the government are of great value. Yet the maintenance of private spheres, in which individual persons and groups are autonomous, is also beneficial to democracy. The democratic principle cannot be extended indefinitely without effectively drying up its own source. Where the people have yielded up the whole of their autonomy to the governing authority, they risk extinguishing their own initiative, including their ability freely to participate in determining the direction and personnel of government. In short, excessive democracy endangers democracy itself.

IV. The Complementary Principles of Authority and Autonomy

In Simon's judgment, authority and autonomy must be seen as complementary. For one cannot exist without the other and both are essential to a healthy and well-ordered society. Only where authority's function is substitutional ought the two to be seen as polarities in tension with each other. But, where authority exercises an essential function, the two are polar only insofar as one falls at the top and the other at the base of a hierarchy. Otherwise, the two presuppose each other and belong together.

Simon defines autonomy as the interiorization of law, that is, the incorporation of the law's precepts into one's own heart and mind (*FAC* 96). A person possesses greater autonomy to the extent that he willingly conforms in his being and actions to the law. That is, insofar as a person becomes what his nature calls him to be, the less necessary it is for a heteronomous authority to impose this from without. This is the foundation for genuine freedom in a society. And if such is the case for individual persons, it also applies to communities of persons. For where a given community acts in accordance with its own nature and seeks a common end appropriate to that nature, the less need there is for it to be instructed or compelled in this direction by another institution or person (*FAC* 46).

It is on this basis that Simon posits a "principle of autonomy" to regulate the relations between the state and subordinate communities. In the preceding discussion, we have seen that he is concerned to demonstrate that there is a place for temporal communities that ought neither to be reduced to individual contract nor to be absorbed altogether into the broader political community. The status of these communities can best be accounted for and protected by recognizing two principles on which society rests. The first of these is the "principle of authority":

> Wherever the welfare of a community requires a common action, the unity of that common action must be assured by the higher organs of that community.

Complementing this is the "principle of autonomy":

> Wherever a task can be satisfactorily achieved by the initiative of the individual or that of small social units, the fulfillment of that task must be left to the initiative of the individual or to that of small social units (*NF* 45).

To hold these two principles in balance results in a hierarchical order in which the authority of the higher institution does not overstep its bounds but, rather, respects the autonomy of the subordinate institutions insofar as they have attained to it.

The vitality of a society is an important consideration here. Vitality requires that the various parts of a society possess an initiative of their own and that they act so as not to require direction from the top. There is a lack of such vitality in a society where the whole alone possesses initiative. Here, subordinate institutions and individual persons are merely lifeless instruments acting on command from above. But a healthy society is suffused with vitality throughout all of its institutions and communities (*PDG* 30). Vitality and autonomy are thus clearly connected, in Simon's view.

V. Concluding Comments

As I observed at the outset, the principle of subsidiarity has been an important theme within Roman Catholic social and political thought since the time of Leo XIII over a century ago. Subsidiarity has historically been part of a larger effort to offer, in a way fundamentally different from individualistic and collectivistic theories, a pluralistic account of the distinct status of a variety of communities within society, or a structural political pluralism. Along with his revered teacher, Jacques Maritain, Yves R. Simon has been part of this effort and, in his writings on the four themes set forth above, has articulated a political theory supportive of such a pluralism.

Ralph Nelson

Freedom and Economic Organization In a Democracy

In addition to the work of Yves R. Simon as Thomist philosopher in such areas of investigation as ontology, the philosophy of nature and moral psychology, and particularly his contribution to political philosophy, there is an aspect of his thought that has been less prominent. I refer to his study of French social thought. Throughout his writings, references to Saint-Simon, Comte, de Maistre and de Bonald, Durkheim and Georges Gurvitch can be found. He is the author of several essays on Proudhon.[1] Not only was he obviously well-acquainted with the leading ideas of Durkheim, but it is significant that his thesis director, Celestin Bouglé, was the successor of Durkheim at the Sorbonne.[2] Furthermore, he was not only knowledgeable about the French tradition in social thought, but he was well acquainted with the literature of German labor sociologists, notably the writings of Werner Sombart

---

[1] Yves R. Simon, "Les idées artistiques et littéraires de Proudhon," *La Démocratie* I:12 (March 25,1924): 553–62; "Le problème de la transcendance et le défi de Proudhon," *Nova et Vetera* IX:3 (July-September, 1934): 225–38; Vukan Kuic's translation of Simon's essay entitled "A Note on Proudhon's Federalism," in Daniel J. Elazar, ed., *Federalism as Grand Design* (Lanham, MD: University Press of America, 1988), 223–34.

[2] "A typical representative of the mentality of the lay university and a disciple of Durkheim, Bouglé contributed to broadening the initial domain of sociology. Instead of being content with sociological explanation, he integrated it in a more extensive explanation which in the final analysis rests on the psychological modifications which are determined in a given environment by the evolution of social facts" (Michel Mourre, ed., "Celestin Bouglé," in *Dictionnaire des idées contemporaines* [Paris, 1964], 257–58).

and Goetz Briefs.[3]

Now, it is not my intention to argue that there was a split in Simon's thought with the Thomist philosopher, on one hand, and the social theorist on the other. If his contributions to theoretical philosophy proceed on Thomist lines, his achievements in practical philosophy combine the employment of Thomistic principles and a deep study of social and political issues. In this regard, "Thomism and Democracy"[4] marks a significant milestone in his intellectual development with its assertion that Thomism is relevant to modern democratic theory and its trenchant examination of the party system in democracy.

What I want to argue is that there are really two facets of Simon's democratic philosophy. In the earlier phase of its genesis, he was primarily concerned with the economic organization of a democracy, or its socioeconomic dimension, while, in the later phase, he was primarily concerned with the political dimension. In *Philosophy of Democratic Government*, both dimensions are examined,[5] and, for that reason, it can be seen as a kind of culmination of his reflections over a considerable period of time on the socioeconomic and political dimensions of democratic life.

It should be noted that the purely political aspects of his philosophy of democratic government have been the subject of considerable commentary—I think, for instance, of two essays of W.J. Stankiewicz;[6] little, if anything, has been said about his reflections on economic organization. Now, it is beyond doubt that the relationship between authority and freedom is central to Simon's philosophy of democratic government. Yet the concern with human freedom is not confined to the political sphere, anymore than

---

[3]In *Work, Society, and Culture*, there are references to both Sombart and Briefs. Simon was particularly influenced by Goetz Brief's treatise, *The Proleteriat: A Challenge to Western Civilization* (New York: McGraw-Hill, 1937). See also Yves R. Simon's translation of the original German edition into French: *Le proletariat industriel* (Paris, 1936).

[4]Yves R. Simon, "Thomism and Democracy," Louis Finkelstein and Lyman Bryson, eds., *Science, Philosophy and Religion*, vol. 2 (New York: Distributed by Harper and Row, 1952), 258–72.

[5]While the political dimension is paramount in the first three chapters, the socioeconomic dimension is broached in the last two chapters.

[6]W.J. Stankiewicz, *In Defense of Sovereignty* (New York: Oxford University Press, 1969), and *Approaches to Democracy; Philosophy of Government at the Close of the Twentieth Century* (New York: St. Martin, 1981).

it is confined to the ethical life. It must be understood in the context of economic organization. Taking economic liberalism and state socialism as opposite and extreme alternatives, Simon examines the factors involved in modern economic life that impede freedom or are conducive to it. Of course, these factors may be viewed in terms of equality (and justice) as well as in terms of freedom, unless the two terms are defined as referring to the same thing. It is characteristic of Simon's approach to distinguish clearly between equality and freedom, while insisting on the close connection between them. Insofar as possible, this paper will focus on freedom alone.

A good starting point for analysis of Simonian thinking on the economic organization of democracy is the *Charles Dunoyer, mémoire*, a thesis completed in 1923.[7] Granted that this is an early work, subject to all the restrictions of a university requirement, still the subject matter and the themes developed provide a kind of overture to his later preoccupation with the world of work. Dunoyer was a representative of economic liberalism at the time of its introduction in France.

As the political revolution in France was followed by the industrial revolution, so economic liberalism followed political liberalism. Charles Dunoyer's thought, says Simon, is located at the "confluence of industrialism and liberalism" (*CDM* 4). Simon asserts that "his ideas constitute the most complete systematic treatment of liberal industrialism" in his day (*CDM* 8). If there was a form of political liberalism in France that was purely critical and negative, Dunoyer's approach seems constructive and positive. Jean Baptiste Say in his *Political Economy*[8] was the leading interpreter of the ideas of Adam Smith in France. Dunoyer, in contrast to his fellow countryman Say, is not noted for his contributions to formal political economy, while Say's law about supply and demand has entered into the classical formulation of modern economics. Incidentally, Dunoyer preferred the term "social economy," though he was closer to Adam Smith than Say was on the issue of the measure of values (*CDM*).[9]

Not concerned with the problem of free choice as such, Dunoyer defined freedom as "the power, the facility of action" (*CDM* 19). This power can be more easily employed when obstacles to its exercise are

[7]I am indebted to Anthony O. Simon for his generous gift of a copy of this thesis.

[8]Jean Baptiste Say, *Traité d'économie politique*, 3 vols. (Paris, 1826).

[9]References to social economy are found on 13 and 16, to Say and Smith on 46–47.

removed. On one hand, nineteenth century criticism considered Dunoyer's definition as one-sided, having simply a positive character and, on the other hand, as Proudhon argued, as having only a negative character, "as if it were only a synonym for the removal of obstacles" (*CDM* 21). It is Simon's contention that there are indeed the two aspects insofar as freedom progresses through the removal of obstacles to its exercise, and that freedom is something positive; it is power.

Simon then notes that "freedom understood in the sense of power is something other than freedom understood in the sense of independence or autonomy" (*CDM* 21), although Dunoyer tended to confuse these two quite different conceptions. Furthermore, Simon notes that the definition of freedom as power does not entail liberalism, for there were socialists as well who accepted a similar definition. Moreover, one significant twentieth century version of liberalism rejects the idea of freedom as power and maintains that freedom means freedom from coercion.[10]

Dunoyer defended "an individualistic conception of life" (*CDM* 17, n.1). Simon observes that "nowhere in his text is there a social aim distinct from individual improvement" (*CDM* 55). In fact, "the unique aim of social activity is individual improvement" (*CDM* 55–56). The government, accordingly, leaves or should leave individuals free to act as they please. However, in this regard, Dunoyer moves from an initial stance against the idea of repressive government to the later view that "such a regime is an essential condition of freedom" (*CDM* 58). So there is both liberalism and authoritarianism in Dunoyer's theory and, indeed, he attempts to reconcile his love of freedom and the sense of order. Simon gives no indication that he thinks Dunoyer succeeded in this intention.

Dunoyer, while a liberal, was no democrat, and he tended to confuse

---

[10]F.A. Hayek, *The Constitution of Liberty* (Chicago: University of Chicago Press, 1960), 16–17. In his commentary on Hayek's conception of freedom from coercion, Raymond Aron makes the following observation: "What is the concrete freedom which serves as the model for this definition of freedom? Obviously, the freedom of the entrepreneur or the consumer: the first is free to take initiative and to combine the means of production, the second free in the use he will make of the buying power provided by his monetary income. But neither the worker in a production line, nor the employee inside a vast organization, nor the soldier who is subject to strict discipline, nor the Jesuit who has taken a vow of obedience is free, according to this definition. Indeed the very nature of industrial society seems inexorably to reduce the number of persons for whom this kind of freedom is accessible, at least in work" (*An Essay on Freedom*, trans. Helen Weaver [New York: World Publishing Company, 1970], 88–89).

democratic and socialistic ideas. His belief in the benefits of free trade for the distribution of wealth led him to the optimistic conclusion that such a system would render socialist systems useless. Summing up Dunoyer's approach, Simon says that he "completed political liberalism by economic and ethical considerations" (*CDM* 92).

Now, out of the commentary, a number of salient themes emerge: the distinction between two notions of freedom (and Simon's early concern with the freedom of autonomy); liberal individualism and its social and economic consequences; and, finally, the relation between freedom and authority, the central theme of Simon's political philosophy.

Now, if the opposition between freedom as power and freedom as autonomy is accepted as central to understanding the issues of freedom in the work world, some of Simon's remarks about a form of economic freedom distinct from the freedom of autonomy fall into place. In a passage in which Simon would seem to invoke Saint Thomas' name (*TLT* 42), he argues for the proposition that property functions as a support for freedom. The person without property is by the same token deprived of power and, in extreme cases, deprived of the means of life itself. Elsewhere, he will argue that property should not be viewed as an instrument of exploitation but "in its essential function as a guarantee of freedom against governmental arbitrariness" or the exploitation of others.[11] Now, a close examination of Saint Thomas' teaching on property does not reveal that he was particularly concerned with property as a support for freedom, though that might not be an unreasonable inference from remarks he makes about wage workers. It is more likely that this idea is one that Simon took over from Proudhon.[12] In any case, while maintaining that one may indeed speak of economic freedom in this regard, Simon is principally concerned with the freedom of autonomy. But it is not the isolated individual who preoccupies him when he speaks of autonomy. Unlike some who would want to discuss autonomy in purely individualistic terms—for

---

[11]Yves R. Simon, *La marche à la délivrance* (New York: Editions de la Maison Française, 1942), 118.

[12]"The last thought of Proudhon on the subject would be nicely expressed by the consideration that much should be forgiven to property on account of what it does for liberty" (*Philosophy of Democratic Government*, 248).

insistance, the freedom of the entrepreneur or the customer—Simon reflects a widely held view in treating autonomy as a social concept. As one commentator on contemporary democratic theory put it, "autonomy in most democratic theory is now assumed to arise only in a social context."[13] To sum up, Simon, while not denying the relevance of a notion of freedom depending upon property as a guarantee, directs all of his attention to the freedom of autonomy that is non-individualistic. In short, the "freedom *from* abusive power" is distinct from "the freedom of a group *to* govern itself" (*PDG* 76).

To define autonomy simply as self-government is insufficient. In an account that owes much to Maritain, Simon notes that freedom of autonomy is a terminal freedom. Properly speaking, it "is constituted by the presence of law within liberty. It is won by an interiorization of the law" (*CF* 18).[14] This is a formulation opposed to the Kantian notion of autonomy but congruent with that of Durkheim, except that Durkheim has a more limited notion of law than Simon. Autonomy can be absolute, as in God, or relative, as in human beings. This occurs when "the spontaneous inclinations of the agent coincide with the exigencies of the law" (*CF* 20). Simon sets out a program when he states that "the sure means of starving despotism out of existence is to realize, at all levels of personal and social life, the fusion of law and freedom" (*CF* 21). We are now prepared to deal with "the quest for autonomy as it should be pursued in the humble and fruitful tasks of daily life" (*CF* 30).

In a series of inquiries stretching over more than twenty years, Simon, starting from an examination of the meaning of the term "work," elaborated conceptions of autonomy in the workplace that precede and parallel what he had to say about autonomy in the political realm. The *Three Lectures on Work* (1938), in which the first account of workplace autonomy was sketched, was followed by "The Concept of Work," *Philosophy of Democratic Government*, and the posthumous *Work, Society and Culture*.[15] The first socioeconomic treatment preceded the first application of the theory of autonomy in the political domain in *Nature and Functions of*

---

[13]Dennis Thompson, *The Democratic Citizen: Social Science and Democratic Theory in the Twentieth Century* (Cambridge: Cambridge University Press, 1970), 14. Simon says, "it follows that it is not in solitude but in the community that the quest for autonomy should be pursued" (*Community of the Free*, 30.)

[14]The original statement dates from 1945.

[15]Yves R. Simon, "The Concept of Work," in Robert B. Heywood, ed., *The Works of the Mind* (Chicago: University of Chicago Press, 1947).

Authority (1940). It is a fair conclusion that Simon was initially concerned with social autonomy and subsequently became concerned with political autonomy. For a Thomist, there seem to be good methodological reasons for proceeding in this way.

The focus in the *Three Lectures* is on the industrial world. In a metaphysical perspective, work is contrasted with contemplation. It is useful activity, geared to the state of the thing being worked on, and involves generosity and motion (thus is subject to the law of change and time) (*TLT* 2; cf. *WSC* 5–8). On each of these points, with the exception of generosity, contemplation differs from work. Of course, there are intermediary forms of activity, particularly mental activity, that involve work. Clearly, there are some paradoxical features to the notion of intellectual work.[16] While it is an error to conceive of mind, as some philosophers do, as a "productive faculty," it would equally be an error to see in manual work "the highest form of activity" (*TLT* 10–11). If autonomy is, as we have seen, "the presence of law within liberty," it first arises in the world of manual labor when one compares "legal fulfillment" and "the order of free expansion" (*TLT* 16). To work as a gardener in order to fulfill a need differs from the same work done as an amusement or pastime. The first concept comprises "activities which fulfill a definite prescription of a biological or national nature"; the second "aims at some human perfection placed outside the sphere of definite prescription" (*TLT* 16). Now, the way in which this affects the worker is that he "finds the fulfillment of his personal being in the very exercise of his generosity," even though it is true that he labors for the work and not himself. Or take the case where there is legal fulfillment without this free expansion, an all too frequent case. What Simon is getting at is "the expansion and felicity of the creative life" (*TLT* 44). In such favorable instances, the law of the object is united with the expansion of the working subject.

Legal fulfillment includes scientific discipline and arts and crafts. The argument turns to the development of what Simon calls "technical culture" (*TLT* 58).[17] As long as the worker is involved solely in execution, and not in the direction of work, he is deprived of free expansion. He is told what to do; he does it, and gets paid for it. But it is obviously a matter of degree. The question of free expansion is a question of access to technical

---

[16]Denis de Rougemont examines these paradoxical features in *Journal d'un intellectuel en chomage (1933–1935)* in a compilation, *Journal d'un époque (1926–1946)* (Paris: Gallimard, 1968), 149–53.

[17]See also Simon, "The Concept of Work," 16.

culture. What is envisaged is the free worker's participation in the direction of work. And, if we are to believe the labor sociologists, the demand of workers is not simply one for higher wages, but has as "its principal origin the heteronomy (*Fremdbestimmung*) of work" (*TLT* 69–70). Simon sums up the problem:

> It is clear that this absence of initiative eliminates any chance for the worker to acquire the wisdom of the social laborer. Prudence having for its content the very use of freedom, the possibilities of a worker culture of a prudential type corresponds strictly to the amount of autonomy possessed by the worker (*TLT* 70).

The perspective here is that of large industry and the possibilities within that sphere of "a broad liberation of worker initiatives" (*TLT* 70). Stated in the language of autonomy, the answer is not in replacing subordinative relations by contractual relations, but by the constant association of two principles:

> *The principle of authority*: whenever the welfare of a community requires unity of conduct in matters where the meeting of minds is uncertain, either in principle or simply in fact, this unity of conduct must be assured by the decision of the higher organs of the community. . . .

> *The principle of autonomy*: in a hierarchical whole, whenever a function can be assumed by the lower without detriment to the object of this function, it should be effectively assumed by it, for there is more perfection in a whole whose parts are full of life than in one where the parts are but instruments crossed by the initiative of the higher organs of the community (*TLT* 70–71; cf. *NF* 44–45).

It seems to me that Simon first sees the issue of autonomy in the industrial workplace arise in the relationship between technical imperatives and the development of a technical culture in those who remain mere operatives and do not share in the direction of work itself. To distinguish this from another dimension of how autonomy is realized, or might be realized in the workplace, let us say that he began by looking at the working group distributively and then looks at it collectively, for autonomy essentially concerns the group.

Well, what is the collective aspect of the search for autonomy in the workplace? The same division of labor that produced "an unprecedented separation between planning and execution," has led to the development of the proletariat as a class of "permanent and hereditary wage-earners" (*WSC* 100). Following Goetz Briefs, Simon wants to distinguish between the proletariat and the working-class and to argue that the former term is not appropriate to the American case.[18] Nevertheless, the problem of autonomy remains, even when one denies the existence of a class of permanent and hereditary wage-earners: "Every community normally tends to achieve autonomy. This is a sort of law: whenever there is a normal community, there is also a tendency toward autonomy" (*WSC* 104). Since the working-class, because of the conditions of modern production, is a community, it has this tendency as well. However, it is a class that once had no autonomy, no power of self-government. The principal institution that contributes to the autonomy of the worker is, of course, the labor union. While Simon has no illusions about the shortcomings of labor unions, he says that

> labor organizations have accomplished the double feat of helping to establish discipline among masses of men and of giving such discipline the higher meaning of autonomy. What this great product of the technological society—the labor union—has done for autonomy is of such exceptional value that any reform which would jeopardize the operation of labor unions or alter their essential constitution is bound to arouse the suspicion of the democratic mind (*PDG* 306).

He goes on to refer to "two essential organs of democratic life—the party and the labor union" (*PDG* 317).

If Simon were maintaining that the present adversarial relationship that characterizes labor-management interactions was sufficient to guarantee the collective autonomy of various groupings of workers, his position would be open to serious objection. The legal relationship between management and labor insures the perpetuation of a basically authoritarian system and the term is used by Simon to contrast that kind of system with a democratic one (*PDG* 142).[19] Simon was clearly interested in going beyond the *status quo* in industrial relations when he treated the issue of autonomy in reference to the labor group considered collectively. The degree of autonomy that has been achieved through the efforts of

---

[18]Goetz Briefs distinguishes between the wage-earner group and the proletariat in *The Proletariat*, 22–23. He did believe that "the creation of a genuine proletariat is now in progress" in the United States (167–68).

[19]"Any method which subtracts the governing personnel from the control of the people can be termed 'authoritarian'."

labor unions would have to be extended, and he suggests the kinds of institutions that might affect this transition. Among the new forms of community life he has in mind are "mutual-assistance societies, consumers' cooperatives, institutes for popular education, factory committees, autonomous workshops" (CF 29). It seems to me that the last of these is the most promising and most in line with the development of workers' movements in Europe since Simon wrote on these subjects. The thrust of his thought seems to be in the direction of self-management within the existing capitalist system, rather than self-management socialism as understood in France.[20] Whether such a transition would be achieved mainly through concern for productivity or occur through greater worker representation on management commitees—by broadening collective bargaining in order to allow for greater participation, by recourse to public legislation, or some other presumably democratic means—is open to question. Simon indicates the need for greater autonomy within a system that continues to require authoritative structures, but he apparently did not think that the task of the philosopher is to elaborate the specific steps by which this might be achieved. This is in line with his general reluctance to enter into the level of decision-making, which should, in his opinion, be left for prudential judgment.

Now, while I have spoken of two dimensions as Simon did, it is obvious that there is a close relationship between the prospect of the workers acquiring a greater technical culture and that of greater worker self-management. Analytically distinct, the two dimensions are joined in actuality. If Simon has made so much of the need for worker autonomy, the principle of autonomy, it should not be assumed that it would operate to the detriment of the principle of authority. The issue concerns the manner in which these two principles will be joined within technological society.

Simon suggests that there is a connection between the absence of self-government in the workplace and the dificulties of the worker in learning to govern himself in his moral and social life. Even though this connection is not a necessary consequence, "it is psychological and likely to be a matter of fact in a majority of cases" (PDG 299).

Up to now, attention has been focused on the industrial workplace. In *Philosophy of Democratic Government*, Simon turns to agriculture, a field hitherto neglected in his analysis of the modern workplace. Since agriculture does not allow for the kind of division of labor characteristic of in-

---

[20]Ralph Nelson, "Emmanuel Mounier, Between Proudhon and Marx," *Science et Société* XXXI:2 (University of Montreal, 1979): 225.

dustry, the opportunities for workers to govern their own work is much greater in it: "All other things being equal, the farm worker finds in the condition of his work an opportunity in training for self-government, both in the technical order and in the human order, which industrial conditions do not furnish" (*PDG* 301). The economic unit he has in mind, however, is not what is now called agribusiness, but the family farm. While there is an old tradition in France glorifying this institution, it is an object of veneration in North America as well.[21] Here, as elsewhere, the lone entrepreneur or worker is not the focus of attention, but the group, that is, the family. However, where the call for greater autonomy in the industrial workplace would be considered a radical idea, at least in North America, the defense of the family farm might be viewed as reactionary, nostalgic,[22] economically unrealistic. The family farm is viewed as a way of life, not simply as a business. Simon is well aware that a certain kind of paternalism may threaten this institution as a center of autonomous work. Yet, that aside, he presents a strong argument for the values of this form of rural life. Of course, this coincides with an old strand of Catholic social thought based on the family unit.

In any case, it is surely a sign of our times that the family farm is greatly threatened today and may not endure much longer as an important aspect of agricultural production. Regardless of the values it embodies, is it likely that an institution that is apparently economically unviable—because of the cost of machinery and other capital investment, not to speak of the risks of farming itself—will be maintained for traditional reasons? It is commonplace to consider the loss of a farm by a family, particularly one that has labored for generations on the land, as a catastrophe, while the demise of an urban family business goes unmourned. While one can agree

---

[21]"At that time, as since, agriculture in France was more than an occupation; it was what with proper solemnity would now be called a way of life," John Kenneth Galbraith, *Economics in Perspective: A Critical History* (Boston: Houghton Mifflin, 1987), 46.

[22]In a chapter entitled "The Nature of Social Nostalgia," Galbraith says: "This manifestation of social nostalgia explains the unique reverence with which, in the United States, we regard the family farm. It is our most important surviving example of comprehensive economic administration by the household. Where, under the pressure of economic circumstance, the family farm gives way to a highly capitalized enterprise with a sizable labor force, we do nothing about it. And almost any farm with less than a million dollars of invested capital or two airplanes can still be called a family farm" (*The Liberal Hour* [New York: Houghton Mifflin, 1960], 108).

with much that Simon says about the family farm, the shortcoming of his treatment of the problem of agriculture in his reflections on democracy and technology is that he does not really examine the effect of technological developments in agriculture on the units of production. This does not mean that we must accept a kind of technological determinism, or assume, as Marx did, that there will be large agricultural factories just as there are large industrial ones. But the conditions of modern agriculture may indicate the need for new forms of association which, while taking into account the laws of agricultural work, will provide new opportunities for self-government. Unless it is believed that the family farm is a more durable institution than I have supposed, this is the direction in which the quest for autonomy in rural life must turn.

Throughout his writings on work, Simon revealed a concern for the secessionist or rebellious tendencies of the working class. To counter this tendency, already an old aspect of the modern industrial order, Simon proposed measures that would provide for the integration of the working class in modern society. This integration presupposed the joint operation of the two principles of authority and autonomy. It would provide not only for the technical culture of the worker, but the increased self-government of the working class. This remains an important issue in the contemporary industrial order.

When he turned his attention to agriculture, Simon quite understandably praised an institution that to a considerable degree had achieved the joint operation of the two principles, the family farm. If the quest for autonomy in rural life can no longer rely on this institution as a basis, than an inquiry faithful to the Simonian project must canvass other possible institutional forms. If it is not the task of the social philosopher to invent such forms, it surely is his duty to show the need for them.

John A. Gueguen

Parallels on Work, Theory, and Practice in Yves R. Simon And John Paul II

This study is an exercise in liberal education understood as an on-going contemporary conversation between outstanding representatives of two traditions of discourse—the one secular and academic and the other ecclesial and pastoral.[1] It is not intended to explicate or comment upon the lectures of Yves R. Simon or the encyclical letter of Pope John Paul, but rather to set them side by side so as to note the common insights that can help us to understand work better than we do and to enhance our capacity to derive more benefit from the specific forms of work we engage in.[2]

In pursuit of this objective, we shall also note that the study provides evidence of an essential compatibility between reason and revelation. Simon's application of Aristotelian philosophy (metaphysics, psychology, ethics, and politics) and John Paul's application of Sacred Scripture (especially the anthropology he finds within it) complement and reinforce each other in arriving at similar conclusions from diverse analyses concerning the meaning of human work in a common context of challenges brought against its authenticity by forces at work in the modern world.

Simon conducts a philosophical analysis that falls into equal parts:

---

[1]This study focuses on parallel passages in Yves R. Simon's *Work, Society, and Culture* and Pope John Paul II's *Laborem Exercens* (On Human Work) (Boston: Saint Paul editions, 1981).

[2]An earlier version of this study was presented at the annual meeting of the *American Maritain Association* at the University of Notre Dame on October 29, 1988. The author is grateful for observations offered by those present when the paper was presented, some of which have been incorporated into this version.

theoretical (lectures 1–3) and practical (lectures 4–6). In the former, he examines work from several related points of view (which he calls psychological-metaphysical and socio-ethical); in the latter, he shows how these standpoints throw light on several aspects of the history of the labor movement, wealth, and culture. Throughout, he proceeds by simple examples, inviting his students to view each question from various angles until an answer emerges. Logically, the practical part comes first, because it suggests why Simon finds it desirable or necessary to take up a definition of work.

In the encyclical, John Paul summarizes and updates the Church's social teaching as it concerns human work. Meditating and commenting mainly upon the Bible, the Pope speaks for the Church's theological analysis of the way social reality impacts upon work in the context of what has been called over the past hundred years "the labor question."[3] He calls upon historical experience and scholarship in the social sciences to show how recent developments in technology, economics, and politics require fresh attention to the meaning of work.

The year 1988 marks the fiftieth anniversary of Simon's monograph, *Trois leçons sur le travail*,[4] and the thirtieth anniversary of his course "On Work and the Workman" at the University of Chicago (Committee on Social Thought). Midway between those two dates, Simon contributed "The Concept of Work" to a Chicago symposium on *The Works of the Mind* (1947). His reflections on the place of work in human and social life belong to a comprehensive set of interests in theoretical and practical philosophy that developed over time in his examinations of knowledge and experience, freedom and community. For Vukan Kuic, who edited the lectures for posthumous publication, they contain "a complete prescription, difficult to fill but realistic, on how it may be possible to save the modern man from himself" (*WSC* xv).

If Karol Wojtyla had heard Simon's lectures, his attention might especially have been caught by a reference to Saint John of the Cross, the subject of his own doctoral dissertation.[5] He would surely agree with Simon's

---

[3]John Paul II, *Laborem Exercens*, 9. [Due to the frequent use of this work in the article, it is referred to by *LE* and placed within the text according to the method adopted for books by Adler, Simon, and Maritain—Ed.]

[4]The three lessons are on "the definition of work," "work and wealth," and "the worker's culture."

[5]Simon also cited Saint John of the Cross in *Critique de la connaissance morale* (Paris: Desclée de Brouwer et Cie, 1934).

praise of the Spanish mystic's insight into the way love links work with contemplation, an even more exalted form of human activity. Simon's course reaches a climax at the end of the theoretical part, where he shows how a worker is motivated by the love of friendship, a form of love where the center of attention lies outside the self. "The great adventure of work," he writes, "is that it promotes precisely such feelings and not only among a chosen few but practically among the whole of mankind" (*WSC* 71). It brings out a "communion in appreciation . . . living within each and all" and "at all times"—an expression suggesting the theme of "solidarity" that is to be found in *Laborem Exercens* and in all of Pope John Paul's social writings and speeches.[6]

Wojtyla would also have understood and respected the difference between Simon's purpose and method, and his own orientation to work. It is not surprising, given that difference, that the two texts under study here contain no footnoted references in common. The encyclical cites only the Old and New Testaments, the Papal and Conciliar Magisterium, and the Common Doctor of the Church, Saint Thomas Aquinas. Simon's lectures never once cite those authorities; his references run from Aristotle to a range of contemporary authorities in the humanities and social sciences, but, in the main, his own and others' experiences underlie the argument.[7]

Linking those diverse approaches is a common awareness of the dangers and difficulties confronting work and workers as a result of modern ideological forces arrayed against the classical and Christian traditions. Simon's thought seems fundamentally inspired by the need to provide a philosophical critique of *laissez-faire* economic theories which treat human labor as just another commodity that can be bought and sold in the market (*WSC* 137). The Pope is sensitive to the same error, which he

---

[6]Cf. *LE* 19–22 and *Sollicitudo Rei* (On Social Concern, 1987).

[7]So far as I can determine, Simon rarely cited Scripture in his published work or paid explicit attention to the social documents of the Church. I have found a few references to the encyclicals of Pope Leo XIII. In Simon's Aquinas lecture at Marquette University—*Nature and Functions of Authority*—he quoted from Leo's *Immortale Dei* (On the Christian Constitution of States, 1885), in a note. The same quotation, which summarizes Leo's general theory of government, is noted in *Philosophy of Democratic Government*, Simon's Walgreen lectures at the University of Chicago. Elsewhere in that work, he notes *Rerum Novarum* (On the Condition of the Working Class, 1891), with reference to freedom, and *Diuturnum* (On the Origin of Civil Power, 1881), with reference to civil government and to sovereignty. As may be expected, Simon often makes use of the work of Saint Thomas Aquinas and other scholastic commentators on Aristotle.

identifies as "materialistic economism" (*LE* 17ff).

In the fifth lecture, "Work and Wealth," Simon cites the Charter of the International Labor Organization as evidence that by 1919 "the principle that human labor was *not* an item of merchandise . . . had been accepted all over the world by most diverse sections of opinion" (*WSC* 132). If further evidence was needed of the failure of *laissez-faire*, it was the practical experience of the Great Depression, when "abundance itself was a cause of poverty. . . . This tragic experience," he goes on, "should have opened our eyes to the immense fact that wealth can never be distributed adequately by means of exchange alone" (*WSC* 139ff). Compensation according to services rendered and distribution according to need—both admirable principles, in his view—become impossible if human labor is treated as a commodity. Moreover, the unmasking of this error will lead to a moral review of all commodities: "From now on," Simon writes, "they too must be evaluated by humane and social standards; . . . the market place will increasingly be judged by rules pertaining to human labor" (*WSC* 138).

John Paul also mentions the I.L.O. in his discussion of the human rights of workers that are threatened by the modern denial of the principle of the priority of labor over capital (*LE* 26). *Laborem Exercens* contains a spirited critique of "economism," which in the early nineteenth century asserted that work is "a sort of merchandise that the worker sells to the employer." Like Simon, the Pope argues that recent developments make this earlier view untenable in theory as well as in practice; it has given way to "more human ways of thinking about work." Nevertheless, John Paul cautions that as long as philosophical materialism maintains an influence in the world, there is danger that this erroneous view of work as "an impersonal force needed for production" will reassert itself (*LE* 17ff).

If the restoration of Aristotelian realism in our thinking about human, and especially social work is Simon's leading purpose in these lectures, John Paul's corresponding objective is a reassertion of the primacy of the person over things—a principle he finds in the "Gospel of work" (*LE* 16, 57, 61). For him, the great need at present is to prevent "the objective dimension of work" (roughly equivalent to Simon's psychological-metaphysical dimension) from gaining the upper hand over "the subjective dimension" (which Simon calls socio-ethical), thereby depriving the worker of his dignity and reducing his inalienable rights (*LE* 25; cf. 14, 15, 17). To prevent the placing of man and his work in such a position of dependence, the Pope appeals for changes in theory and practice in line with a conviction that labor has primacy over the means of production and over capital (*LE* 32, 34).

Those familiar with the personalist character of Karol Wojtyla's life work will recognize here that the Pope's interest in work is instrumental to his prior concern for man, the subject of work, for man as worker is first man as man. Work must be attended to because it lies at the heart of the human question, especially in its social dimension. The entire first decade of John Paul's pontificate has seen a sustained and multidimensional pursuit of the truth about man in light of the Church's knowledge of the Man-God, Jesus Christ. When the Pope looks at work "from the point of view of man's good," he sees that it is "probably *the essential key* to the whole social question" (*LE* 7, 10).

This link between man as a whole and man as worker is what gives the ethical and social character of work a special urgency—for both pope and philosopher—in the present circumstances of technological and economic development. The "very important conclusion" John Paul draws from theological-anthropological analysis of work is that work must be "for man," and not man "for work" (*LE* 17); the worker must know at all times that he is working in the first place "for himself," and not for "the economy" (*LE* 38). The Pope adds that this is why private ownership is preferable to public; Simon concurs: "Personally, I prefer free distribution through independent institutions rather than directly through state institutions" (*WSC* 141).

After treating this central theme of the personal, or subjective, character of work and the worker, John Paul moves on to the way work supports family life—a matter Simon also insists upon. For the Pope, "the family constitutes one of the most important terms of reference for shaping the social and ethical order of human work." It does this, in large part, by serving as the primary educational agency in human development: "The family is simultaneously a community made possible by work and the first school of work . . . for every person" (*LE* 24ff).[8] Later, he derives practical conclusions from this thesis (for example, the family wage) (*LE* 46).

Simon takes up the family in lecture 3, "Man at Work." He observes that in modern times there has been "an enormous separation between work and family life," in contrast to Aristotle's observation that "what is daily an essential in the life of work is performed within the family unit." Here "the extremely precarious bonds of love and affection which are supposed to hold families together are constantly strengthened by the members' association in the daily actuality of work. . . . Working together, they all share also in the sociability of the worker. Their unity, in other words, is brought about by their common tasks, which most naturally in-

---

[8]This is further developed in *Familiaris Consortio* (The Role of the Christian Family in the Modern World, 1981), part iii.

volve a division of labor" (*WSC* 89, 77ff). The natural sociability of work done in common (the Pope would say "solidarity") lays a basis in the elementary human association for stability in community life, by strengthening the bonds of love and friendship in the most natural way. What John Paul ascribes to person, Simon ascribes to nature. The philosopher hopes, incidentally, that the shortening of the workday will allow more time for working at home in the presence of the family (*WSC* 83).

After treating the family, *Laborem Exercens* moves on to the broader sphere of social relationships. This third "sphere of values" connected to work is "a great historical and social incarnation of the work of all generations." As in the family, this heritage passes from generation to generation by means of education (*LE* 24ff). Past work keeps adding to the patrimony of the human family and contributes to the building up of culture.

Simon dwells at greater length on this matter of "the right conduct for the individual in his relations with members of social groups to which he belongs." He applies socio-ethical analysis to historical materials in an effort to discover "the right order to be established in the uses of human freedom" (*WSC* 56), and in the final lecture enlarges on many implications for culture. For Simon, "the principle of the social utility of work" is "an essential part" of his theoretical definition (*WSC* 109). "I insist," he had said at the outset of the lectures, "that work cannot be defined without reference to society. . . . The man who does nothing but speculate" may be engaged in something intrinsically more valuable than working, but he does no work "because he does not render a service to society. To qualify as work, an activity must not only be honest but also socially productive" (*WSC* 31, 38ff; cf. 55, 110).

While Simon asserts with John Paul that "the end [of work] is not in wealth but always in man," and that "the real wealth produced by work is above all destined to serve," he develops more fully what the Pope calls the "objective dimension" of work (*WSC* 118, 121). This is understandable in view of the Pope's greater attention to the human person than to implications for work, which Simon finds so interesting in the Aristotelian focus on human nature. John Paul is surely not indifferent to those implications; at one point, he asserts that "the moral obligation of work" flows from man's nature, which is thereby maintained and developed, as well as his responsibilities to family and society—to what he refers to as "the indirect employer" (*LE* 39ff). But what John Paul notes in passing, Simon brings out in its psychological-metaphysical fullness.

Perhaps the most eloquent passages deal with philosophical distinctions between work and contemplation, and between work and art. In the former case, we are shown how "the terminal character of contemplation

[is] in sharp opposition to the mere usefulness of work," that is, to the transformation of physical nature for human purposes. This utility of work is what Simon refers to as "a metaphysical characteristic of work: Work is never a terminal activity"; or, as John Paul puts it, work is always something transitive—for it "always leads to something else" (*WSC* 109ff). This is a metaphysical characteristic in that work involves a "compromise with the law of what is," with "pre-existent data" (*WSC* 74, 76). While art "is always an activity of free development," work occurs under the constraints of being, of the existing state of things, and is thus "an activity of legal fulfillment"; it is "always something serious" (*WSC* 31, 74, 76).

In contrast to both work and art, contemplation "is always an end in itself and can thus never be useful. In fact, it is better than useful" (*WSC* 13). Simon hopes that this distinction might lead to a new "ethic of the worker" which replaces "resentment of the contemplatives" with a recognition of "the goodness of things that have nothing to do with social utility." Aristotle justifies contemplative life "because he has an idea of the good that is . . . desirable for itself because it is an end in itself" and hence "better than useful" (*WSC* 55).

Still, Simon does not want us to agree with Josef Pieper that leisure for art and contemplation is the "basis" of culture. A good it surely is, but the activity leisure permits, in Simon's more socially or politically sensitive view, transcends culture and benefits mainly the individual. Conditions that facilitate work are what provide the real foundation for developing social life. In a passage I find somewhat prophetic, Simon says at the conclusion of his lectures: "The real basis of culture . . . is to be found rather in activities in the performance of which a workmanlike disposition is indispensable. . . . Holding out an ideal of culture based on freedom from work inevitably leads to a disorderly exaltation of the flowery element of culture, and this makes for subjectivism, arbitrariness, and an attitude of frivolous aversion to nature and its laws." Therefore, "the immediate task before us appears to be the development of a theory of culture centered not on leisure but on work in the broadest sense, including moral, social, and intellectual, as well as technical and manual work" (*WSC* 185ff).

That John Paul would agree with this is evident in the very first sentence of the encyclical: "Through work man must . . . contribute to the continual advance of science and technology and, above all, to elevating unceasingly the cultural and moral level of society within which he lives in community with those who belong to the same [human] family" (*LE* preface, 5). He indicates, too, that more and more of the weight of this responsibility will fall upon persons who work with their minds, as machines come to replace what for centuries has been the principal form of work.

The Pope carries forward this observation in a quasi-poetic meditation on the spirituality of work that draws upon his theological sources. Having explained how work enters into the salvation process, he finds a particularly apt passage in Vatican II's *Gaudium et Spes* (On the Church in the Modern World):

> When a man works he not only alters things and society, he develops himself as well. He learns much, he cultivates his resources, he goes outside of himself and beyond himself. Rightly understood, this kind of growth is of greater value than any external riches which can be garnered.... Hence, the norm of human activity is ... that it should harmonize with the genuine good of the human race and allow people as individuals and as members of society to pursue their total vocation and fulfill it (*LE* 61).[9]

Simon treated this subject in the context of the worker "as a psychological type" whose exclusive concern is with the thing to be produced and hence is a kind of lover. Ultimately, workers whose interest is absorbed in things strictly external to themselves, as they observe the metaphysical laws cited earlier, coincide with lovers as a psychological type (*WSC* 66ff, 70). Simon goes even farther to assert that "the good worker and the lover of truth ... have much in common, and the promotion of their understanding could do a great deal for the reformation of our concept of culture" (*WSC* 187). When I am "struggling toward what is good for my fellow men," I am "simultaneously struggling ... toward an order of wisdom." Hence, "it is even clearer that social action in the community at large must be combined with the psychology of the lover if it is to be genuine. We all expect social workers to be animated by love because when they are not so animated social work is necessarily perverted. How could it be social work if it is not coupled with love for one's fellow men?" (*WSC* 70). So "there is such a thing as love ... in struggle," as Simon had said when he introduced the notion of love in his first lecture. "And there is such a thing as love in presence and joy.... The higher, the more perfect, the more genuine form of love exists ... in presence and by way of rest" (*WSC* 7). Through love, work and rest enter a unity that is at once metaphysical (in origin) and cultural (in end).

A final problem, however, remains to be met, and that is what Simon calls the "irksomeness" of work (*WSC* 31ff). The Pope, too, observes the "heavy toil" that sometimes accompanies human work, both physical and intellectual (*LE* 22).

Simon deals with this problem by simply excluding irksomeness from

---

[9]This passage is quoted from sec. 35 of *Gaudium et Spes*.

his theoretical definition of work. While it must be admitted that there is "a permanent foundation for irksomeness" in work because it is "legal" and not "free" activity, still, the frequently onerous and sometimes oppressive character of work is not "essential" to it (*WSC* 31ff).

John Paul, I think, is able to do better than this: "In spite of all this toil—perhaps, in a sense, because of it—work is a good thing for man." It is good *because* it is irksome, a *bonum arduum* in the terminology of Aquinas. On this last point, the Pope is able to go farther, because he associates work with virtue, a virtue he calls industriousness, a part of the cardinal virtue of fortitude. This virtue brings out the goodness in toil and enables work to perfect man in spite of its irksomeness and even its oppressiveness. Hence John Paul adds that there is a "moral obligation to link industriousness as a virtue with the social order of work" (*LE* 22–24).[10] Simon's understanding of moral virtue as "habitus" makes him want to exclude virtuous activity from any association with work. Yet, almost in the same breath, he admits that "these things are profoundly mysterious" (*WSC* 19, 24).[11] John Paul's resources give him an advantage over the Aristotelian philosopher when it comes to things mysterious. And so, at the end of the encyclical, where he meditates on work in the context of the Cross of Christ, we can see why, for him, toil "goes with" work (*LE* 63).[12] Perhaps, if Simon were to look at the matter in that light, he might be able to admit that industriousness is a facilitating "habitus" for human work after all. For, as a Christian and Thomist, he knew that, for all the greatness of philosophy, there is a brighter light than reason, a stronger force than nature.

---

[10]The reference is to Saint Thomas Aquinas, *Summa Theologiae*, I–II, 40, 1 and 43, 2 ad 1.

[11]Cf. *The Definition of Moral Virtue*, especially chap. 3. It may be significant that one of Simon's rare citations of Scripture is Saint Paul's "We see now through a mirror in an obscure manner . . ." (1 Cor. 13:12) in *A General Theory of Authority*.

[12]Cf. *Salvifici Doloris* (On the Christian Meaning of Suffering, 1984), where he does for pain what he does for work in *Laborem Exercens*.

Part III
Jacques Maritain

John Hellman

Maritain, Simon, and Vichy's Elite Schools

I. Forming Youth Leaders:
August 1940 to June 1941

During the early years of the war, the Vichy regime tried to revolutionize French young people with elite schools in an effort to transform the country through a "National Revolution." One of those schools, the Ecole Nationale des Cadres d'Uriage, was particularly prominent and sophisticated—a surrogate for the old Ecole Normale Superièure, which, despite its very limited enrollment, had produced an impressive number of the leaders of the now defunct and discredited Republic. From August 1940 to June 1941, the Uriage school evolved from the relatively modest ambition of training instructors for one of the new scout-like youth movements,[1] to becoming a "spiritual university" geared toward forming the elite of France's future leadership. As we shall see, there was a peculiar and somewhat paradoxical relationship between Jacques Maritain, and Yves R. Simon, and these now forgotten Vichy initiatives.

During the early 1940s, Simon told Maritain that their Thomism had failed as a guide to confronting the political situation in Europe. Simon was reading books on the French revolution, and he urged Maritain, too, to "rethink his past," especially his past attitude toward democracy. What disturbed Simon, first of all, was the shocking behavior of some of their friends during the war (eg., Father Garrigou-Lagrange, distinguished authority on Saint Thomas and celebrant of the Maritain retreats at Meudon a few years earlier, had become a firm champion of Franco and

---

[1]The *Chantiers de la jeunesse.*

Pétain, declaring support for de Gaulle a mortal sin for Catholics). In fact, there were problems with the attitude of a whole Catholic generation toward fascism. Simon, and eventually Maritain, too, wondered over the wisdom of their having concentrated their own energies at promoting a Thomist renaissance in their country, as the political situation steadily worsened.[2]

Jacques Maritain's influence in the 1920s and 1930s was not only in inspiring young philosophers such as Simon, Mortimer Adler, Etienne Borne, or Emmanuel Mounier, but also in more broadly shaping a new collective religious mentality. His popular books, such as *Antimodern, The Primacy of the Spiritual, Three Reformers,* and *Integral Humanism,* his efforts to shape a Catholic counterculture in reviews such as *Sept, Temps Présent,* or *Esprit,* the Meudon discussion and study circles, were all important for this. Internationally renowned and respected as a Catholic philosopher, theologian, and political theorist, Maritain was also a respected commentator on the arts, a social critic, and an expert on medieval thought who also lived as a conspicuous and charismatic ascetic, as a sort of lay cardinal, in the most rarefied intellectual and literary circles of Paris and New York. He was eventually venerated as a moral guide if not some kind of living saint by his contemporaries,[3] and so his attitude toward fascism in general, and toward the kind of clerico-quasi fascism around Pétain in par-

---

[2]Simon lamented, for example, that Christian and Thomist moderation of his earlier denunciation of the Italian invasion of Ethiopia that had rejected the idea of violent resistance to fascism. For further details on the events mentioned in this paragraph, see my essay, "Yves R. Simon, Jacques Maritain, and the Vichy Catholics," in Yves R. Simon, *The Road to Vichy, 1918–1938,* revised edition (Lanham, MD: University Press of America, 1988), vii–xxxiv.

[3]A typical anecdote: Paul Martin, Sr., later a distinguished Canadian politician, retains, as one of his most vivid memories of student days at Saint Michael's College at the University of Toronto during the 1930s, observing the great Jacques Maritain serving the morning Mass of a humble young priest in a campus basement chapel "as if he were just anyone" (interview with the author). In North American Catholic circles, where serious Catholic thought was largely imported, having Maritain around seemed the next best thing to having Saint Thomas Aquinas himself.

ticular, was of some importance.

At Vichy, the metamorphosis of young people was to be the thrust of the "National Revolution," a transformed elite among them was deemed essential to achieving this goal. Catholics were to be crucial to this effort;[4] on September 6, the new governmental organization created a "Secrétariat général à la jeunesse" with a young, devout engineer, Georges Lamirand, as "secrétaire général."

A thirty-four-year-old Catholic cavalry officer from a traditionalist provincial aristocratic background, Captain Pierre Dunoyer de Segonzac, received permission on August 12, 1940, to create a special school in a château near Vichy. It was to transform 140 junior officers into the first cadres for the "Chantiers de la Jeunesse."[5] With the requisitioning of a new château in the mountains above Grenoble and the arrival of a new cohort on October 5, 1940, however, Segonzac's school was no longer merely a leadership school for the "Chantiers" but, rather, a "Centre supérieur de formation des chefs," with what soon appeared to be the grandiose ambition of constituting an alternative sort of "Ecole Normale Supérieure," to replace the old secularizing and anti-Catholic one, and of creating a fresh kind of elite for a new kind of France.[6] The Catholic influence was graphically represented by the fact that the group of ninety-five original trainees

---

[4]Jean Ybarnégaray was given the new position of "Le Secrétariat d'Etat à la Famille et à la Jeunesse," created on July 12, 1940. He had been a right-wing deputy and the vice-president of Colonel de la Rocque's Parti Social Français (an organization dominated by Catholics), and he soon hired many Catholics.

[5]W.D. Halls, *The Youth of Vichy France* (Oxford: Oxford University Press, 1981), 311–12.

[6]The Ecole Normale Supérieure had long been a bête noire for French Catholics, for it had "long been the hatchery of France's liberal academic and even political elite," having "not only nurtured the secular sociology of Durkheim and the socialism of Jaurès and Lucien Herr," but also "served as headquarters of the pro-Dreyfus camp during the Affair." Cf. Paul Cohen, *Piety and Politics. Catholic Revival and the Generation of 1905–1914 in France* (New York: Garland, 1987), 19. By the late 1930s, French Catholics held the ENS responsible for an over-representation of Jews and Protestants among France's intellectual and political elites. Once the Catholics had the political backing, they turned to creating alternative institutions.

would number ten seminarians, . . . and even a Cistercian monk![7] Captain Dunoyer de Segonzac was an ardent Catholic, had contacts with the energetic "Latour-Maubourg" Dominicans[8] (the publishers of several reviews to which Maritain contributed), and deemed the French Catholic intellectual renaissance an inspiration for his school.

The school's dramatic new setting was the romantic "Chateau Bayard" near the alpine village of Saint Martin d'Uriage, on a high plateau above Grenoble. This imposing seventy-room historical edifice, whose first constructions dated from the twelfth century, was requisitioned, along with neighboring properties, including several chalets placed at the disposition of the married instructors. The school chaplain, the Abbé René de Naurois, would play a decisive role in its early ideological orientation. He was a disciple of Maritain's close friend Père Bernadot, founder of the erudite *La Vie Intellectuelle*, as well as of the more popular *Sept*. Despite his ties to intellectuals, Naurois was basically an activist,[9] who had been a militant member of *Esprit*'s activist auxiliary, the "Third Force," and had led *Esprit* group trips to Germany in the 1930s.[10] Naurois contributed to the distinctive religious element in the Uriage "style."

What was to be the general orientation of the new Ecole Nationale des Cadres d'Uriage? In an article on "youth movements" in Europe, one of the young instructors promoted the idea of a distinctly French experience

---

[7]The idea of even a few seminarians in the prewar ENS, with its high-powered rationalism, is hard to imagine. For these, and many other details regarding the Uriage school, I am much indebted to Bernard Comte's doctoral dissertation, *L'Ecole Nationale des Cadres d'Uriage. Une communauté éducative non conformiste à l'époque de la révolution nationale (1940–1942)* I & II (Lyon, 1987), 1203 pp. (in this case, 111 and 335). As M. Comte mentioned in his text, I do not agree with his general view of the overall significance of the Uriage enterprise.

[8]The convent and publishing offices of the avant-garde French Dominicans were located on the Boulevard Latour-Maubourg in Paris, near the Invalides.

[9]M. Hubert Beuve-Méry remembered him as "an odd sort of curé who looked more comfortable in battle fatigues with grenades strapped about his waist than in a cassock" (interview with the author).

[10]One of these, during Easter vacation in 1938, is described in Jacques Madaule's memoirs, *L'Absent* (Paris, 1973), 113–14. The young Frenchmen were invited to dinner by the *Deutsche-Französische Gesellschaft* and to visit a National Socialist *Ordensburg* (elite school) in the Baltic Sea.

over against the Italian and the German.[11] At this time, the Study Bureau of the "Secrétariat Général à la Jeunesse" was itself putting out a literature that referred to the famous reactionary writers of the nineteenth century such as Joseph de Maistre and Charles Maurras, but also to the authors of the Catholic revival—Péguy, François Perroux, Mounier, Berdyaev . . . and Jacques Maritain—and calling for a "purely French" youth option, a "Catholic Order."[12] And the Uriage school was to be just a beginning: in December 1940, Georges Lamirand proudly announced that he had created almost sixty "Ecoles des chefs" that rivaled one another in vision and enthusiasm. But at the head of them all was Uriage, the "université spirituelle de la jeunesse."[13]

II. The Study Group and the New Christian Order

The Abbé de Naurois encouraged *Esprit* director Emmanuel Mounier and the personalist philosopher Jean Lacroix, as well as Père Henri de Lubac, to help elaborate the Uriage ideology. And as it was being hammered out, in a crucial debate over "the future of French youth," Mounier's "communitarian personalism" surfaced as the most popular doctrine there. So, from relative obscurity, as a marginal radical Catholic writer, Mounier became *the* philosopher of the "spiritual university" of France's National Revolution. Displaying the school's greater ambitions, Segonzac and Naurois announced to the first evening fireside gathering of the December 1940 cohort, that all men, whatever post of command they would be responsible for in the outside world, whether functionaries or engineers, professor or lawyers, would submit to a training period at the school as part of a process of effecting the total transformation of France.[14]

At this point, a decisive, remarkable personality joined the staff of the school as director of studies. Hubert Beuve-Méry had been at *L'Institut français de Prague* from 1928–38, as well as correspondent for the prestigious newspaper *Le Temps* (whose confiscated facilities he would use, after the war, to create *Le Monde*). A vigorous and manly Catholic, a dedi-

---

[11]The sociologist Paul-Henri Chombart de Lauwe, cited in Comte, *Uriage*, 172.

[12]P. Ordoni, *Tout commence à Alger*, 106–15, cited by Comte, *Uriage*, 182.

[13]This is what the Uriage school was called in an official publication. See Comte, *Uriage*, 187.

[14]Comte, *Uriage*, 230.

cated alpinist convinced that the French were no match for the Nazis he had seen on the march in eastern Europe, Beuve-Méry had encountered similar thinking at the progressive Catholic weekly *Temps nouveau*,[15] directed by Maritain's close friend Stanislas Fumet, as well as at Mounier's *Esprit*.[16] After having held a French cultural and foreign affairs post of the French government in Lisbon for six weeks, Beuve-Méry returned to France to take up the position of director of studies at the Uriage school in June, 1941. Some months before, in an essay analyzing National Socialism, Beuve-Méry had argued that "over against the deprivations of intellectualism, of individualism, of liberalism, and of capitalism, over against the watering down and deviations of Christianity . . . before degenerating . . . into corruption and cruelty, [National Socialism] helped give men . . . a taste for life and the courage of sacrifice, the feeling of a solidarity and of a certain grandeur."[17] Soon, Beuve-Méry began setting forth a vision of a new, more virile Christianity, a personalist humanism, which could inspire the work of the men of Uriage.

By spring of 1941, the Uriage school had drawn the elite of France's young Catholic intellectuals:

- Hubert Beuve-Méry, founder of France's most important newspaper;

- Henri de Lubac, later to become one of France's most important postwar theologians and cardinal in the Catholic Church;

- Emmanuel Mounier, director of *Esprit*, France's most important Catholic intellectual review;

- Jean Lacroix, perhaps France's most important postwar personalist philosopher.

These talented, dedicated, and energetic young intellectuals were put together in a château with the flower of the younger members of the French officer corps and an apparent mandate to transform France's whole educational system, and, with it, French society. In any case, the naively enthusiastic general secretary, Lamirand, was delighted with Uriage and would remain a firm supporter . . . whatever the young people there thought of him. (On visiting Uriage, Lamirand began shaking hands

---

[15]He wrote a column for this journal under the pen name "Sirius."

[16]Maritain had played a key role in founding this. See my *Emmanuel Mounier and the New Catholic Left, 1932–1950* (Toronto: University of Toronto Press, 1981).

[17]Hubert Beuve-Méry, *Vers la plus grande Allemagne* (Paris, 1938), 100–01.

warmly with the cadets, looking each individual directly in the eyes in good "personalist" fashion. So, as a joke, several of the trainees, having passed to the other side of the hall, climbed down a drain pipe only to reappear at the door again ... and receive another "personal" hand-shake.)[18]

The "Uriage spirit" was first formulated, and then diffused, in the teaching given to the trainees and later passed on by them in the different schools in which they taught. After that, there was a publicly circulated, popularized periodical: *Jeunesse ... France!* There were also the Uriage Study Group's efforts to achieve a formal expression of their ideas, particularly in the Charter set down in late 1941, and also the alumni network set up by the school, the "Equipe Nationale d'Uriage." At Uriage, philosophers, heirs of Péguy, Blondel, and Maritain, with their dream of a spiritual revolution, met young army officers, heirs of Lyautey, with their own idea of a patriotic education geared toward disciplined and efficacious action. But always, at Uriage, the spiritual dimension drew everyone together. Père de Lubac described the "Catholic renaissance" as an element in the "present work of reconstruction" in France; citing Beuve-Méry, he conveyed the "dream of a generation of young Frenchmen who would take Christianity seriously."[19] Beuve-Méry, for himself, spoke of a "communitarian order" over against "anarchic individualism" and the "reign of money." In portraying what was distinctive about Uriage in *Temps nouveau*, Beuve-Méry described the school doctrine as contained in the

---

[18]Comte, *Uriage*, 320.

[19]Père de Lubac cited Beuve-Méry's article "Révolutions nationales, révolutions humaines," which had been published in *Esprit* (March 1941): 281–84. It is possible that de Lubac's hopes for a Christian renaissance growing from such somber times were encouraged by the cosmic optimism of his close friend and fellow Jesuit, the evolutionist Pierre Teilhard de Chardin. Mimeographed copies of Père Teilhard's speculations circulated at Uriage, and de Lubac wrote of his own hopes for a spiritual revival in France to the paleontologist, then in exile in China. Beuve-Méry's idea of creating elites who would be crucial once the inevitable authoritarian revolution came to France had already been noted in *Esprit* before the war. See *Esprit* 80 (May 1939): 302–03.

speeches of Pétain, but said "its method, its spirit" constituted its originality.[20]

The Uriage Charter, set down in fall of 1941, seemed a sort of "rule of life of a community," in which references to a "collective experience" eclipsed references to the Marshall and to the objectives of the National Revolution. The fundamental commitment of the school was to "the service of the spiritual," but, while only "a religious faith" could give "full value to that affirmation," a "man of good will" deciding to "transcend himself toward the ideal," could nurture an authentic interior life. The foremost authority on Uriage has described the first chapter of this Charter as very much reflecting "the vocabulary and structures of thought familiar to the readers of Jacques Maritain."[21] The visionaries of Uriage—consciously avoiding "the capital sin of caste spirit"—recognized that, for national renovation, the first condition was the "determining and putting in place of authentic elites." But how could one create these new elites in a France dominated by the Nazis? The correct sense of "strength" was regularly debated by the Christians at Uriage. In 1941, Etienne Borne showed the similarities and differences between the sort of "heroic" morality then being vaunted in France and true Christian morality. Père de Lubac analyzed the notion of a "virile order." Dunoyer de Segonzac rejected the notion that Christianity necessarily devirilized men.[22]

---

[20]*Temps nouveau* (August 15, 1941). This review was suppressed, along with *Esprit*, soon after the appearance of this article, as part of a struggle for the ideological orientation of the National Revolution. Dunoyer de Segonzac's pretensions and radical Catholic rhetoric had attracted people. Sympathizers of the *Action Française* feared for their own influence over the young.

[21]Comte, *Uriage*, 380.

[22]Etienne Borne, "D'un héroisme chrétien" in *Jeunesse et communauté nationale* (Cerf, Rencontre, n. 3, 1941). Pierre Dunoyer de Segonzac, "Réponse: Le christianisme a-t-il dévirilisé l'homme?" *Jeunesse de l'Eglise* 2 (1943): 78–82.

III. The Uriage "Style"

Was Uriage as uplifting as its instructors imagined it to be? One former trainee described his "growing discomfort in that 'community,' which seemed to have something of both the regiment and the monastery about it with . . . neither the interior liberty which . . . the army left to soldiers, nor the personal space which monastic silence provided. . . ."[23] But there were admirers, too. The extreme-right writer Alfred Fabre-Luce found the idea of an Order in the air at Uriage in fall 1941: "The carefully chosen youth of Uriage are like a first cell of a new world. . . . From a union of young and ardent young men, in a sublime setting *from which women are excluded* [emphasis my own], was germinating a force which endures. To the France of Pétain, will survive, if necessary, an Order of Knights of Uriage."[24] Again: "On that hill, I dreamed . . . of an Order of Knights who would maintain lofty values in the vulgarized 20th century world."[25] In fact, chivalry was evoked in the symbol marking Ecole Nationale des Cadres publications: a lance-bearing knight, mounted and armored from head to foot, his face entirely hidden in his mask. Here was a medieval ideal of honor and generosity over against the individualism and the materialism of a bourgeois and urbanized modern era. The influence of Berdyaev, with his book predicting *A New Middle Ages*, and of Maritain, combined with Péguy to inspire these initiatives. Maritain had backed Belgian Raymond De Becker's *Communauté* movement in 1933–34, an effort to create an explicitly Catholic "order" of laymen oriented toward the purification of its members while also supporting their political or social initiatives.[26] Another ecumenical, communitarian-style endeavor of the period—although itself directed by clergy, not laymen—was the famous Protestant monastic community of Taizé, near Lyon, which has promoted

---

[23]Interview recorded in Comte, *Uriage*, 397.

[24]Alfred Fabre-Luce, *Journal de France, 1939–1944*, definitive edition, vol. II (Geneva, 1946), 387. The original text is from 1942.

[25]Alfred Fabre-Luce, *Vingt-cing années de liberté*, II: *L'épreuve (1939–1946)* (Paris, 1963), 95. This text dates from twenty years later.

[26]Etienne Borne, "D'un héroisme chrétien."

charismatic multinational ecumenical gatherings of young Christians to this day. Some of these spiritual initiatives were less explicitly "medieval" than others, but all tended to assume that Western Europe had entered into a "New Middle Ages," probably for a long time, and one had to attune accordingly.

A year after the creation of the Ecole Nationale des Cadres d'Uriage, its directors enjoyed an attractive community life in an impressive retreat setting (facilities which the advocates of personalist revolution, at *Ordre Nouveau* or *Esprit*, did not yet have),[27] a task (the training of young men), a network of affiliates, and a method. They also enjoyed high-level government and Church endorsement and the encouragement of a whole network of prewar counterculture groups. Convinced of the insufficiency of the purely intellectual selection criteria of the *grandes écoles*, Uriage sought candidates "selected for their leadership abilities" or "remarkable simply for their aptitude to command."[28] The Uriage school alone (without its affiliates), during the first fifteen months of its activity, "formed" about 1,000 young men in ten normal sessions, and 600 in special sessions.[29]

The intelligentsia at the Ecole Nationale des Cadres regularly thought about their role in an international perspective. In his lecture on "a Christian explanation of our times," Père de Lubac criticized contemporary illusions and called for the development of a truly "Catholic" spirit after

---

[27]After the war, however, the *Esprit* group would build a community, which exists to this day, in the grouping of romantic old buildings in "Les Murs Blancs" at Chatenay-Malabry, near Paris, buildings acquired on the eve of the war. Mounier, Henri-Irenée Marrou, Jean-Marie Domenach, and Paul Ricoeur have been among the best known inhabitants.

[28]Dunoyer de Segonzac, "A la recherche des chefs," *Jeunesse ... France!* (September 22, 1941).

[29]Comte, *Uriage*, 419.

centuries of individualistic and rationalistic deviation ... a "human revolution." Père de Lubac's had something of the trans-cultural cosmic optimism of his friend Père Teilhard de Chardin, and he could have sketched the vast horizons of Teilhard's evolutionary metahistory at Uriage.[30] Hubert Beuve-Méry was, characteristically, more down to earth in his conferences, as he stressed the positive qualities of the Portuguese youth movements he had observed firsthand.[31] This was not so surprising because several French Catholic intellectuals in the 1930s had also evinced a sympathetic interest in the Portuguese model. Maritain, for example, was read and admired by Dr. Salazar and had visited Portugal on the dictator's personal invitation. Salazar represented a relatively "soft" Catholic authoritarianism, firmly "spiritualist" and anticommunist, capable of making its own sort of peace with a fascist Europe. Portuguese efforts to promote spiritual values among the young had to seem an attractive alternative to Nazism, to Bolshevism, and to the "materialism" of East and West for many French Catholics. The Uriage leaders, on their alpine plateau, seemed to think that France, too, could transcend republicanism, liberalism, and democracy, and create a relatively humane and Christian authoritarian regime, nurtured by "the primacy of the spiritual," in a lucid, critical acceptance of a European New Order.[32]

---

[30]Since, in Teilhard's evolutionary philosophy, "everything which rises must converge," fascism and National Socialism, however rough and aberrant at present, had necessarily to contribute to the inevitable spiritualization of mankind in the "noosphere." This was a useful perspective for trying to "Christianize" fascism or Nazism, but less encouraging to resisting totalitarianism in the name of individual liberty. Like so many others of his generation, Père Teilhard argued for the "personalizing" of the individual through communitarian involvement.

[31]Comte, *Uriage*, 466.

[32]Catholics had become so critical of "individualism" and "liberalism" by the late 1930s that they voiced little regret over their apparent disappearance from the European scene ... even if it was a scene dominated by Adolf Hitler. Nevertheless, Professor Comte tries hard to prove that, in contrast to the gist of several of their public pronouncements, the Uriage leaders never believed that international fascism would win the war.

IV. Life on the Mountain

The style of humanism that the Uriage school was trying to promote is well illustrated by the authorities, or literary references, alluded to in the lectures given there. Charles Péguy was most often cited; after him, Vigny, Montherlant, Saint-Exupéry, Malraux, Pascal, or Dostoevsky. Despite the grandiose pedagogical ambitions of the school, contemporary scientific thought was ignored, as were the questions that it raised about the human condition.[33] Georges Bernanos (who, like Maritain, had evolved from sympathy for the extreme right to antifascist, anti-Vichy polemics) was not cited at all, but Jacques Maritain often was—especially for his catchwords "primacy of the spiritual" or "integral humanism." In fact, poet Pierre Emmanuel thought that Maritain should be delighted by what was happening there, as he wrote the latter on September 27, 1941:

> . . . great movements are taking form in France: some . . . are rich with hope and promise. . . . In the youth movements whose leaders are among our friends there is . . . enthusiasm in discipline and hope for the future. L'Ecole des Cadres d'Uriage . . . is forming true men, in whom the feeling for spiritual reality is not stifled, but rather exalted, because it is considered in its relation to the most ordinary and everyday realities of political and social life.[34]

Emmanuel's assumption that Maritain might be pleased with Uriage is understandable if one considers Maritain's conceivable contributions to the style of the place:

(1) Maritain had helped precipitate general criticism of the "individualism" and "rationalism" of the modern world in his polemical works *Antimoderne* (1922) and *Trois réformateurs* (1925);

(2) he had eloquently called for the "primacy of the spiritual" (*Primauté du spirituel*, 1927);

(3) he had juxtaposed the "person" to individualism in the name of a "true humanism" that would herald a new Christianity (*Humanisme intégral: Problèmes temporels et spirituels d'une nouvelle chrétienté*, 1936);

(4) he had celebrated the Middle Ages, medieval virtues, aspects of the medieval *mentalité*, in his crusade for the philosophy of Saint Thomas

---

[33]Comte, *Uriage*, 473.

[34]Pierre Emmanuel to Jacques Maritain (September 27, 1941), cited and translated by Bernard Doering, *Jacques Maritain and the French Catholic Intellectuals* (Notre Dame: University of Notre Dame Press, 1983), 201.

Aquinas;

(5) he helped create communities of Christian elites—in the groups that met in his home in Meudon, in religious orders, and in concert with the reviews to which he contributed;

(6) he was a charismatic layman living an "antimodern" life of asceticism, purity, and chastity.

Even if Maritain would have been shocked by Uriage, his writings did contribute, at least to some extent, to what was distinctive about the school.

What was daily life at Uriage? The trumpet sounded at seven and the trainees had five minutes to gather in shorts in front of the château from where the physical education instructor led them across the park, with all of the instructors, Segonzac at their head, invariably participating. For twenty minutes, there were exercises of various sorts, then jogging and running at full speed, and finally the return to the château, chanting and in step, while all the while being exhorted by the coach "Allons garçons!" and "Secouons-nous!" Each student had his day set out on a chart divided into quarter-hour segments, color-coded for each activity. They were required to go everywhere in step, because, according to Segonzac, "to go from one point to the other in order and in rhythmic step is the best way to move quickly, harmoniously, buoyantly." But a trainee who was late for a meal—even if he had been performing a service for an instructor—had to stand and sing alone at his place before he could take his seat.

"Le vieux chef"[35] met with each candidate on arrival and "with his clear look and patient voice assessed his intentions." Cadets recalled Segonzac, interviewing a very promising prospect for membership on the staff, suddenly breaking off the interview and ushering the candidate unceremoniously to the door: the young man had wanted to know, first of all, how much he would be paid each month.[36] While singular dedication was expected of the staff, Segonzac also had a unique notion of the role of intel-

---

[35]This was the pet name given to Segonzac by the trainees, who were, themselves, only a few years younger than the "chefs" of Uriage.

[36]Comte, *Uriage*, 481, 486–87.

lectuals: "We should commission the intellectuals of the National Revolution without delay," he urged in March 1941; "Let's choose them preferably in good physical condition, good fathers of families and capable of jumping onto a moving streetcar."[37]

V. What Happened to Uriage?

It is highly unlikely that Jacques Maritain was pleased with initiatives like Uriage, for he was far more critical of Vichy privately than publicly. Yves R. Simon, for his part, was outraged by the Vichy involvements of their friends and pressed Maritain to denounce treasonous complicity with the values of the occupant. The Maritain-Simon letters during the late 1930s and the first two years of the Pétain regime show a growing sense of alienation from some of their closest friends over an increasing "softness" towards fascism in reviews like *Esprit* and *Temps Présent* in France . . . or even in *The Commonweal* in the United States.[38]

The Uriage School continued until the outright support of Vichy for the Nazi war effort, and the occupation of all of France by German forces in late 1942. In total, about 4,000 men had passed through it before it was closed down at the end of that year.[39] But even before the final disbanding of the school there had been tensions with the government. In fall 1941, for example, Maritain's old protegé Emmanuel Mounier was barred from the school as a result of animosity at Vichy toward the Christian personalism at Uriage by both some "Action Française" sympathizers (such as Henri

---

[37]"Intellectuals," *Jeunesse . . . France!* (March 8, 1941). Jacques Maritain would have probably been eliminated on all counts; Yves R. Simon, who had a tubercular leg, on one or two. Segonzac's idea seems to have been taken seriously. There was a conscious effort at Uriage by mountaineer Beuve-Méry to form intellectuals who were in top physical condition. Like Segonzac, he seemed to equate stoical virtues with Christian virtues.

[38]For more details on this matter, see John Hellman, "Yves R. Simon, Jacques Maritain, and the Vichy Catholics" in Yves R. Simon, *The Road to Vichy, 1918–1938*, revised edition Lanham, MD: University Press of America, 1988), vii-xxxiv, or "The Road to Vichy. Yves R. Simon's Lonely Fight against Fascism," *Crisis* V1:5 (May 1988): 30-37.

[39]Halls, *Youth*, 312.

Massis) and certain committed pro-Nazis.[40] The school became more and more sensitive to the internal power struggles in the Vichy regime, and identified, more and more, with old Marshall Pétain (as he was, or as they imagined him) over against the Pierre Laval clique. The directors of the school seemed more and more independent, charting their own course of National Revolution. As an historian of the regime remarked, Uriage was "the history of an alternative Vichy, one that might have been."[41]

By the end of December 1942, when the school was closed, the German disaster in the Russian campaign was apparent, and the occupation of all of France made Vichy's pretense at independence no longer credible. With the war turning against the Germans, and fear of communist domination of the Resistance growing, Dunoyer de Segonzac went to Algiers in early 1944 to explore the possibility of putting "his men" at the service of de Gaulle but, not altogether surprisingly, was rebuffed.[42] The Uriage network, without turning directly against the Marshall, organized more and more overtly for armed combat. Late in the war, Segonzac was given a command in the Free French forces, and, with several of his lieutenants, participated in the liberation of France. Several Uriage alumni lost their lives in liberating their homeland.

The Uriage château was taken over in early 1943 by an eccentric Acadian-American with a Ph.D. in Thomistic philosophy, M. de la Noüe du Vair, who lived there with his wife and many children like a great feudal lord. He turned the château, flying pennants with du Vair coat of arms from the battlements, into an aristocratic training school, in which everyone attended daily Mass, for the notorious *milice*. Subsequently, these white-gloved militia cadres, fearing Western Christian civilization threatened by an insurrection of the atheistic communists, did their best to help the Gestapo track down members of the Resistance. There are anecdotes of devoutly Catholic *milice* members saying the rosary together before facing Resistance firing squads.

At the end of the war, the members of the old Uriage circle came to power to a remarkable extent in France, not only in journalism—as Beuve-

---

[40]For example, Pierre Pucheu and Paul Marion, who wanted French youth remodeled along frankly National Socialist lines with less Catholic influence.

[41]Halls, *Vichy*, 324. This is also the judgment of H.R. Kedward, *Resistance in Vichy France* (Oxford: Oxford University Press, 1978), 209.

[42]Among other things, Dunoyer de Segonzac had denounced as traitors the French officers in Syria who supported the Free French.

Méry, using some Uriage alumni and the confiscated facilities of the collaborationist *Le Temps*, built *Le Monde* into one of the world's great newspapers—but also in book publishing, film, and various branches of religious, cultural, and academic life. In general, the men of Uriage were unrepentant about their past, and, to the horror of "resisters" like Bernanos, Maritain, and Simon, several became pioneers in postwar "dialogue" with the French communists. For Maritain, Bernanos, and Simon, the Stalinists were not essentially different from the Nazis, and they were bitterly critical of the new "ecumenism" that grew out of the Uriage experience.[43] The rise to prominence of National Revolution veterans as anti-American "progressive" Catholics in France after the war had something to do with Bernanos' bitterness,[44] Maritain's only returning to France for brief periods in the immediate postwar period, and with Simon's decision never to set foot on his native soil again.[45]

[43]See the concluding chapters of my *Emmanuel Mounier*.

[44]See, for example, his *Français, si vous saviez!* (Paris: Gallimard, 1961), 172, in which he explicitly denounces this development.

[45]The author is grateful to McGill University and to the Sciences and Humanities Research Council of Canada for their research support.

Robert Royal

Creative Intuition, Great Books,
And Freedom of Intellect

Nietzsche—one of the bad boys of great books lists—once remarked: "Every idea has its autobiography." This provides me the initial link for Creative Intuition, Great Books, and Freedom of the Intellect in my title. During the Stanford controversy about required readings in Western Culture earlier this year, I was reading Jacques Maritain's *Creative Intuition in Art and Poetry*. Before beginning his philosophical analysis of intuition in that work, Maritain distinguishes the characteristics of Indian and Chinese art on the one hand from those of the art of the West on the other (*CI* 10–21). He draws these distinctions generously, but sharply, based on categories of a self-conscious inhabitant of the West. My own spark of intuition jumped from Maritain's powerful and magnanimous *method* to the very weak and condescending arguments about some generic need to study non-Western culture issuing from Palo Alto. And, in the same flash, I saw the deep connection of this controversy to maintaining—or perhaps achieving again—a vibrant, high, and free common culture.

Let me begin with a little further autobiography. I feel honor-bound to confess at the outset my own prejudices, if that is what they are. As an undergraduate, I attended a prestigious university, one of those described by Allan Bloom in *The Closing of the American Mind*. My not-so-*alma mater*, however, goes Bloom's typical institution one better; it is so open and tolerant that it prides itself on having no requirements at all. A student must only complete a certain number of courses to graduate and must work out with a faculty member something called a "concentration" (a postmodern term for a major). The abdication of educational leadership is, for me, therefore, a vivid memory.

All the university's promotional material touts this "New Curriculum" (even though it is now over fifteen years old) for its "flexibility." Now, for a student of the classical philosophy of education, this term "flexibility" may not immediately inspire awe. Plato and Aristotle seem to have thought it not worth mentioning. In fact, most theories of education until the last few decades would have thought mere flexibility good only in so far as it permitted better approaches to well-defined and dynamically pursued disciplines. The idea that flexibility in and of itself could be grounds for choosing a school had to wait for the lucid tranquillity of the Vietnam War era to raise its shining banner on the campuses.

To be fair to the university in question, which I shall not name, the reputation for flexibility has made it one of the two or three most popular colleges in the country. The admissions office is happy, the administration delighted, the faculty (for once) satisfied, and the fund-raisers breathless at their success in luring the eager high school students of America with promises of flexibility.

The only fly in the ointment is the effect on those of us who by now have had our four years of flexibility and have gone on as other generations into the world, where the very term concentration is misunderstood and bosses are occasionally less flexible than the average Ivy League professor. Some of us who continue to work with our brains also reflect occasionally on what good and harm all this flexibility did us. A recent poll of alumni found that, in spite of all the huffing and puffing in university materials and the applause from guidance counselors' offices around the country, only about half of the university's graduates say they liked their four years because of the flexibility, and about the same number say they didn't like their four years because of the flexibility.

In my experience, people who wanted to learn at this institution (I leave the merely idle aside for some future sociological study) fell into two large categories. The first knew little, but were constantly being told they were the best and the brightest. They left the ivied halls happy and still mostly ignorant—some, the kind of feminists who make stern criticisms of Western civilization, but seem to know nothing that happened in the West prior to the 1950s. These, I am sure, along with the engineers, premed students, and so forth, make up the bulk of those who were delighted to be flexible.

The other large group, I think, seriously wanted an education, and finding none available in any systematic way, went about picking up odds and ends and reading into interconnected subjects with the passion, but also the unavoidable eccentricity, of the autodidact. These people found great books—I certainly did—but they tended to order them in personal, idiosyncratic ways that make discourse about them, even with one another, very difficult. As a result, if I remember rightly, we for the most part did our reading and conversed little with one another. Perhaps it would have been too painful to find that there was so little commmunity of thought, even among the few people trying to do some thinking.

Having been through this experience, I am probably in a better position than most people to appreciate the inestimable value of great books courses and courses in Western civilization (I will use the terms interchangeably for the remainder of this essay, even though I know there are great differences between the two). But I think it necessary to keep in mind some principles that Maritain would have introduced into this debate. Let's begin by way of what I believe the Schoolmen called *remotion*. I want to make clear what mere lists of the monuments of Western culture are *not*.

I. What the Great Books Are Not

First, while great books nourish our ethical and social roots, they are not, as Jacques Maritain already saw in the 1940s, salvation from our current cultural crisis;[1] the decay is too great for that. To say that they are sufficient to our moral predicament is to argue that some secular canon, like the canon of Scripture, is sufficient. *Sola scriptura* is a bad principle in either realm.

Some advocates of great books give the opposite impression—that passionate reading of crucial texts alone will give us the guidance we need to get through the dark wood of contemporary life. The best refutation of this view that I know of is Saul Bellow's novel *Herzog*. The character who gives his name to the book writes brilliant intellectual analyses of great Western books—as well as letters to their authors—but his own life is far more troubled than that of the average person. Commenting on this novel, Bellow rightly identifies *the* modern problem as first of the soul rather than the intellect.

> To finish with *Herzog*, I meant the novel to show how little strength "higher education" had to offer a troubled man. In the end he is aware that he has had *no* education in the conduct of life (at the university who was there to teach him how to deal with his erotic needs, with women, with family matters?) and he returns, in the language of games, to square one—or as I put to myself while writing the book, to some primal point of balance. Herzog's confusion is barbarous. Well, what else can it be? But there is a point at which, assisted by his comic sense, he is able to hold fast. In the greatest confusion there is still an open channel to the soul. It may be difficult to find because by midlife it is overgrown, and some of the wildest thickets that surround it grow out of what we describe as our education. But the channel

---

[1]In his study *Education at the Crossroads* (New Haven: Yale University Press, 1943), Jacques Maritain suggests that the reading of great authors is the usual path of acquiring natural morality (p. 68). But he rightly observes later that already in the 1940s, "The normal way ... does not suffice in the face of tremendous degradation of ethical reason which is observable today" (p. 94).

is always there, and it is our business to keep it open, to have access to the deepest part of ourselves—to that part of us which is conscious of a higher consciousness, by means of which we make final judgments and put everything together. The independence of this consciousness, which has the strength to be immune to the noise of history and the distractions of our immediate surroundings, is what the life struggle is all about. The soul has to find and hold its ground against hostile forces, sometimes embodied in ideas which frequently deny its very existence, and which indeed often seem to be trying to annul it altogether.[2]

A second preliminary point on great books, which follows from the first, is a contradiction of one of the main strands of Western high culture. *Contra* some great books proponents, I would argue that the unexamined life *is* worth living. Such a life may be virtuous and valuable without the Socratic *exetasis* entering into the question, especially when education is likely to lead to the wild thickets that Bellow mentions. We all know simple people who, without being learned, are wise and good *per modum inclinationis*. America generally depends on this repository of simple virtue for its basic functioning. Unless great books programs make it clear that they have the philosophical breadth to account for this, they tend to discredit themselves as elitist studies with arrogant and unwarranted claims.

Third, to return to the ecclesial parallel for a moment, we should be clear that there is no list of *the* great books, because there cannot be. My colleague at the Ethics and Public Policy Center Edwin Delattre, the president-emeritus of Saint John's College at Annapolis and Santa Fe, rightly changed the materials of those schools during his tenure in office to indicate that great books, not *the* great books were read there. I would go still further and say there *should* not be such a list. The canon of Scripture is defined by proper authority at a given moment. The landmarks of human history, intelligence, and creativity cannot be defined once and for all. They are either open to new arrivals and discovery of lost or overlooked eminences—in short, to active intelligence—or they are a series of fossils. Intellectual authority plays a crucial role in defining what is worthy of study and Yves R. Simon has brilliantly examined that role. But I will return to this point later.

All the misconceptions and exaggerated hopes about great books are understandable reactions to the cultural chaos in which we find ourselves. In current conditions, what could be more desirable than a manageable set

---

[2]Allan Bloom, *The Closing of the American Mind* (New York: Simon and Schuster, 1987), pp. 16 and 17.

CREATIVE INTUITION • 185

of readings that define what an educated person should know? In many cases, such programs probably do a good job, though I must say from personal experience that many people I meet who have been through these programs or teach in them show a good deal of narrow sectarian spirit and far less catholic intellectual tastes than I would have expected. This is a problem that does not even take us to the main questions of intellectual depth and power—the tough questions of sheer competence, both for teachers and students. Perhaps these phenomena are the counterbalance to the excessive flexibility of many educational institutions.

II. The Importance of the Less than Great

One of the most striking aspects of Maritain's reflections on the products of creative intelligence is precisely his catholicity and willingness to study less-than-great books. If you read his *Creative Intuition in Art and Poetry*, for example, you are overwhelmed with its philosophical and esthetic insight. But, even more important, you are struck with how much more "modern," in the best sense, Maritain is than most of those who prescribe great books for the ills of current culture—even thirty-five years later. Perhaps this is because he is so confident in certain truths that he finds them simultaneously antimodern and ultramodern,[3] i.e., timeless. Maritain illustrates his arguments with passages from and reflections on Apollinaire, Cocteau, Gide, the surrealists, Rouault, Chagall, Debussy, Hart Crane, Eliot, and Baudelaire, among others. His lively appreciation of true poetic intuition, that profound freedom of the intellect, leads him to understand sympathetically what is alive and what is unique in modern works that most great books advocates would think beneath their notice.

Maritain does not find these works beneath his notice. He rejects the kind of prudish classicism that he calls *misoneism*.[4] Instead, he shows why, under modern philosophical and social conditions, these works are what they are. In so doing, he explains the non-representational aspect of more purely poetic modern work from a rare philosophical and psychological depth. These works have their rationale, and their rationale is modern. As he puts it, it "is difficult for a modern poet not to be the child of modern

---

[3]Jacques Maritain, *Antimoderne*, in *Oeuvres Completes*, vol. II (Fribourg: Editions Universitaires Fribourg Suisse, 1987), 928.

[4]*Ibid., loc. cit.*

man" (*CI* 335). This method is a good corrective to the kind of great books program that eschews all discussion of context for fear of historicism or relativism.[5]

In any case, Maritain never commits the sectarian's error of dismissing work simply because it is not comparable to the greatest of the past. Even less great contemporary work is important to us because it gives us the sense of living creation that past work usually cannot. Furthermore, it is the job of intelligence to understand why modern work is what it is. Maritain beautifully presents the case for the greatness of Dante's *Divina Commedia*, for example. Dante is not only one of the greatest poets who ever lived, but he has the advantage of innocent self-assurance and the luck of a solid culture behind him. Maritain defends modern writers who lack these advantages: "it would be nonsense to require from modern poets a 'greatness,' an objective intellectuality and universality of theme comparable to those in Dante" (*CI* 399). Modern poetry gathers together for us all those bits and fragments of contemporary life into poetic intuition that hints at more *for us* at times than do the abstractly "great" works.

The reverse side of this perceptiveness is that Maritain knew early on what many more of us have come to realize in the last few decades: there are transcendently great works that must be actively appropriated if we are to make contact with the fullest range of human life we can appreciate. And, for this need, study of great books is crucial. The curriculum of a very fine school based on a modified *paideia* program defines this part of its program as the "Habitual Vision of Greatness,"[6] a striking way of putting it.

III. The Centrality of Intuition

Creative or poetic intuition bears no little importance to this full range. As Maritain sees it, the poetic and the mystical are somewhat akin, in that they are authentic human dimensions that regularly pass outside of our everyday experience without losing touch with the regulations of intelligence. In Maritain, true poetry and mysticism are never mere flights of the spririt that make their own laws as they go. Rather, he associates both with what he calls the human preconscious. He seems to think that poetic intuition is linked in some ways with the more usual function of the agent

---

[5]Cf. Maritain, *Education at the Crossroads*, 71: "The great books should be accompanied by enlightenment about their historical context and by counsel on the subject matter."

[6]See the brochure of the Trinity School, South Greenlawn Avenue, South Bend, Indiana.

intellect in transforming phantasms into intelligible material for the possible intellect. The difference in poetic intuition is that the human faculty does not merely grasp the object as material for discursive reason. Instead, by a kind of connaturality, it *creates* an object that trails its roots in God's larger creation and shows its affinities with Being Himself (*CI* IV). How this occurs is not entirely open to our discursive mind; but that it does occur we are sure, as anyone who has ever really "gotten" a poem can attest. Perhaps the best way to convey this point is to quote a poet, as Maritain does. In "Maid Quiet," Yeats says "The winds that awakened the stars/Are blowing through my blood." *That's* poetic connaturality.

At first sight, this may merely seem of interest to esthetics and that part of the great books course that deals with poetry or art. I think this view is a mistake, as did Maritain. And we might recall here a sentence from Saint Thomas that Maritain quotes frequently: "*Ex divina pulchritudine esse omnium derivatur*" (*AS* 31).[7] He elaborates this formula in *Creative Intuition in Art and Poetry*:

> A kind of poetic intuition can come into play everywhere—in science, philosophy, big business, revolution, religion, sanctity, or imposture—when the mind of man attains to a certain depth or mastery in the power of discovering new horizons and taking great risks.
>
> There is poetry involved in the work of all great mathematicians. Secret poetic intuition was at work in the primary philosophical insights of Heraclitus and Plato, Aristotle and Thomas Aquinas, Plotinus, Spinoza, or Hegel; without the help of poetry Aristotle could not have extracted from experience the diamond of his fundamental definitions; in the background of all the ideological violence of Thomas Hobbes there was something which poetry had taught him, his awareness that he was the twin brother of Fear. Poetry helped Francis of Assisi, and Columbus, and Napoleon, and Cagliostro (*CI* 238–39).

I quote this passage at length because I think it confirms an important insight that the truly great thing in these diverse figures, before the more humble application of discursive tools, is this larger human insight that makes great the work not only of a Homer, or Dante, or Shakespeare, but of a Newton, Einstein, or—Cagliostro. Prudence, the virtue of art, and science all have a deep and common root in this view.

If our students are not awakened to this greatness of conception, this light flooding things from the preconscious or agent intellect or some other

---

[7]The citation is from Aquinas' *Expositio Super Dionysius De Divinis Nominibus*, c. 4, lect. 5.

source, they may be tempted to think that the figures we hope they will familiarize themselves with are merely "clever" thinkers, or, still worse, convenient political props for the Western system.

It is no accident that the radicals who chant, "Hey, hey, ho, ho, Western culture's gotta go" at Stanford have put themselves in the same position as the Soviet cultural bureaucracy. Whenever the free play of intellect—a freedom, I repeat, Maritain reminds us is not mere license, but a freedom of connaturality with reality—is subordinated to a political orthodoxy, the human prospect narrows. This should not come as any surprise to us, even if the political vision claims to be human and broad. Politics by nature is only a part of human life, but precisely the part we are most tempted to substitute for the higher things, which occupy only a tenuous hold on the modern world.

I have already mentioned my worries about the sectarianism I have encountered both among teachers and students of *the* great books, but that problem pales in comparison with the recent threat to the freedom of intellect reflected in the politicization of the teaching process. The advocates of this politicization argue that the choice of what to study has been politically determined already: we just are not yet conscious of it. This is a minor charge, one that should be kept in mind to make us wary of unintentional blindness, but it entirely misses the main point of education. Education is not simply an indoctrination in correct political views. The radicals themselves are always decrying that. But, in fact, the free play of intellect, that unpredictable arrival of poetic intuition in a really well-wrought work, is constantly now being submitted to political tests.

IV. The Hospitable Canon

I am in favor of keeping our vision of truly great books open to the arrival of new masterpieces. But the current plea for opening up the list shows how feeble the alternatives are on the one hand, and how strong the West is on the other. Writing a blank intellectual check to non-Western cultures without specification of what work is worth studying, strikes me as condescension of the worst sort. We do not insist that students simply study some work from Britain, or Germany, or France, as a sop to those who think these nations important. We read Shakespeare, Montaigne, and Goethe, and would want to read them in whatever tongues they had written.

The current weakness of many Western intellectuals in the defense of the West has two causes, one legitimate and one not. The legitimate reason for wanting to look beyond Western culture is that what goes by the name is not even a full representative of the West—only a modern ghost of the riches actually within Western traditions. Hutchins and Adler mentioned this in the introduction to their series of great books.[8] The desire to break the stranglehold on what passes for *the* Western tradition is not only just, it is devoutly to be wished.

Another stream plays into this one, however. There are many who want to go outside Western traditions because they think them deeply racist, sexist, imperialist, and so forth. The irony that these terms have been developed in the West, because we are concerned to answer the legitimate question that they raise, is unknown to the cultural radicals. Around the time that the controversy was raging at Stanford, for example, an Indian scientist wrote in to a Washington magazine to say, "Nearly all the knowledge of the past glories of these non-Western cultures—in which their intelligentsia take such great pride—is the result of Western scholarship. These cultures, for all their greatness, have little history and and no archeology. So they owe a great debt to Western culture."[9] This debt is so great, in fact, that it induces great resentment—something that we should understand, but reject sympathetically.

One of my colleagues gave a speech recently in which he mentioned that he and his daughter have put their desks next to one another at home under a bust of Aristotle so that they can study together. A woman in the audience rose after his presentation to express her puzzlement that he would have anything to do with Aristotle since he regarded women as by nature inferior and also believed in slaves. My friend replied, as is quite true, that the remedies for these blind spots may be extracted from Aristotle himself, and that it would be a shame if so much intellectual treasure were discarded because of some errors.

I myself spoke in Washington last year, to a group of students from Notre Dame University, and one woman confidently informed me after my presentation that the Bible, Plato, Aristotle, the Romans, the Fathers of the Church, Aquinas, and many other major Western figures right up to the present were hopelessly "sexist." "I've already looked into them," she said with finality. Look into them for a few more years, I said, and then let me know who else is more worth reading. I'm not waiting for a reply.

I think the great books or Western civilization programs leave themselves open to these ignorant attacks if they try to present themselves as what they are not: as some sort of ideal intellectual order. If, instead, some of the

---

[8]Robert Maynard Hutchins, ed., *Great Books of the Western World*, vol. I, *The Great Conversation* (Chicago: Encyclopedia Brittanica, 1952), chap. 9, "East and West," particularly 70–71.

[9]*Insight*, April 11, 1988, 4.

figures just mentioned are presented as moments of great human intuition involved in the ongoing human task of better understanding and enriching human life—that enjoying Shakespeare does not mean you cannot enjoy some non-Western dramatist of equal power and depth—mere honesty will lead most students to see the obvious.

V. The Complexity of Translation

On this point of non-Western figures, I'd like to make a clarification. I've spent a good deal of my formal education learning Greek, Latin, and several modern languages. I'm familiar with philosophical, historical, and literary works in original texts. My experience leads me to believe that to read great books in English translations and to think you are getting most of what you need from them is a chimera. To take a crucial example, the Greek term *eudaimonia* is not exactly the same as *felicitas*, and neither is what we call loosely *happiness*. I still dip occasionally into classical scholarship and I'm repeatedly surprised at how little most of us see when we read the text of Homer or Virgil. The worlds they represent need varied exposition and hard study at the original languages: no easy task. Otherwise, we are simply using our great forebears as mirrors for our ignorant selves. And these works are supposedly in our Western tradition.

I can believe, on the basis of my own reading, that highly important works exist in other cultures. I think of Confucius or the Bhagavad-Gita. But the quick insistence on non-Western works, without specification of what we are talking about, is likely to be far less intellectually respectable than even a superficial reading of a great Western book in translation. Are the advocates of these additions interested in them because they are great human achievements, or just because they are non-Western? As William James might have put it in his much understood phrase, what is the cash-value of these non-Western works? Even if this question can be answered, how are students really to understand these works without large chunks of time being devoted to linguistic, historical, and cultural matters? We already have plently of difficulty teaching works drawing on concepts within our own general culture.

We should be wary of a second problem of translation also. It is the very core of modern cosmopolitanism to believe that all works are transparent to the modern eye. There is great reason to doubt this. Many works, I would place the Bible among them, require strenuous and long habituation before we even begin to understand them adequately. In his recent book, *Whose Justice? Which Rationality?*, Alisdair MacIntyre puts the case forcefully:

> The type of translation characteristic of modernity generates in turn its own misunderstanding of tradition. The original locus of that misunderstand-

ing is the kind of introductory great books or Humanities course, so often taught in liberal arts colleges, in which, in abstraction from historical context and with all sense of the complexities of linguistic particularity removed by translation, a student moves in rapid succession through Homer, Sophocles, two dialogues of Plato, Virgil, Augustine, the *Inferno*, Machiavelli, *Hamlet*.... If one fails to recognize that what this provides is not and cannot be a re-introduction to the culture of past traditions but is a tour through what is in effect a museum of texts, each rendered contextless and therefore other than its original by being placed on a cultural pedestal, then it is natural enough to suppose that, were we to achieve consensus as to a set of such texts, the reading of them would reintegrate modern students into what is thought of as *our* tradition, that unfortunate fictitious amalgam sometimes know as "the Judeo-Christian tradition" and sometimes as "Western values." The writings of self-proclaimed contemporary conservatives ... turn out to be one more stage in modernity's cultural deformation of our relationship to the past.[10]

Whether he is right or not about the original locus of the problem—that part of his argument is historically doubtful—MacIntyre develops a very interesting idea of tradition in his latest book which may help us in our reflections here. Modern cosmopolitan culture thinks of itself as a neutral observer of all particular traditions, says MacIntyre. In fact, however, it has turned into one more tradition, and a tradition with so many internal problems and self-contradictions that we are justified in looking upon it with a cold eye. There are competing main traditions, at least in the West: those deriving from Aristotle, Augustine, Aquinas, and Hume. We might want to add to MacIntyre's list Kant as well. MacIntyre ultimately favors the blend of Aristotle and Augustine carried out by Aquinas, but his view of this blend is different from the usual Thomism.

As he views Saint Thomas, Thomist thinking is an open-ended advancing tradition that establishes itself on a broad ground of reality and seeks to incorporate new material and the solutions of new problems into the tradition. The good Thomist will not only internalize Thomas' views, he will move them forward in ways that Aquinas could not have foreseen, but would have approved. The very idea of a "tradition"—a handing down of wisdom and knowledge requires this dynamic. A culture *is* the incarnation of such a tradition. Culture provides us with a starting point for thinking without which progress is not possible both for lack of a place to stand and for the infinite complexities that would overwhelm any inquiry

---

[10]Alasdair MacIntyre, *Whose Justice? Which Rationality?* (Notre Dame: University of Notre Dame Press, 1988), 385–86.

we think we can undertake *de novo*. As G.K. Chesterton put this, "culture is the mental thrift of our forefathers."

VI. Taking Our Bearings

Recognizing that we can only make intellectual progress as part of some tradition is anathema to the modern *paideia*, though it is practiced by all those who belong to the modernist tradition. The principle value of great books, as I see it, is that they help us to locate ourselves among the traditions. I don't think I'm alone in having had the experience of reading some great text that suddenly explains where basic beliefs I have long held took their origin. Granted, most undergraduates will leave such a program with little idea of what it all means. Some will think they understand everything on this brief acquaintance. But those who learn what large task really lies ahead will be worth the failures of the program.

This leads me to another serious modern problem: how do we deal with the mass of secondary materials that have now proliferated around every subject? Each person knows and can know only a small part of even his own field. What does this mean for the organic nature of culture?

I think the work of the chemist turned philosopher Michael Polanyi is very useful here.[11] Polanyi did fine work, not only on epistemology, but on the idea of tradition, the scientific tradition in his case. When a discipline is in good condition, as science is in our time, the vast network of individual researchers and writers organizes itself into a self-criticizing mechanism that resolves small-scale problems. As regards the grand scale, Polanyi's vision is similar to Maritain's in that he sees the big advances in science as not merely the result of logical increments, but also as the effect of scientific intuitions that take a great step beyond the available evidence without being mere fantasy. Einstein, Heisenberg, and other great figures of twentieth century science all had intuitions of theoretical truths long before data could be obtained to confirm or falsify these truths.

The difference between natural science and what we may broadly call culture, however, is that modern culture is not in good condition. Its subject matter differs from natural science in a way that calls for a different method of procedure. Failure to recognize this has led to theories like deconstruction, which assert that because a text is unknowable in its totality it is unknowable period. In some ways, I would argue, this is merely a reflection of the situation in which many professors find themselves:

---

[11]See Michael Polanyi, *Personal Knowledge: Towards a Post-Critical Philosophy* (Chicago: University of Chicago Press, 1962).

they are constantly inundated with a flood of contradictory readings of texts and events. It's no wonder that their characteristic *deformation professionelle* is to regard them as all plausible without possibility of rational choice among them.

Such a predicament underscores the need for a developing tradition of reason that will preserve us from the perturbations of mere logic. I disagree profoundly with those great books advocates who would seek to save the situation by throwing out secondary materials entirely—a recommendation unfortunately embedded in the original great books program. I do not know how I personally would have benefitted from not reading secondary materials, and I assume others would be equally crippled by this limitation. One of the tasks of modern teaching is to show students what is and is not important among the secondary material. If I can revert to my ecclesiastical metaphor, we need to have an idea of who are the good expositors and theologians of the developing secular canon if we do not wish to be cultural fundamentalists.

The best reason for seeking to avoid this fate is that, as in religion, there *is* no valid reason for such a narrow conception of human culture. We may forgive its advocates, who are reacting to what they quite rightly see as cultural chaos. But, as in religion, the answer to chaos is not fundamentalism. The answer to chaos and fundamentalism alike is today, as it has always been, catholicity, in the sense of universality, supported by legitimate authority. In this, the great books will be helpful to us, but not if we sin against the light.

VII. The Question of Authority

And, as in ecclesiastical matters, we must at some point confront the question of authority. I am not a deep student of Yves R. Simon, but I have found *A General Theory of Authority* very helpful. The experts on Simon may recall that he says in that work that "when the issue is one of action, not of truth, the person in authority has the character of a leader; but when the issue is one of truth, not of action, the person in authority has the character of a witness" (*GT* 84). This is very good and distinguishes between two functions, both of which the university educator must possess because he is involved both in the action of teaching and learning, as well as in the pursuit of truth.

These functions have been ill served by a false conception of teachers and students as merely and equally pursuing truth. As Simon says elsewhere commenting on the relationship of liberty and authority, both are necessary and only prudence can correctly determine the degree to which each is needed in given circumstances (*NF* 5). Unfortunately, many of those called to authority in modern higher education have abdicated, refusing either to lead or to witness. An administrator at my *alma mater,* admittedly an extreme case, explained a couple of years ago why there are no requirements at the university: "We admit highly intelligent and very motivated students to this institution. The least we can do for them when they arrive here is to get out of their way." As a parent of young children who struggles to make ends meet, I think I speak for many when I say, "If this is true, why bother to send children to such institutions at all?" Although this is an extreme form of an attitude present in higher education today, it is a pure sample that shows better than anything else the root of the problem.

My administrator, and thousands like him not carried by their own emotion to make explicit the principle, thinks universities and their faculties have no responsibility to lead, in Simon's sense. They do not see learning as an action that may be performed better or worse, in which an experienced leader might have anything to say to new arrivals. Such educators make themselves into mere technical facilitators, or less, not leaders in a great tradition.

One of the odd things about teaching that allows such a confusion to occur is that it lies on the borderline between action and truth. The action of teaching truth calls for educational leadership. We have always tacitly acknowledged as much by creating institutions that require certain types and levels of performances, by empowering teachers to evaluate student achievement. The authority of truth, Simon's witnessing, is the essential element in education, but only after students have been *led* to the essential *foci* of significant action—the perennial human questions reflected in the wisdom of the race.

Some people are quick to blame the cowardice of current education for the failure to lead and to witness. I think educators have simply been hoodwinked, like much of the rest of the society, into believing that authority is in and of itself evil, that we are all pretty much on a plane of equality, and any privileging of some persons or some ideas over others sets us inexorably on the road to totalitarianism. On this view, authority must be authoritarian.

This is almost the precise opposite of the truth. The petrification of intellectual life for political reason, a danger more likely to come from broad anti-Western forces today than from the tradition itself, is a tyranny already in place in some institutions and threatening others. At Stanford, a coalition of black, Hispanic, and Asian students were reported to have called the Western Culture course a "year-long class in racism." The irony here, of course, is that it is only in Western or Western-style terms that African tribalism, Asian caste systems, and Western slavery may even be rejected under the label "racism." But even worse is the uninformed and presumptuous reduction of the immense fruit of Western history, matching the achievements of any known human culture, to a paltry political category.

Only a properly constituted authority may begin to address this youthful presumption and ignorance. Great books programs try to correct prejudice of this sort by teaching what it means to be a "truly educated person." I have no objection to this goal, but the somewhat priggish tone of the phrase may put off the very people who need teaching most. Instead, I would approach the problem by quoting the authority of a non-Westerner, Confucius, on his own path to wisdom. He said:

1. At fifteen, I wanted to learn.
2. At thirty, I had a foundation.
3. At forty, a certitude.
4. At fifty, knew the orders of heaven.
5. At sixty, was ready to listen to them.
6. At seventy could follow my own heart's desire without overstepping the t-square.[12]

The Chinaman's geniality and self-deprecating humor not only give us a better idea of the lifetime task of learning, they also remind us that the ultimate end of education is not merely to have the right political views nor to become a "truly educated person," but to know and *listen to* the orders of heaven.

---

[12]Ezra Pound, *Confucius: The Unwobbling Pivot, The Great Digest, the Analects* (New York: New Directions, 1928), 198.

Michael Novak

The Philosophical Meaning of American Civilization in World History

In the panorama of world history, what is the meaning of the American Revolution? In most of the world today, Professor Arendt notes, intellectuals and activists take their beginnings from the French Revolution of 1789.[1] That revolution is echoed in Victor Hugo's novel, *Les Miserables*, set in 1832, and it has established a romantic paradigm for later revolutions from China to Nicaragua. Most of the world's intellectuals forget the American Revolution of 1776. They ignore its terse and eloquent Constitution of 1787, its quiet Bill of Rights of 1792. In his Instruction on Christian Liberty, even Cardinal Ratzinger cited the historical importance of 1789, while totally ignoring 1776.

Notwithstanding its neglect by romantic revolutionaries, Professor Arendt calls both the "colonization of North America and the republican government of the United States perhaps the greatest, certainly the boldest, enterprises of European mankind."[2] Abraham Lincoln, in a terrible period, called it "the last, best hope" of humankind. Jacques Maritain said that, of all civilizations, American civilization comes closest to the proximate practical ideal he had imagined for the future of true Christian humanism (*RA* 174–75). Maritain challenged those of us in the next generation to make articulate the inarticulate ideology of this American civilization, for our own sake and that of humans everywhere (*RA* 118).

---

[1]Hannah Arendt, *On Revolution* (New York: The Viking Press, 1965), 49.
[2]*Ibid.*, 49.

Lord Acton called the U.S. Constitution one of the half-dozen greatest landmarks in the entire history of liberty. He thought that the principle of federalism, designed as a structural device for dispersing power and protecting liberty, was a breakthrough of world-historical importance.[3] Alexis de Tocqueville published his own observations on the startling innovations that American civilization had already introduced into the course of history, as if guided by the hand of Providence, innovations for which Europe had better ready itself.[4] His account was written after the American experiment had already proved itself in the sixty years between 1776 and 1836.

The American framers, too, especially Madison, had quietly noted the originality of their designs, recognizing that history offered them "no model" on which they could completely draw, no prior design that they could imitate.[5] They were testing, in Hamilton's words, whether for the first time in history a people could form a government from reflection and choice, or whether governments must forever be formed by accident and force.[6] They called their experiment, of whose successful outcome they were in some serious doubt, *Novus Ordo Seclorum*. It was a "new order." There was no precedent for it. Well, what *was* new about it? In their eyes and in the eyes of observers overseas?

If we are ever to explain America to Europe, to the rest of the world,

---

[3]Lord Acton, *Lectures on Modern History*, intro. Hugh Trevor-Roper (New York: Meridian Books, Inc., 1961), 295.

[4]Alexis de Tocqueville, *Democracy in America*, the Henry Reeve text, ed. Phillips Bradley (New York: Vintage Books, 1945), vol. 1, 7.

[5]The Americans accomplished, Madison wrote, "a revolution which has no parallel in the annals of human society. They reared the fabrics of governments which have no model on the face of the globe." Alexander Hamilton, James Madison, John Jay, *The Federalist Papers*, intro. Clinton Rossiter (New York: New American Library, 1961), No. 14 (104).

[6]*Federalist* No. 1 (33).

and to ourselves, we urgently need a philosophy of American civilization. Its spinal cord would certainly be the human capacities for "reflection and choice" that are the inner spring of "natural liberty." The preliminary form of this philosophy is already adumbrated in what the framers—and Tocqueville—sketched out as "the new science of politics."[7]

Long before Leo XIII was to articulate the foundations of modern Catholic social thought, the American framers were inventing institutional architecture for the "system of natural liberty." Like Catholic social thought, the framers rooted themselves in Greek and Roman thinking about virtue, character, and the natural order of liberty, including intellect ("reflection") and will ("choice"). Like Catholic social thought, they maintained a profound awareness of human waywardness, ambition, envy, and destructiveness. To paraphrase together several passages of *The Federalist*, one might write: "What is the history of governments if not a melancholy reflection upon the history of human vice?"[8]

In many ways, American social thought drew upon Christian and classical sources quite congenial to Catholics; in some ways, though, it was generations in advance of Catholic social thought and, indeed, of the social thought of Europe and the other continents. Recall what Catholic popes and bishops were saying around 1790, around 1830, and even at the time of *The Syllabus of Errors* (1863). Compare all these to the thought of Madison and Jefferson, Tocqueville and Lincoln.

Among countries as among individuals, God often raises up the distant, the disdained, the small, and the as yet uncelebrated, to advance out of obscurity and to lead the way. So it occurred, Tocqueville argued, that the distant civilization in the wilds of America had been chosen to lead sophisticated Europe and the entire world.

---

[7]Tocqueville, *Democracy*, 7.

[8]See, e.g., the whole of *Federalist* No. 6, for Hamilton's reflections on human evil. While appealing to "experience, the least fallible guide of human opinions," and to "a tolerable knowledge of human nature," he writes: "A man must be far gone in Utopian speculations who can ... forget that men are ambitious, vindictive, and rapacious. To look for a continuation of harmony between a number of independent, unconnected sovereignties situated in the same neighborhood would be to disregard the uniform course of human events, and to set at defiance the accumulated experience of ages" (54).

I. The American Proposition: Murray and Maritain

American civilization was original both in the minds of its founders and in the objective view of distant observers. But in which precise discoveries lay its originality? What exactly are the intellectual contributions of American thinkers to the international body of "social thought"?

Let there be no doubt that the American contribution is intellectual. It represents one of the world's greatest achievements of *practical philosophy*. Its *speculative* dimensions remain to be worked out by philosophers so inclined. Such dimensions are indispensable. Yet, in the actual unfolding of American intellectual life, they have so far been left inarticulate, no doubt for reasons good and bad. They are, nonetheless, present in classical American texts as truths taken for granted, explicitly cited, but hardly fully displayed or intellectually defended.

Consider, for example, Jefferson's ringing, historically pregnant passage: "We hold these truths to be self-evident," that is, truths so firmly held (at least *by us*) as to need *for practical purposes* no further argument. Argument they certainly need; but not necessarily in the heat of creating the workable institutions that would give them *practical expression* before an attentive world. As befits men trying to shape the beginnings of all future world history, the Framers concentrated on showing that these truths do in fact work. It would be idle, they knew, to offer a metaphysical program for liberty, justice, equality, and growing prosperity among peoples, if such a program should end in miserable failure. The republican idea of self-government had already fallen into historical opprobrium. For this reason above all, the first defense it needed was practical, not speculative.

"It is classic American doctrine," John Courtney Murray wrote in the very first sentence of *We Hold These Truths*, "immortally asserted by Abraham Lincoln, that the new nation which our Fathers brought forth on this continent was dedicated to a 'proposition.' " And a proposition of this type is both "the statement of a truth to be demonstrated," and also "an operation to be performed. Our Fathers dedicated the nation to a proposition in both of these senses." The American Proposition is at once doctrinal and practical: "It presents itself as a coherent structure of thought that lays claim to intellectual assent; it also presents itself as an organized political project that aims at historical success."[9]

Moreover, this American Proposition "rests on the forth-right assertion of a realist epistemology. The sense of this famous phrase is simply this: 'There are truths, and we hold them, and we here lay them down as the basis and inspiration of the American project, this constitutional commonwealth' " (WH viii–ix). The American framers thought that "the life of man in society under government is founded on truths, on a certain body of objective truth, universal in its import, accessible to the reason of man, definable, defensible. If this assertion is denied, the American Proposition is, I think, eviscerated at one stroke" (WH ix).

Father Murray then points to the challenge that the American Proposition has put to Catholic social teaching: "A new problem has been put to the universal Church by the fact of America" (WH 27). The kind of pluralism represented by the American experiment had no model or precedent in Catholic history. In Europe, pluralism was forced on warring factions by history; in America, pluralism was the rule from the beginning of national constitutional life. Despite this novelty, American Catholics, yesterday as today, "participate with ready conviction in the American Proposition," and "accept on principle the unique American solution to the age-old problem" of religious diversity (WH 28).

The reasons for this acceptance cut deep. Underlying the American Proposition are radical beliefs: in the sovereignty of God over all political life and in "the tradition of natural law as the basis of a free and ordered political life" (WH 41). Murray pointedly adds: "Historically, this tradition has found, and still finds, its intellectual home within the Catholic Church. ... Where this kind of language is talked, the Catholic joins the conversation with complete ease. It is his language. The ideas expressed are native to his own universe of discourse. Even the accent, being American, suits his tongue" (WH 41).

The paradox, for Murray, is that "a nation which has (rightly or wrongly) thought of its own genius in Protestant terms should have owed its origins and the stability of its political structure to a tradition whose genius is alien to current intellectualized versions of the Protestant religion, and even to certain individualistic exigencies of Protestant religiosity." The contents of the American consensus "approve themselves

---

[9]John Courtney Murray, S.J., *We Hold These Truths: Catholic Reflections on the American Proposition* (New York: Sheed and Ward, 1960), vii. [Due to the frequent use of this work in the article, it is referred to by *WH* and placed within the text, according to the method adopted for books by Adler, Simon, and Maritain—Ed.]

to the Catholic intelligence and conscience." This has remained true, even when other Americans over the generations have come to distance themselves from the tradition of natural law (*WH* 40–43).

Moreover, Jacques Maritain himself derived one of his most central insights in political philosophy from analogous reflections. Like Murray a man of Catholic "intelligence and conscience," steeped in the materials of Christian philosophical history, Maritain felt unexpectedly at home in America. His earlier negative views, derived from European biases, were dissipated by his daily experience, as he details in *Reflections on America*. Here it was that he discovered the key difference between a "secular common faith" founded on *speculative* principles (which, under conditions of genuine religious liberty, would be impossible to bring about) and one founded on *practical* principles (sufficient for civil pursuit of the common good). Indeed, his personal intellectual contribution to the founding of UNESCO and to the writing of the Universal Declaration of Human Rights produced by UNESCO, extended into the international arena the vision of *practical* pluralism he had learned from the American experiment.[10]

II. The Proposition and Its Betrayal

The American Proposition, as Father Murray has shown, sets a very high standard, from which a failure of moral virtue or intellectual conviction is a serious falling off. Therefore, a distinction is needed in order to clarify what it is that one is defending when one defends the American Idea (the American Proposition): a distinction between the Proposition and the Practice. On the one hand, the American Idea is *embodied* in a living system of laws, customs, institutions, traditions, and virtues. It is no mere Platonic idea. On the other hand, the American Idea cannot be identified with everything that some Americans (even a majority) happen to think or do. The American Proposition is not identical to "the American way of life" or even "the American dream." There is a great deal to be criticized, lamented, and fought against in American practice, not only in our day but in every past generation of American history. The crucial point, however, is that the American Proposition carries within itself—in its homage to the Creator and in its appeal to natural law—the standards of judgment by which our people's failings may be brought under critical fire. The phrase,

---

[10]See, e.g., both his exchange with Sidney Hook in *The Nation* (1945), "The Pluralist Principle in Democracy," and his Inaugural Address to the Second International Conference of UNESCO, "The Possibilities for Cooperation in a Divided World," reprinted as chapters 12 and 13 in *The Range of Reason*.

"nation under God," has traditionally been invoked, not only by ardent preachers, but also by the nation's duly elected officers, to bring the nation to the bar of transcendent judgment.

Indeed, from the far left and the far right, and from all points in between, Americans have always felt at home in the sermonic form of rhetoric, castigating the nation's sins, and insisting upon repentance and reform. Quite deliberately, the nation's Founders intended to keep open this channel to invoking divine judgment in the name of a "higher law." Americans are uncommonly fond of telling one another, in one breath, "This is a free country" and, in another, "There should be a law against that." Practices or laws current in any one generation are not taken to be self-justifying; they are held to the measure of a higher and more exacting standard.

Not only is it true that the American Proposition holds American institutions and practices under the judgment of the law of God and the law of nature. It is also true that the American Proposition not only legitimates, it almost demands, that the citizens of the United States hold themselves and their fellow citizens under vigorous and incessant criticism. There is hardly any activity that is more characteristically *American* than criticizing the actual goings-on of this Republic—criticizing the Congress, the President, the Courts, the military, the bankers, the rich, the movie stars, the athletes, the press, the unions, churchmen, and the vices and blindnesses of fellow citizens. There is not a taxi driver in New York who can't do all of this between Manhattan and the airport and hardly stop for breath.

That the Framers intended this is indicated by two (among other) signs. First, the depiction of the *Novus Ordo* chosen with care for the Great Seal of the United States is that of a pyramid deliberately left uncompleted. This was intended to indicate that such goals as "liberty and justice for all" transcend the labors of any single generation and, indeed, of all generations cumulatively. The Framers wished to invoke the memory of the people of Israel wandering in the desert, going out from Egypt toward the Promised Land. In an important way, the American experiment was held to be, analogously, under the same scorching judgment of the Almighty as the first Israel. The people of America were imagined to be the second Israel. The point of view from which this was done, of course, was civil and natural, not precisely religious. The Framers were not trying to claim a sacral history, nor to coerce all citizens into an established state religion. But what they did want to borrow from the history of the Hebrew people was public recognition of the sovereignty of God above and beyond all politics and culture. It is this point that Father Murray has shrewdly seized upon in the founding documents.

Second, one of the "truths we hold" in Jefferson's classic rendition in the Declaration of Independence is that *each generation* of citizens has the same right as the founding generation, viz., to live under laws and institutions to which it has given its reflective consent. This truth signifies in a powerful way that, in passing judgment on the current state of their public order, each generation may repair to nature and nature's God. *That* is the substratum of conviction on which its rights are based. "To secure these rights, governments are established among men." Governments, that is, laws and institutional arrangements, are indispensable for the securing of rights in actual practice. But the actual practice remains always under scrutiny.

Thus, nothing is more in keeping with the American Proposition than a profoundly felt sense of laboring under the judgment of the Almighty. No degree of material prosperity shields the nation from this searing judgment. No degree of military might or worldly preeminence can deflect this judgment. It would never be enough for America merely to be rich, or merely to be powerful. (Often in history, the rich and the mighty have been humbled.) To fulfill its own stated principles, America must be faithful to the laws of nature and the laws of God.

On no other ground are the rights claimed by its citizens established. Indeed, this is a blessing for which, even amidst the fratricide and carnage of the Civil War, the Congress of the United States saw fit to require President Lincoln to proclaim a public holiday of Thanksgiving to Almighty God. Similar invocations of gratitude to Providence have been a constant motif of public speech throughout our history—in the Constitutional Convention, in the *Federalist*, and in a long line of Inaugural Addresses of our Presidents. Such expressions of public religion are no more than what they claim to be, expressions of a "civil" religion. There was, and is, no religion of a higher order that is nationally established. Such expressions flow, nonetheless, from the religious imperatives of the natural law.

Therefore, all those citizens today who are sickened by what they see around them as rampant materialism, the neglect of the moral virtues, the exaltation (under the name of "liberation") of selfishness and "looking out for number one," etc., are not in violation of the American Proposition when they proclaim the obligations inherent in the law of nature and the law of God, as these have been made known to them. Those, too, who protest against the aggressive denial of the warrants of natural law and the law of God—for example, by professors, jurists, and journalists of a set of convictions usually described as "militantly secularist"—do not have to step outside the American Proposition to make such a protest. On the contrary, better than those who deny, those who affirm the law of nature and the law of God stand foursquare within the American Proposition.

It is, then, the American Proposition that we defend, not the betrayals of it that have been so common in every generation of American history. It is the high standard, not the multitude of sins. And yet, in history, Christian faith itself teaches us that we must not be dismayed by the powerful presence of sin in our midst, even in our own hearts. Thus, those who sought to build here a "New Republic" recognized that there is no point in designing a Republic for saints. There are not enough saints at any one time, in any one place, to constitute a Republic. Our forebears built for sinners. That is why they took such care with checks and balances, with the division of powers, with the division of systems, with empowering against every ambition a counterambition, and with remedies against the maladies inherent in the democratic idea itself.

No doubt, then, we are not the first generation to find ourselves up to our *kiesters* in the flaws, corruptions, vices, and self-destructive impulses of our kind. *"O Tempora! O Mores!"* is not an original expression. Nonetheless, some tempering comments are in order. Both on the left and on the right today, fierce partisan passions lay stinging flagellation across the back of this Republic. The poor country is flayed for faults real and imagined. What is missing in these jeremiads is calm, critical judgment. And also the presumption of innocence. A country, too, is innocent until proven guilty.

Aristotle warned us that in politics we must be satisfied with "a tincture of virtue." Thus, in flaying America for its many faults, we do well to remind ourselves of the limits of moral possibility. We have no right to demand absolute moral perfection. Moral wisdom counsels judgments concerning "more" and "less." It is proper to ask: *Compared to what?* Compared to the transcendent standards inherent in the American Proposition, yes, the nation asks to be, and deserves to be, severely judged. But even here, mercy ought to temper judgment; if justice is the sole measure, what nation in what era could stand?

Moreover, some respect ought to be shown for the limitations of historical existence. Thus, moral judgments about the United States today must be understood in a comparative context. Was the United States in earlier generations morally better than it is today? Which other nations, today or in the past, show a higher level of moral practice? If one does not answer the question, *Compared to what?*, one's moral seriousness is suspect. Since no nation and no people has ever met the full standards of nature's law and God's law, to measure the moral seriousness of judgments about existing nations or peoples one needs to weigh them against other real alternatives. Otherwise, moral judgments will seem hyperbolic.

Consider two examples: (a) If one judges the present generation harshly, would one actually prefer the United States of the 1930s, or 1850s, or 1770s? In what respects? With what reservations? (b) If one thinks the people of the United States today lacking in moral virtue, which people today does one hold to be their moral superior? On what evidence? The very size and complexity of such judgments induce an appropriate humility. They bring ethical discussion down with a thud to earth. Distinctions become necessary. After the case for the prosecution is made, the case for the defense will need to be heard. Evidence is required from both. Jacques Maritain's *Reflections on America* proceeded in this spirit. In reflecting on America, he kept Europe (past and present) in mind. His wise distinctions altered forever the way I would respond to accusations that Americans are "materialistic" or "consumerist" (a word not in fashion then), and "bourgeois" (in its continental connotations).

Maritain's methods teach us to make several distinctions in these matters. (1) There is a difference between the way American life is presented in the *media* and the way it is lived by our neighbors, colleagues, relatives, and local communities. Maritain regularly contrasted the ideas about the America he had learned about in France with his actual experiences with neighbors and strangers in this land. (2) There is a difference between the "new class"—the mores, manners, beliefs, and symbols of our better-educated elites who figure so powerfully in the media—and other bodies of Americans, less visible in the media, but known to us in our parishes and local environments. When one hears generalizations about "Americans," or even "yuppies," it is useful to see if they fit one's Uncle Emil or one's nephew Joe, just graduated from law school and living in an urban setting. Quite often, they don't. Maritain was always testing his preconceptions in this way. (3) It is useful to distinguish within "ideal types"—such as "Americans," "yuppies," "the rich," "the homeless," "welfare mothers," etc.—any number of varieties and subtypes, including vivid counterexamples. (4) Above all, it is useful to distinguish between the American Proposition and the failures of mere mortals to live up to it. Maritain, like a good philosopher, tried to capture the ideals, the spirit, the *finality* of the American people and our institutions.

These lessons from Maritain bring me back to the beginning. Our Framers claimed no specifically *American* rights, but only rights inherent in *all* human beings. Our Framers believed in objective truths; they were not relativists. For example, Abraham Lincoln affirmed that the right of human beings to govern themselves is a right "applicable to all men and all times." He knew well that such a right was not being secured at that time for most human beings on this planet, but that, he believed, was a lapse of moral principle. He was willing to shed vast amounts of blood to uphold that principle, within his responsibilities to the Constitution and to the Union.

Today, by contrast, many Americans, who have casually absorbed a principle of moral relativism, think that the American Proposition is *not* morally superior to that of Vietnam or Honduras or the USSR, but is merely "relative" to our culture; it's merely "ours."[11] Such a standpoint empties morality of meaning. It reduces morality to a mere "hurrah" for our side. It denies that persons capable of understanding reasons, and of making reasoned choices, deserve to be ruled only with their own consent. It denies the American Proposition, whose warrants are the laws of nature and nature's God. Abandon those warrants, and you have eviscerated the American Proposition—first as an intellectual theorem, but also as a political experiment. That makes a mockery of many brave efforts expended, of many profound intellectual and institutional discoveries nobly carried out, and of such hallowed spots as Gettysburg, to name but one patch of blood-drenched earth. Criticize American practice to your heart's content. But do so wisely, recalling the American Proposition to which, in such criticism, you will necessarily be obliged to repair. Those, in particular, who wish to criticize the alleged materialism, secularism, relativism, and consumerism of certain sectors of American life will find the American Proposition convenient for their purposes.

III. Five Propositions for Exploration

Setting aside our past failures, and advancing into the future, I would like to propose five ways in which the American Proposition has launched into the world new ideas, new institutions, new ways of doing things. It is the vocation of American intellectuals, Catholics especially, to be of service in the desperate search of our worldwide contemporaries for a foundation in natural law for the international community, in which women and men of radically divided religions and secular faiths seek ways of practical cooperation. That the speculative divisions on this planet are immense is a fact. That there are practical principles for common action available for international expression is a lesson Maritain invited us to pursue.[12]

In addition, a revolution in communications (including television, VCRs, and electronic networks) has occurred since the deaths of Murray and Maritain. This revolution has given new reality to worldwide standards of public behavior and speech. The reputations of leaders and regimes, submitted to universal and instantaneous inspection, are assailed

---

[11]See Hadley Arkes, "Moral Obtuseness in America," *National Review* (June 16, 1989): 33.

[12]For the distinction between speculative and practical ideology, see *The Range of Reason*, 180.

by worldwide public opinion. What was formerly hidden is now brought into the light of universal judgment. The imperatives of natural law now run beyond the complete control of local, protective ideologies. When tyrants abuse their citizens, worldwide opinion condemns them.

With this in view, I have listed five world-historical breakthroughs of the American experiment, with implications for an ordering of international freedom according to natural law.

(1) *Religious Liberty.* "On any showing," Murray writes, "the First Amendment was a great act of political intelligence" (*WH* xi). But what is its profound meaning? What is its universal bearing?

Liberty of conscience, Pope John Paul II has often said, is the first of all fundamental rights.[13] It goes to the heart of human identity. Still, there are not lacking many Americans, even Catholics, who profoundly misunderstand the *social* dimensions of the First Amendment. The words of that amendment are deceptively simple: "Congress shall make no law respecting an establishment of religion or prohibiting the free exercise thereof." Now it may well be that some Protestants conceive of religion in a wholly individualistic and private manner. Yet in 1792, there were also Catholics and Jews in America, whose conception of religion as a community of faith and obligation was not thereby disfranchised. Congress is expressly prohibited from establishing a Protestant conception of religion, by the first clause, and from barring the free exercise of Catholic, Jewish and other conceptions of religion, by the second.

In the generation preceding ours, perhaps too much attention was given by philosophers, lawyers, judges, and public discussion generally to the "no establishment" clause, and far too little to the "free exercise" clause.[14] But, more deeply still, the "no establishment" clause is in itself violated by interpreting it solely in a Protestant, individualistic sense. Thus, if our public dialogue in the United States has in fact been warped by infidelity to the basic neutrality of the express language of the First Amendment, the fault lies not in our stars but in ourselves. We have failed to deepen our own intellectual heritage, and to press it in the public

---

[13]See *Redemptor Hominis*, 17. In a letter to Kurt Waldheim at the United Nations, the Pope wrote that "religious freedom ... is the basis of all other freedoms and is inseparably tied to them all by reason of that very dignity which is the human person." See also the discussion in George Weigel, "Religious Freedom: The First Human Right," *This World* 21 (Spring, 1988): 39–44.

[14]This is the gravamen of the Williamsburg Charter on Religious Liberty. See *This World*, No. 24 (Winter, 1989): 54–101.

square. In that case, we have been inhibited not by lack of liberty, but by lack of intellectual perspicuity, hard work, and courage.

This failure has international implications, for most of the world thinks rather in communal terms of human identity, than solely in individualistic terms. Religion, for most humans, grounds *social* obligations and *public* expression. The First Amendment prohibits the coercion of any consciences by an establishment of religion; but, in the same stroke, it also prohibits the coercion of those consciences for whom religion does impose social and public obligations. The latter must enjoy the rights of free exercise, so long as they do not seek to coerce the free exercise of the consciences of others. These principles allow for considerable variation in structures and arrangements among various nations of diverse histories. Equivalents to the "First Amendment" in other national constitutions need not take precisely the American form. Nonetheless, under pain of violating this "first of all human rights," the practice of all nations must respect the existing variety of conceptions of religion and conscience, and permit their free exercise, privately as well as publicly.

(2) *The Social Question.* Always close to the heart of Jacques Maritain and Yves R. Simon was the growing desire of the poor of the world—whom they often spoke of in European terms, as "the workers"—to live a more prosperous life, above the level of mere subsistence (or less) to which from time immemorial they had been condemned.[15] Still, Hannah Arendt in *On Revolution* observed correctly that it was the American experiment that showed Europeans for the first time, and through them the whole world, that the poor are not inevitably enchained in poverty, but, under well-designed institutions, do better their conditions massively. This American success turned generation after generation of poor immigrants into a large and thriving middle class, and created for Europeans a crisis of conscience. If *les miserables* are not confined to everlasting misery by God or by fate, but by ill-designed institutions, then nineteenth-century Europe was obliged to confront its own massive "social problem,"[16] which had been ignored for centuries. By European intellectuals and activists, this problem was misidentified as a crisis of industrialization and capitalism. For it was precisely to "capitalist" America and to centers of industry in Europe (and elsewhere) that the desperately poor rural masses were flee-

---

[15]See, e.g., Maritain's discussion of the working class in *Integral Humanism*, and Yves R. Simon, "Socialism and the Democracy of the Common Man" in *The Community of the Free*, 137–72.

[16]Arendt, *On Revolution*, 15.

ing in search of opportunity. Indeed, had there not been an example of how "huddled masses yearning to breathe free" could find a better life, the worldwide "rising expectations" of the poor could hardly have been awakened. Expectations would have remained as they had ever been; and the life of vast majorities would have remained "solitary, poor, nasty, brutish, and short."

In this respect, the social history of the last two centuries deserves a second look, from other than an anticapitalist point of view. One would think that American Catholic intellectuals, so many of them recent descendants of the world's most miserable and poor, would inquire more deeply into the design of institutions that allowed their families to escape from immemorial poverty. Some among them might prosecute the following systematic inquiry: Through which *institutions* was the poverty of our families alleviated? How did it happen that they did not long remain poor?

The answer to such questions cannot be merely "hard work"; our ancestors had also worked very hard in the lands whence they emigrated. The answers are surely both systemic and practical. Such lessons have, indeed, gained in informative power, as other economic experiments on the international scene repeatedly fail. Socialist leaders in the USSR, Hungary, Poland, China, and elsewhere speak more often these days of markets, private property, incentives, enterprise, personal initiative, and the privatization of earlier nationalized industries. Surveying the conditions of his native Poland during his lifetime, Pope John Paul II linked to the fundamental right of religious liberty a second fundamental right to "economic initiative."[17] He justified this right in terms both of the person and the common good.

(3) *Creativity and Enterprise.* Imbibing the lesson of Adam Smith (but not the philosophy of *laissez-faire*) that "the cause of the wealth of nations" is discovery and invention, the American framers led the world in listing among the "rights" of Americans (in art 1., section 8 of the Constitution) the right, for a limited time, to the fruits of their own inventions and discoveries, "in order to promote the sciences and the practical arts"—i.e., for purposes of the common good. Alexander Hamilton's superior knowledge

---

[17]*Sollicitudo Rei Socialis*, reprinted in *Aspiring to Freedom: Commentaries on John Paul II's Encyclical 'The Social Concerns of the Church'*, ed. Kenneth A. Myers (Grand Rapids: William B. Eerdmans Publishing Company, 1988), 16.

of economics, furthermore, prompted him to establish institutions of enterprise, manufacture, and commerce that turned the Northern states, at least, away from the Jeffersonian and Madisonian emphasis upon the yeoman farmer, and enabled the North to move far beyond the rural poverty in which the South was so long enmired.[18]

At the risk of some repetition, let me again emphasize that American Catholic scholars have been remarkably slow in grasping the secrets of the economic system, first invented in America, that propelled their ancestors from poverty and misery to reasonable affluence. Sitting as they do on vast resources of historical research for grasping *How the West Grew Rich,*[19] in this first of the "developing nations," American humanists have had remarkably little to say to the billions of the world's poor struggling today to discover and to build systems that liberate the vast majority of the poor from poverty. Such systems must include institutional supports in which to learn and to exercise the moral-intellectual virtue of economic enterprise, such as institutions that afford cheap and easy incorporation of small businesses, credit for the poor, venture capital, universal education, and research and development. Without the Homestead Act, and the Land-Grant College Act, the rapid development of the American West would hardly have been conceivable. For economic development springs from institutions that inspire and support the capacities for creativity and enterprise endowed in all humans by the Creator, in whose image they are made.

(4) *The New Science of Politics.* The American Proposition that government is properly "of the people, by the people, and for the people," must necessarily call forth from among the people new virtues, to be added to the classic tables of the virtues. This theme—that a new form of politics requires new virtues—was dear to Alexis de Tocqueville, who understood quite well the classic, aristocratic virtues of the European past. In ancient societies, citizens needed reserves of sheer endurance and patient resignation. In the new republic, by contrast, citizens faced new and unprecedented civic and economic responsibilities, for which ancient virtues of resignation could not be sufficient. They needed civic responsibility, enterprise, and initiative. They needed new forms of civic cooperation and practical cooperation. They also enjoyed—and needed—a personal sense

---

[18]See Forrest McDonald, *Alexander Hamilton: A Biography* (New York: W.W. Norton & Company, 1982).

[19]See Nathan Rosenberg and L.E. Birdzell, Jr., *How the West Grew Rich: The Economic Transformation of the Industrial World* (New York: Basic Books, 1986).

of belonging to a great common and public project, that of creating a new society. They were inspired by American institutions with an unprecedented ambition and bustling energy, which was remarked upon by such Catholic visitors from abroad as Crevecoeur and Tocqueville. Whereas ancient tables of the classic virtues had frowned upon "utility," Tocqueville shrewdly observed, Americans speedily made it both an instrument of effecting the common good and of raising the levels of common life to standards (material and spiritual) never before attained.[20]

In brief, new thinking on the moral virtues appropriate to political and economic life in free republics is urgently needed. It is not the case that the older virtues lose their appropriate roles; rather, they must be complemented by a new panoply of virtues, appropriate to the full civic responsibilities that citizens assume in becoming a sovereign people. The new scope of moral virtue is, therefore, larger and more demanding than before, not less demanding. Liberty is in this way a heavy moral burden. Moreover, without the practice of these specific new virtues, the institutions of the new republic cannot function. Worse, they will fall into desuetude and decadence. On that front, we face no little threat today, since in many places the moral capital of the past is being spent without replenishment. The "new science of politics" cries out for a "new science of the moral virtues," appropriate to new institutional arrangements.

(5) *Curing Democracy's Diseases.* The American Framers proved to be far wiser than the leaders of the French Revolution in several ways. One of the most important was that the Americans, unlike the French, saw clearly the diseases to which democracy is prey, and against them devised a host of remedies. Perhaps the briefest way to state the difference is that the Americans were realists, whereas the French prided themselves on an ideological reconstruction of society. This may explain why the American

---

[20]"In the United States there is hardly any talk of the beauty of virtue. But they maintain that virtue is useful and prove it every day.... [The Americans] enjoy explaining almost every act of their lives on the principle of self-interest properly understood. It gives them pleasure to point out how an enlightened self-love continually leads them to help one another and disposes them freely to give part of their time and wealth for the good of the state" (Tocqueville, *Democracy*, 525–30).

Republic flourished during the next fifty years, while the French did not: it was born without the bloodbath that the French Revolution lustily championed. Unlike so many other revolutionaries, the American Framers died peacefully in their beds, revered and celebrated, as were Thomas Jefferson and John Adams when they both died on the fiftieth anniversary of the Declaration of Independence, July 4, 1826.

The American framers saw clearly that even democracy may be tyrannical. They rightly feared "the tyranny of the majority,"[21] recognizing from history that personal and minority rights would not be safe in the hands of majorities. They understood quite well the sudden passions—and the demagoguery, rhetorical and otherwise—to which majorities are prey. They were not willing to exchange a king for an unchecked majority, one tyrant for another. Therefore, even while retaining the principle of majority rule, they contrived to find ways to protect limited government, and most especially private and minority rights. To the idea of majority rule, they added a rather large number of republican checks and balances. Eschewing a utopian democratic idea, they sought to construct a democratic *republic*.

Among the most original of remedies to democratic diseases was an insight of which Madison was especially proud, "the enlargement of the orbit."[22] Whereas earlier sages had argued that democracy is attainable only within a small state—ideally, for Aristotle, a forum small enough to be within the reach of a single human voice—Madison hypothesized that a democratic republic could best survive within a very large territory. He

---

[21]"When a majority is included in a faction, the form of popular government . . . enables it to sacrifice to its ruling passion or interest both the public good and the rights of other citizens" (*Federalist* No. 10, [80]). See also Tocqueville, *Democracy*, vol. 1, Chapter XV, especially the section entitled "Tyranny of the Majority."

[22]See *Federalist* No. 10 and the discussion of Madison's thought in Marvin Meyers, *The Mind of the Founder: Sources of the Political Thought of James Madison*, revised edition (Hanover: University Press of New England, 1981), xxvii–xxx. See also Martin Diamond, *The Founding of the Democratic Republic* (Itasca, IL: F.E. Peacock Publishers, 1981), 70–78.

therefore argued that the very large expanse of the existing American states (and others to be added) was not, as the ancient wisdom had supposed, an impediment to success; on the contrary, it was a necessary condition.[23] The reasons for this advantage, made out of a seeming disadvantage, were several. Among the most important are these. First, the larger territory would include a broader range of diverse interests, parties, and habits of life, with the result that the number of checks upon any tyrannous majority would be multiplied. Second, although a small community might more easily fall under the sway of a demagogue, or powerful family, or particularly talented set of forceful personalities, it would be far more difficult for such local powers to extend their sway over citizens in other communities, whose livelihood has a different basis and whose habits of life are different. Democracy may require a small compass, he argued; a republic requires a large.[24]

But there must also be other remedies to the diseases to which democracies are prey. A limited, constitutional government divides the fundamental human social systems into three, by two major subtractions from the power of earlier states. First, moral and cultural powers concerning conscience, information, and ideas would be excluded from control by the political powers. The church, press, and other institutions of the intellectual and spiritual life would be separated from government control. Second, to an unprecedented degree, the economic system would also be separated from direct political control. In short, the project of *limited* government entails a diminution of political power regarding the moral and the economic bases of the life of free citizens. Powers of conscience and economic initiative will thereby have larger fields of liberty than under preceding regimes. All three systems—political, economic, and moral-cultural—will be interdependent, of course, since all citizens are simultaneously political, economic, and moral beings. Moreover, each system will quite properly operate as a check upon the other two. As a whole, the system will be a properly "mixed" system, composed of all three subsystems. The (relative) *in*dependence of each is secured by this original design, as is the *inter*dependence of all three.

---

[23]"The two great points of difference between a democracy and a republic are," wrote Madison: "first, the delegation of the government, in the latter, to a small number of citizens elected by the rest; secondly, the greater number of citizens and greater sphere of country over which the latter may be extended" (*Federalist* No. 10, [82]).

[24]See *Federalist* No. 14, (100) and No. 10, (83).

Next, in similar fashion, the political system will be itself divided into its three independent, yet interdependent, parts: executive, legislative, and judicial.

Again, federalism will introduce yet a further system of checks and balances, inasmuch as every participant state will retain its sovereignty, even while delegating to the national (federal) government certain limited powers, sufficient to the pursuit of the general welfare. This conception of dual sovereignties functions as a principle of subsidiarity, bringing government closer to the governed in their smaller political units.

Beyond this, Madison and the other Framers were fertile in thinking up other "auxiliary precautions." Calvinist in background, although on the creative and optimistic side of Calvinism, both Madison and Hamilton knew that their task was to found a Republic that would work among sinners like themselves. Such a Republic would depend mightily on the virtue of its citizens and its leaders. But to depend solely on virtue would not be realistic, since even the most virtuous sometimes sin, especially when power is entrusted to them, and since a majority must be expected to rank no higher than in the middling ranks of the virtuous. Thus the need for "auxiliary precautions" is present throughout society in its every part, not alone in government:

> This policy of supplying, by opposite and rival interests, the defect of better motives, might be traced through the whole system of human affairs, private as well as public. We see it particularly displayed in all the subordinate distributions of power, where the constant aim is to divide and arrange the several offices in such a manner as that each may be a check on the other—that the private interest of every individual may be a sentinel over the public rights. These inventions of prudence cannot be less requisite in the distribution of the supreme powers of the State.[25]

Democracy, in short, even democracy in its republican form, cannot be imagined as a paradise, a dominion of the righteous, a realm where troubles cease, conflicts disappear, and vigilance against sin and error are no longer needed. On the contrary, without virtue republican self-government is not remotely possible. But even virtue needs the social support of checks and balances, and against its lapses government offices need to be so designed that the interest of officeholders in their own success requires them to be jealous of the boundaries between their power and that of others. In this way, each becomes a sentinel simultaneously of his own interest and the integrity of the Republic.

---

[25]*Federalist* No. 51 (322).

A realistic vision such as this, far from being incompatible with a healthy Catholic sense of sin, almost perfectly expresses it. Sin has not totally corrupted human nature; but it has wounded it. Therefore, a regime of virtue is possible, but it can never be expected to be total, and "occasions for sin" should be diminished by the very structure of social institutions. The democratic republic is a high achievement, only insofar as it contains remedies against its own inherent flaws.

IV. Conclusion

We have not yet succeeded in erecting a fully American expression of "Catholic social thought," informed by the political wisdom that is our providential inheritance. For that reason, much of Catholic social thought, as it is preached in America, lacks power to convince. Its accents seem European, not American. Its analyses seem not nearly as advanced and sophisticated in matters of political economy—or even in "the new science of politics"—as they could be. As more and more nations choose the route of democracy, and must then confront the diseases to which democracies are prey, the American experience will become an ever more valuable resource. For the democratic republic is not merely an ideal; it is also a web of institutions, habits, carefully constructed balances, and "auxiliary precautions." The democratic revolution is moral or not at all. But it is designed, as well, to cope with human waywardness.

The five points of American originality listed above might easily be added to. What is most striking about American Catholic writing in books and journals in the years since the groundbreaking work of Maritain and Murray, however, is the relative absence of serious reflection upon Madison, Jefferson, Hamilton, Lincoln, and other significant figures in American social thought. It is as though our own patrimony as Americans is still remarkably closed to us. Since the American Proposition rests on concepts such as natural law, virtue, character, human frailty, and the transcendence of God, which are for Catholic lungs familiar air, this relative indifference to our patrimony may in the future be held as a fault against us. Nonetheless, Tocqueville did predict that one day American Catholics would be among the best prepared to defend the American Idea. The vindication of that prediction is within our grasp, if we but meet our responsibilities.

Matthew J. Mancini

Nominalism, Usury, and Bourgeois Man

Jacques Maritain's carefully worded final written testimony was paradoxically a preliminary sketch as well, written in both fear and hope: fear of not being able to get the thoughts down before he died, and hope that they would be taken up, debated, and criticized. I refer, of course, to the utopian project called "A Society Without Money,"[1] a strange and disturbing essay, without doubt the most revealing of Maritain's last writings. It is philosophy written *in extremis*, giving us the privilege of a remarkable moment of perception into the dying philosopher's innermost concerns. And what we find there can properly be termed amazing. For the essay in which he discloses his "obsession," as he calls it, the subject that "haunts" him on his deathbed, and which at the cost of "a vast and fearful effort" of his flickering energies he managed to commit to paper before his exhausted and broken ninety-year-old body failed him at last—this essay is a condemnation of usury.

It seems ironic, at the very least, that Maritain yearned for so long to give himself to a life of prayer and contemplation, but that when at last he was able to do so, he devoted his final intellectual energies to the most worldly of all concerns—money.

In "A Society Without Money" Maritain again, as he had done for four decades, analyzed the divergence of theory and practice that obtains under the capitalist treatment of money. To Bernard Doering we owe a thorough and sensitive description of the biographical context of this piece, combined with an orderly presentation of Maritain's earlier writings

---

[1]Jacques Maritain, "A Society Without Money," *Review of Social Economy* 48 (1985): 73–83.

on the subject.[2] I can only commend Doering's study, and I will not add to or criticize it here. What I will attempt is a critique of Maritain's own analysis, which in turn will lead to some inferences I will make as to the place of interest in his sociopolitical thought.

"A Society Without Money" is not primarily a utopian tract about tokens and work, vacations and travel, but is first and foremost a long-delayed continuation of *Freedom in the Modern World* (1936), where he addressed directly and at length the question of usury. Maritain's arguments in the essay evince no real development in forty years, but do contain significant further clarification.

It was in *Religion and Culture* that Maritain first discussed the nature of money's perverse transformation into a *"living organism."* The place to begin our analysis, therefore, is with that brief, richly suggestive appendix called "The Fecundity of Money" (*RC* 56–57; *FMW* 126–33). Here Maritain, like Marx, pointed to the reversal of values that takes place under modern conditions of production.

Maritain meticulously expounds the question. What is at issue, he points out, is not the productive relation between money and the means of production, by which capital funds are invested in plant and equipment and receive a return in the form of profits. "No fault can be found in such a scheme." The evil arises because the reality diverges from this neat *theoretical* picture. *In practice*, modern productive forces are not harnessed to a human end, not primarily treated as a means to the end of producing useful commodities. On the contrary, money itself has been transformed into an end. The object of the productive process is thus to multiply currency. Money has, as it were, risen in revolt from its proper subordinate role as a means and a measure of wealth and has usurped the throne in the kingdom of ends.

The theory is unobjectionable: money feeds production because it is used to purchase capital equipment. Profit from that production is a normal and legitimate share of income. But the practice bears no resemblance to the unobjectionable "scheme." Goods are treated as means to the fructifying of money, which is now perceived as a *"living organism."*

In this transposition, the essentially instrumental nature of money has been lost. While production is a fruitful, organic process, money is inanimate, "barren," as the ancients used to say, and a mere measure of

---

[2]B. Doering, "The Economics of Jacques Maritain," *Review of Social Economy* 48 (1985): 64–72; Doering, "Misappropriating Maritain," *Commonweal* 112 (1985): 105–09.

value. It is the sign, not the signified.

The problem with Maritain's account in *Religion and Culture* is that he takes the argument of Aristotle, that money is *by nature* merely a measure of value and in itself "sterile," and subjects it to no further criticism or analysis. For him this is all there is to say about money. In book I, chapter X, of the *Politics*, Aristotle says:

> Very much disliked also is the practice of charging interest; and the dislike is fully justified, for the gain arises out of currency itself, not as a product of that for which currency was provided. Currency was intended to be a means of exchange, whereas interest represents an increase in the currency itself. Hence its name [*tokos*, offspring], for each animal produces its like, and interest is currency born of currency. And so of all types of business this is the most contrary to nature.[3]

John T. Noonan and others have shown how Saint Thomas' definition of money led him to conclude that interest transgresses the principle of commutative justice—the principle of equal valuation in exchanges:

> St. Thomas ... fastens upon the statement [of Aristotle] that money is a measure.... As it is his custom to treat the essences of things, he will always consider money, formally, as a measure.... Money, thus formally considered, is conceived as having one constant, fixed value—its legal face value. Like other measures, money is considered independently from the things it measures, and as fixed and stable in its measurement.[4]

And, indeed, in the sense that Saint Thomas seems to be using the term, commutative justice was in his day often violated in money loans. In the modern regime of finance, however, interest can actually be said to serve the ends of commutative justice, insofar as it provides compensation for the future as well as the present value of the funds advanced. In other words, by adding a factor of time to present value, interest can be thought of as a just payment for a scarce factor.

---

[3]Aristotle, *Politics*, revised edition, trans. T.A. Sinclair (Harmondsworth, 1981), 87.

[4]John T. Noonan, *The Scholastic Analysis of Usury* (Cambridge, MA: Harvard University Press, 1957), 52. Two other works were of special value for the perspective of this essay: Joseph A. Schumpeter's thorough and sympathetic account of the Scholastics in his classic *History of Economic Analysis*, ed. Elizabeth Boody Schumpeter (New York: Oxford University Press, 1954), 82–94, esp. 92–94; and the judicious study by a Jesuit economist, Thomas F. Divine, S.J., *Interest: An Historical and Analytical Study in Economics and Modern Ethics* (Milwaukee: Marquette University Press, 1958), esp. 36–63.

Why did Maritain not see this fundamental and commonly understood point? To comprehend precisely why the feeding of money by profits constitutes a reversal of means and ends, we must first direct our attention to the distinction, inherent in the Thomistic understanding of the virtues, between two spheres of human action, the *factibile* and the *agibile* (*FMW* 193–214; *AS* 7–22, *TRA* 21–46). Following this, we will examine Maritain's and Thomas' analyses of usury. After recasting the argument in the language of modern economics, we will come full circle to the passage on the fecundity of money, and observe that what "haunted" Maritain was not capitalism as such, but rather what he called "the nominalist decline" of philosophic thought (*FMW* 128, n. 3).

In briefest summary, the factibile concerns the realm of "poetic" or productive activity, "the application of human reason to the elaboration of some material" (*FMW* 197). Its object is making things, and its characteristic virtue is art.

The *agibile* appertains to the domain of moral activity, of free will. It concerns the use to which things are put. Its end is the act to be done, while the virtue corresponding to this sphere is prudence.

- *factible*: sphere of action = production; end = thing to be made; virtue = art

- *agibile*: sphere of action = morality; end = act to be done; virtue = prudence

Maritain cites the *Summa Theologiae*, II-II, 66, 2, to explain this distinction and to uphold individual property. Turning to the passage, we find Saint Thomas pointing out mankind's "twofold competence in relation to material things," and thus distinguishing between caring for the earth's resources (*procurandi et dispensandi*) and making proper use (*usus*) of them. As concerns the first, from a purely practical standpoint (not as a matter of natural law, but as a rational inference from it), the fashioning of earthly goods demands that the agent in control of the materials be an individual. But in regard to the second, acting morally with respect to the thing made requires that its use benefit the multitude. Thus, while production demands individual ownership, morality requires that the use of goods "must . . . be of service to all" (*FMW* 196).

- *factible*: sphere of action = production; end = thing to be made; virtue = art; goods = held in private

- *agibile*: sphere of action = morality; end = act to be done; virtue = prudence; goods = used for community

What has happened to money in this exposition? In order to incorporate this troublesome outsider into the discussion of the economic order, we must examine briefly the hoary topic of usury, the Church's repeated condemnations of which, Maritain wrote, "stand at the threshold of modern times like a burning interrogatory as to the lawfulness of its economy" (FMW 117).

A momentous change in the Church's attitude toward usury occurred during the eleventh century, when it began to be treated as a sin of injustice rather than uncharitableness.[5] To exact more in return than had been lent at the outset was a form of theft, a violation of the right to private property. In our own day, however, usury, "the sovereign mistress of the bourgeois world," reigns over economic and social life (FMW 129). But usury must be sharply distinguished from profit. Again, Maritain's source is the Summa; this time the well-known question on usury, II-II, 78. That this question contains the verdict on both usury and profit, the latter being an innocent return, is highly significant.[6] The antiusury argument is based on the fact that money is a "fungible" good whose use constitutes its consumption—like (to use the classic examples) wine or oil:

> In such cases, the use of the thing should not be considered separately from the thing itself so that when someone is given the use of the thing, he is given the thing itself. . . . If someone wants to sell wine and to sell the use of wine, he sells the same thing twice or sells what does not exist—a clear sin against justice. . . . We call this usury.
>
> [Moreover] according to the Philosopher money was devised to facilitate exchange, so that the proper and principal use of money is its use or expenditure when exchanges are carried out. Therefore it is wrong in itself to receive a payment for the use of a loan of money—which is called usury.

To summarize the argument thus far, this time having recourse to modern economic terms, we might recall from the principles of economics that each of the factors of production, land, labor, and capital, receives a return—it has a price. To the so-called "primary" inputs, land and labor, go

---

[5]Noonan, Scholastic Analysis of Usury 17, 30–31.

[6]Thomas Aquinas, Summa Theologiae, II-II, 78, 2 ad 5: "Somebody who lends money hands over the possession of it to the borrower, and with it the attendant risks and the obligations to make complete restitution, from which it follows that the lender is not entitled to ask for more. Somebody, on the other hand, who entrusts his money to a merchant or a craftsman in a sort of partnership does not hand over the ownership, and so it is still at his risk that the merchant trades or the craftsman works. The lender is, therefore, entitled to ask for a part of the profit of the undertaking in so far as it is also his own." See also II-II, 77, 4.

factor prices called rent and wages, respectively. Maritain considered wages to be a kind of substitute payment for the dividends received by capital, and he seems never to have attacked the wage system as such. I know of no references to rent in his works, but justifications of it are found in the same question of the *Summa* that treats usury.

But the case of the "secondary" input, capital, is more complicated. For just as there are two sorts of capital, so there are two categories of factor prices for it. Capital considered as equipment, factories, machinery, and the like—man's art that enhances productivity—receives profit. To financial capital, the funds that are advanced in order to facilitate the purchase of the equipment and so forth, there goes interest. In Maritain's analysis, then, of these four factor prices, three—rent, wages, and profit—he considered legitimate. But the fourth, interest, which unfortunately dominates the entire structure of modern economic life, serves to strangle civilized life itself (*FMW* 129).

Can Maritain really be saying that interest-taking in any form is always wrong? Remarkably, as he revealed forty years later in "A Society Without Money," the answer is an unqualified Yes.

To understand fully the reason for Maritain's perplexing obsession with interest, we must re-examine the language of the passage on the fecundity of money.

There, we remember, Maritain maintains that, while the theory or "scheme" of capitalism is unimpeachable, in practice it works in a manner "absolutely different." Money is treated as a fertile, living being, so that—and here I believe is the key phrase—"the *sign* money predominat[es] over the *thing*, commodities useful to mankind." What does he mean by this?

In the essay "Sign and Symbol," Maritain developed the distinction between what he called the "magical" and the "logical" sign. The magical is "a sign *for the imagination* taken as a supreme arbiter or *dominant factor* of all psychic life," whose sphere is the Dream, and whose medium is "the living ocean," the "nocturnal regime of the imagination." For persons whose cultural matrix precludes the daylight realm of the Logos, "the presence as to knowledge of the signified in the sign becomes ... a presence as to reality, a physical interchangeability, a physical fusion, and a physical equivalence of the sign and the signified."

What Maritain calls "the logical sign," by contrast, exists "*for the intelligence* (speculative and practical) taken as the *dominant factor* of the psychic regime."[7] The practical sign is a particular kind of logical sign helping to direct as well as denote the activities of individual persons as both makers and moral agents.

When "Sign and Symbol" is approached from the angle of the economic ideas I have just expounded, it becomes clear that money is properly regarded as one of those practical signs, "invented," says Saint Thomas in his discussion of happiness, "by the art of man for the convenience of exchange and as a measure of things saleable."[8] By virtue of its having been created by man's art, we can say that money is a *practical sign in the realm of the factibile*; it is property. At the same time, this practical sign must also be agibile, guided by the virtue of prudence to the common good.

But what do we find in the concrete operations of contemporary economic life? We see that, in direct contrast to its proper role, money stands outside the domain of the Logos altogether. It has, in practice, neither a factibile nor an agibile status. Instead, it functions like some hideous fertility goddess, being constantly fed by the output of the social economy. It has been perverted from a logical into a magical sign.

Thus we can see that Maritain's remarkably vehement attacks on capitalism stemmed not from any consideration of economics per se or even primarily from considerations of justice (although these latter are certainly important). Rather, they take their place in what, from one angle at least, could be characterized as Maritain's lifelong philosophical vocation: the attack on nominalism.

The fact that nominalism lies at the root of capitalism's evils is evidenced by the language of Maritain's excoriations of bourgeois man, which are notable for a comparative absence of references to injustice or exploitation. The problem with the bourgeois, Maritain said, was his detachment from things, his alienation from the world of real objects. Like Descartes, whom Maritain charged with committing the "original sin of modern philosophy," what bourgeois man wants is "independence from things" (*TR* 77). Thus arises his narcissism: his polity evinces "no real common thought—no brains of its own, but a neutral, empty skull clad with mirrors" (*MS* 110). And why? Because, like primitive men under the sway of the magical sign, he is absorbed by the signs of things, rather than things themselves. "A whole idealist and nominalist metaphysic underlies his

---

[7]Jacques Maritain, "Sign and Symbol," in *Ransoming the Time*, 217–54; quotations on 228, 232.

[8]Thomas Aquinas, *Summa Theologiae*, I-II, 2, 1.

comportment. Hence in the world created by him, the primacy of the sign: of opinion in political life, of money in economic life." And so capitalist society is one "not of men but of money and paper, of symbols of wealth, a society whose soul is the desire to produce more titles possession" (*IH* 78, 164).

So, in the end, Maritain's attitude gives equally cold comfort to both left and right.

That "A Society Without Money" evinces no modification or retreat whatsoever from his earlier censures of capitalism must be clear to anyone who reads it. But persons on the left ought to pause before embracing Maritain's conclusions, for his critique is seriously vitiated by several factors.

First, and most damaging, it rests on a fundamental misunderstanding of the nature of the regime of finance—and not, it should be pointed out, just capitalist finance, but that in any mode of production. Regardless of where or how the value of output is distributed, as long as a factor is scarce in relation to demand it must have a price. As Thomas F. Divine, S.J., writes, "Capital, like all scarce factors, has a marginal value determined by the demand for its services relative to its supply."[9]

Second, when Maritain merely considers capitalism in the abstract, it is clear he sees it as a system of wages, rents, and profits. That is, and I believe this is crucial to his mental picture of capitalism, he views interest as *extrinsic* to the system. Capitalism as such is an acceptable form of political economy. In fact, by doing an informal content analysis, I have found that, conceding a number of significant counterexamples, in the overwhelming majority of the scorching passages in which Maritain condemns capitalism, he is actually attacking not the "mode of production" itself, but rather the social structure that that mode has spawned, and in particular, of course, the contemptible figure of the Bourgeois.

So the trouble with capitalism is bourgeois man, the narcissistic nominalist, who is actually presented in a 1947 passage as exploiting even the capitalists themselves: "Manipulating as masters of the signs of other people's riches, [they] enslave the fortune of the world to their financial feudalism."[10]

The tableau of modern capitalism in Maritain's possibly unique view is thus as follows: land, labor, and capital in a regime of private investment

---

[9]Divine, *Interest*, 231.

[10]Jacques Maritain, *Raison et raisons* (1947), 253; quoted in Doering, "Economics of Jacques Maritain," 70.

and return receive their legitimate shares of income in the form of rent, wages, and profits. Outside and, as it were, above this system stands the bourgeois, now revealed as a usurer, paradoxically a creation of that very system—a manipulator of signs, who perverts this otherwise unexceptionable mode by subordinating it to the realm of money. Something organic is made to subserve something sterile in the monstrous belief that the money itself can create. But only nature (and human societies are natural) is fecund. Money only gauges that fecundity.

At the same time—and this is the final irony—it is equally true that Maritain's theoretical approval of capitalism is useless to the right. For this image of the system is not one that any serious analyst can credit. To say that capitalism is acceptable, as long as you don't have to pay interest, is to ignore both an essential part of the overall market mechanism and the historical developments of the last century, especially in the United States, where finance capitalism was pioneered by John Pierpont Morgan and his minions. The contemporary economic system could not exist without interest, without a bourgeoisie.

Maritain even condemned communities of nuns and priests for keeping passbook savings accounts.[11] Given the strength of his conviction, we can only assume that, when Pierre Villard fell among the other thousands of corpses on the Western Front in 1917, and willed his huge estate in equal shares to Jacques Maritain and Charles Maurras, Maritain chose to invest his portion in stocks rather than bonds—in investments yielding legitimate profits rather than illegitimate interest.

At the end of "A Society Without Money," Maritain, with all the old humility and generosity, confesses to the doubts that teem in his mind as soon as the most fundamental questions about his proposals arise. And he expresses the hope behind the essay: that a trained economist might one day be attracted by these thoughts and develop them further.

I am not that trained economist, but, to me, the essay discloses an amazing sight—the aged philosopher poised to undertake a new project altogether, setting down his preliminary notes, assessing where he is at the beginning of a long road, and hoping for that familiar thrill of disputational jousting, this time from a good economist—but knowing, too, that the road he was about to take led to an altogether different destination.

---

[11]Maritain, "Society Without Money," 82.

Joseph J. Califano

Modernization of the Law of
The *Prise de Conscience*

Maritain's and Simon's notions of the maturation of man's moral conscience provides us with a balanced and fertile view of human progress: a view of human history that enabled Maritain and Simon to avoid the prevailing ideological distortions common to many popular theories of modernization. Their penetrating insights into the forces at work in human history enabled them to develop a rich notional framework for engaging in an interdisciplinary dialogue on the nature of modernization and man's moral development: a dialogue between philosophers and those psychosocial theorists in sociology, psychology, and cultural anthropology who give primary significance to the role of symbolic actions in the evolution of man's moral perspective and man's identification of the good. These psychosocial interaction theorists give one a reason to be hopeful that the deterministic view of human action may be waning in the above-cited disciplines.[1]

For Maritain, the law of the *prise de conscience* is the law of man's growth in awareness of good as a sign of human progress (*PH* 69). For

---

[1]In 1986, an interdisciplinary group met in Seville, Spain, and issued the "Seville Statement," endorsed and published by the American Psychology Association and the American Anthropological Association for an early study. Cf. H.D. Duncan, *Interaction Structures and Strategy* (Cambridge: Cambridge University Press, 1985) and H.D. Duncan *Symbols and Social Theory* (Oxford: Oxford University Press, 1969).

Simon, in the evolution of moral conscience, we observe the evolution of the knowledge of good and evil, so that morality has risen to a higher state in the persons of its most perfect representatives (*FAC* 183). I would describe the process as the maturation of man's deliberative moral knowledge and a perfection of his deliberative will through history: a process in which man, as a trans-objective subject (*DK* 93ff), develops a more precise understanding of the natural moral law.

However, for Maritain and Simon there is a built-in ambiguity in certain notions, such as moral progress, which involves the inherent danger of making serious misjudgments (*MS* 1). The risk of misjudgments arises because a notion such as "progress in human affairs" involves one in thinking in terms of very influential and ambiguous common notions of history; such notions appear to involve one in a commitment to either an optimistic or a pessimistic view of human nature, history, and the future. Simon described the situation well when he described optimism and pessimism as confused effective ideas, having an enduring influence in human events precisely because they are confused. Since optimism and pessimism are ambiguous ideas, they find easy entrance into the obscure half-rational sphere of the human mind, where systematic thought mingles with images and emotions. This is "the nursery of general attitudes, states of mind, ideas relative to the future and to the meaning of history" (*MS* 146). Such concepts are loaded with emotional judgments that determine how men view politics, political parties, and the actions of world leaders.

Both Maritain and Simon realized that, for man to understand his nature and his vocation as a moral agent, he must raise to a level of philosophical understanding such common notions that have arisen from the contingent needs of human history. The balanced perspective that Maritain and Simon had of history enabled them to recognize that it was the false optimism of the eighteenth and nineteenth centuries that had led to the nihilistic revolt and debilitating pessimism of the twentieth century. This was the case because the eighteenth and nineteenth centuries were committed to the notion of necessary progress, one called for not only by reason of human exigencies and man's vocation to be virtuous in the use of his freedom, but also because human history manifested deducible necessary laws, intellectual as well as economic, which would insure *de facto* as well as *de jure* progress. All that one had to do was let the process of modernization of thought and economics take their natural course and the future and improvement of man's lot was guaranteed (*MS* 148). All the evil of repressive governments and social injustices would disappear, if only man did not interfere with the predetermined forces at work in historical processes. This was true whether one identified modernization with capitalization, as do libertarians, or collectivization, as do the Marxists. They both preach a secular gospel founded on myths they share in common. They both rob man of his awareness of his creative freedom and his vocation as a moral agent.

The result of the above is that philosophy becomes replaced by ideologies, ones with a secular eschatology of an economic utopia that modernization is supposed to realize. I define an ideology as a secular religion having the following characteristics: (1) a body of doctrine producing a systematic body of beliefs and a value system; (2) a secular priesthood or organized elites who claim to be the ultimate interpreters of human events; (3) an absolute adherence to the absolute truth of the believed doctrines, regardless of actual events (the ideologue thereby seeking to impose upon the doctrines the character of divinely revealed truth); and (4) the absolute conclusion that there is only one simple means available to procure the common good (when, in fact, there are several means or a mixture of a multiplicity available). The ideologue removes all genuine notions of prudence, civic friendship, and final causality from human affairs and the life of man. Autocephalic notions of freedom and the good (or good action) replace any notion of moral development as the interiorization of an objectively true moral law. The good in this context must become only an individualistic, ephemeral phenomenon. Polytheism is thus resurrected in the name of progress; this is true for both the individualists and the collectivists.

The ideologues, who claim that absolute adherence to their doctrines is necessary for the realization of modernization, require the suppression of whatever does not conform to their ideology. Therefore, ideologies in their successive generations become implicitly, and then explicitly, totalitarian. Liberalism and relativism appear, at first sight, artfully to avoid this dilemma, but their common denial of the possibility of attaining truth forces them, in the end, to become a most oppressive form of totalitarianism. Relativism must lead to the conclusion that only through coercion can a consensus be maintained, since a common attainment of the truth is excluded in principle.

When one confronts the ideologue with historical facts that do not support his ideology, the universal response is that one is either paying too much attention to facts or one is paying attention to the wrong facts. The ideologue argues that this is the case on the ground that the pure system he believes in has never been permitted to operate. The libertarian argues that the absolute right to free association and the unlimited right to the appropriation of property have never, in their pure forms, been permitted to have full reign.[2] The collectivist argues the same for pure socialism, whether Marxist or some other variation,[3] both argue that salvation is to be found through the absolutizing of an economic system, and that progress is to be assured through man's becoming freed from his freedom.[4]

Out of ideologies of debilitating pessimism and relativism, there arose the ideology of positivistic methodology: a new variation on an old theme, where one tries to set the limits of human understanding, as did the rationalist and the empiricist. This ideology limits the study of history, by definition, to exclude all judgments related to progress or retrogression. These are judged to be unscientific, because all such judgments involve an evaluation of historical facts. This ideology proposes that the historian be an accountant of facts, one who makes no value judgments: an accountant who is incapable of drawing up a profit and loss statement or a balance sheet. This assumed value-free or ethically neutral view of history and human action (one devoid of any notion of final causality) obliterates any hope of developing an intelligible understanding of man's nature and his relationship to others. In this context, the only possible rationale for human rights is human conventions and legislative law.

Nihilism is the only possible consequence of the above viewpoint. It results in a kind of historical nominalism, in which history is viewed as displaying successive, discrete, and encapsulated epochs of time that are not intrinsically related to one another. No analogies, similes, or lessons can be drawn from one period to another. We cannot, therefore, learn anything applicable to the present from history. We are not only condemned to relive the mistakes of the past, but we could never recognize it as a reliving

---

[2]Cf. T.R. Machan., ed., *The Libertarian Reader* (Totowa, NJ: Rowan and Littlefield, 1982) and John L. Wriglesworth, *Libertarian Conflict in Social Choice* (Cambridge: Cambridge University Press, 1985).

[3]Cf. D. McLellan, ed., *Marx, The First Hundred Years* (London: Francis Pinter, 1983) and Peter Wosley, *Marx and Marxism* (London and New York: Tavistock Publications, 1982).

[4]The libertarian cites examples of Horatio Alger stories, where free, enterprising individuals succeed. The universalizing of such stories presents us with a very selective history indeed, and fails to mention all those instances where enterprising individuals, through no fault of their own, suffer the greatest degradation and even death. Likewise, the collectivist will bring forward examples of economic enterprises, etc., that succeed in supporting his perspective, but will fail to take note of the degradation that has resulted from a blind belief in his ideology.

of the past. Modernization has produced such a transformation of human beings, as well as their world, that all historical periods in time must be studied as if they were different solar systems, energized by different suns and having different bases for their existence. This is not essentially different from viewing historical periods as producing human beings that are alien to one another, like those who are described in science fiction, where our oxygen-based life encounters intelligent life based on some other principle.

This last view, which appears to be the fashionable one today, is the most problematic. This ideology of positivistic methodology claims to be optimistic about what a methodology can produce in and of itself. However this ideology, in the end, is just as pessimistic as the others, since it narrows man's knowledge and vision to the minuscule. This has led either to a determinist or situationist view of human actions. The former obliterates human freedom; the other denies what Maritain and Simon both sustained, namely that true freedom comes from the mastering of our liberty.

A common error characteristic of all ideologies is that they produce a false optimism, for they foster the belief that there are easy answers to fundamental questions about human development. In fact, the simplest of the questions requires generations of hard work to answer. Every genuine inquiry begins with what appears to be a simple question. Yet a genuine answer usually requires that one answer a multitude of more difficult and complex questions, ones that arise out of attempts to answer the original question asked. For example, look at the questions that have arisen out of Mendel's asking why some peas were wrinkled and others were smooth, or what eventuated out of Heisenberg's inquiry into why water wets. Only the dull of mind believe that there are easy answers to fundamental questions. Such questions are easy to ask, but difficult genuinely to answer.

The ideologue, who is easily made into an optimist, is as easily made into a nihilist when he experiences the bitter disillusionment that follows upon his realization that his easy answers solve none of his easily asked questions. With the death of a blind belief in necessary progress comes the nihilistic belief in necessary decadence (FAC 173). Having eclipsed human freedom completely, the ideologue cannot identify or distinguish good or evil in human action, for to do so would refute absolutely the ideologue's principle of necessary progress.

Maritain and Simon both understood the creative and annihilating capacity of human acts in light of the reality of human freedom. It was precisely because they recognized this dual capacity that Maritain and Simon were able to give credence to the reality of both the goodness and the malice in the record of human acts in history. Thus, to understand the law of the *prise de conscience* or the evolution of moral conscience, one must also recognize that good and evil are not divided in human history. Good and evil grow together in human history as two internal movements that advance in time. There is an intrinsic ambivalence in historical developments that does not allow any period of history to be either absolutely condemned or absolutely approved.

For Maritain, the above reflects the law of the fructification of good and evil, which deals with the development of the relationship between ethics and politics in the process of history (*PH* 59). The above law states that, if we consider history over a long enough period of time, then we can see that justice and rectitude tend in themselves to the preservation of human societies, while injustice and evil tend in themselves to the destruction of human societies. If virtue increased in proportion to power, then only good would increase as a result of the increase of power that modernization has placed in the hands of men. However, the facts are that any increase of power is equally susceptible to misuse, as well as proper use, depending on the goodness or malice of men (*PDG* 267ff). Also, any intrinsically evil or unjust situation that demands correction can lead to a change that improves the situation or merely exchanges evils. Revolutions that exchange one set of destitution for another, and where the oppressed become the oppressors, are not progressive but decadent. History provides us with many examples of revolutions producing constitutions that express *de jure* progress guaranteeing human rights, but an ideological perspective that denies *de facto* implementation. This is clearly the case in the Soviet Revolution and others patterned after it; even totalitarian regimes give *de jure* lip service to democratic principles and justice.

If we cease to identify progress as a kind of necessary *de jure* or *de facto* process involving the whole of humanity (*PDG* 179), then we can understand Maritain's and Simon's guarded optimism (or genuine pessimism), and the veracity of the notion of the maturation of man's moral conscience that follows from their guarded moral optimism.

A further difficulty progress confronts is that, once a new moral insight is attained, it must still propagate itself in the human community at large (*PDG* 189). A deepening of man's moral awareness has to overcome a unique set of psychological and sociological barriers for its general acceptance. It is very difficult for an authentically new insight to overcome the inertia inhibiting moral awareness that arises out of collective habits of judging human action from the moral point of view. The tendency towards the acceptance of familiar ways of evaluating human actions is a difficult barrier for men to overcome. Men of the best intentions have often enough led themselves and others astray because of such an inertia.

Recognizing the realities of the human condition and the creativeness of human freedom, we can also recognize that, when moral maturation occurs, it can be mixed with error and evil. For example, the women's rights movement, which properly recognized that women should not be viewed either as property or as never attaining to adulthood, has gone astray by identifying the recognition of women's rights with the appropriation of absolute power over the life of the unborn child. Thus, one observes that there is progress in moral insight mixed with a distortion of the original insight.

While we have appeared to move beyond the ideological belief that economic success depends upon a necessary connection between labor and destitution (i.e., that only the threat of destitution will cause people to work) (*PDG* 185), we have not as yet moved beyond the economic ideologies of work to bring about social justice. The dawn of the belief that war is not to be looked upon as an acceptable means of executing foreign policy will challenge the realist and globalist theories of international relations.

What enables the human person to overcome the barriers to moral maturation is the union of the fact that man is a trans-objective subject with man's capacity to perform originative acts of freedom (*RR* 68–69). The person is a trans-objective subject, who, because of his or her dianoetic and ananoetic vision of reality, is able to perform originative acts of freedom: acts that make a person capable of transcending the models of reality we construct and the ideologies they produce; acts through which one turns away from evil and towards the good; acts that transcend the whole world of empirical convenience, the mother of ideologies (*RR* 68–69). Man's originative freedom is a unifying activity of his cognitive and appetitive powers, ones that enable him to grasp the "is"—from which the ought reasonably follows. The burden of proof to the contrary falls upon the subjectivizers of human knowledge, whose theories of truth must presuppose the realist notion of truth.

It is in this context that the economic knowledge we have obtained and the technological proficiency we have gained can become united to and a part of the mastering of our liberty. They can be united to the kind of grasp of the human reality that produced a Gandhi, yet also to the distortion of the human reality that produced a Hitler.

Man does move in these two orders of good and evil, the orders of symbolic action: one of hope and creative use of his freedom and one of nihilistic negation of the human realities. A genuinely good symbolic act, an act that purifies the means we employ to attain our ends, is one that hurls a rock at an impervious, idol-filled world and shatters it with a single blow.

The charge can be made that Maritain's and Simon's notions of the natural law and the common good are too vague. This, in reality, is a misinterpretation of their thought, since the common good is discovered concretely through the historical maturation of human moral consciousness. The natural law and the common good are not capable of detailed *a priori* exposition. The perennial principles, once discovered, require the virtue of prudence and the originative acts of freedom rooted in man's vision as a trans-objective subject to make more precise our understanding of the natural moral law and our precise concrete realization of the common good.

The growth in our awareness of the moral law leads the way to the mastering of our liberty. The growth in our awareness of the moral law is what moves us to seek the purification of the means we use to attain our ends (*FMW* 139ff). Many prize modernization, yet the destruction of our environment by imprudence—in the way we industrialized and employ energy systems—clearly shows that ideologies, rather than originative acts of freedom, have led the way. The risk to the whole planet caused by the senseless destruction of the Brazilian rain forest, and the concomitant loss of one of the main sources of drugs to cure everything from leukemia and heart disease to skin rashes, is irrational and violent in an immeasurable degree. The fact that our taxes paved the road that made such a disaster possible is even more incredible. The irrational destruction of one of the most fundamental parts of the world's ecological system is clearly an ideology of modernization gone mad. The destruction of the rain forest will cause droughts in our farm belt that will threaten our food supply, and the melting of the ice caps will produce the flooding of our coastal shores, and the salinization of many water supplies.[5] The imprudent destruction of the rain forest in the name of modernization is more likely to destroy human life than a nuclear war. Negotiations with the Brazilians to purify their means of development is an international necessity for the national security of every nation.

Another disturbing fact, involving the security of every nation, is the number of nuclear reactors, whose cores are deteriorating at an ever-increasing rate.[6] We have no means, even theoretically conceivable, by which these reactors can be safely decommissioned and dismantled. Unfortunately, the prevailing view is that, if we throw enough money at the

---

[5]See *World Resources 1986 Report,* by the World Resources Institute and the International Institute for Environment and Development (New York: Basic Books, 1987).

[6]J. Edmonds and J.M. Reilly, *Global Energy Assessing the Future* (New York: Oxford University Press, 1987).

problem, we can buy a solution; but the question remains whether the solution we buy will be the one that we can tolerate environmentally. The decision to build reactors the way that we did can be compared to building the most elaborate car conceivable, but not designing brakes into the system: a situation that resulted from another kind of ideology, the ideology of a technocratic culture.

The philosophies of men like Maritain and Simon are brilliant, in that their guarded moral optimism or authentic pessimism never caused them to lose sight of the necessity of a constant vigilance against the temptation to fall into despair when confronted with the failure of men to remember what is genuine progress in human affairs. Maritain and Simon were men who knew with certainty the necessity of men of every age to strive towards the concretization of the unity of liberty, truth, and justice in man's shared world. Such a unity is never complete in this wounded world, where man can easily lose sight of the fundamental realities of human existence. What has been won by blood and sweat can easily be lost, because men can always leisurely withdraw from the realities of life and their moral vocation: a withdrawal that is a negation of the final cause of man's liberty, a withdrawal that can cause many to replace the hard-earned awareness of the realities of life with mythologies of their age and the illusion that they can live in comfort without a constant concern for the above. Thus, they fail to see that there is no safety in human affairs, nor are there any guarantees provided by human history. Every generation, as it were, must fight to preserve what little gains have been made by those who have gone before and struggle to get a little closer to where we ought to be: that is, to seek to concretize the requirements of a unity of liberty, justice, and truth. We must be guided by an awareness of intergenerational justice.

The philosophies of Maritain and Simon are singled out by the fact that they are imbued with a unified philosophy of history. Their view of history is cautiously hopeful in regard to the future of the human race and causes us to remember our future will be won or lost by our capacity to recognize the realities of our freedom and to exercise our freedom in a way that purifies the means we employ to attain our ends. We must do the above in terms of a richer and more precise notion of justice; only when we choose to modernize in terms of a proper vision of the common good will genuine human progress be realized.

John P. Hittinger

Approaches to Demoractic Equality:
Maritain, Simon, and Kolnai

Yves R. Simon states in *Philosophy of Democratic Government*:

> During the phase of democratic struggle against the old aristocratic and monarchical order, liberty and equality are considered inseparable. . . . The will to be free and the claim for equality seemed to be but two aspects of the same enthusiasm. . . . But soon a split takes place within what was the Third Estate. The Fourth Estate has arisen, with a new claim for equality—a claim which sounds unintelligible to its former allies of the bourgeoisie. . . . The formula which attributed basic unity of meaning to freedom and equality seems to have been lost as soon as the defeat of the old hierarchies was certain (*PDG* 195–97).

Tocqueville argues that equality, and not freedom, was the aim of modern democracy all along. As much as freedom and equality share a common ground, they diverge at many points. He understands the challenge to liberal democracy to be the protection of freedom and excellence in the face of its egalitarian trends.[1] Simon, too, concludes the issue of equality, and its relation to freedom, is too vital to be dodged. Simon and Maritain are known for their attempts to embrace the modern liberal tradition and its egalitarian dynamic; they attempted to purify and elevate it in terms of the Aristotelian-Thomistic political science. Thus, they represent a new

---

[1]Alexis de Tocqueville, *Democracy in America*, trans. George Lawrence, and ed. J.P. Mayer (New York: Harper and Row, 1969). See Marvin Zetterbaum, "Alexis de Tocqueville," in Strauss and Cropsey, eds., *History and Political Philosophy*, 3rd edition (Chicago: University of Chicago Press, 1987), 761–63.

orientation of Catholic political philosophy, which hitherto had been somewhat sceptical of the liberal tradition in politics. Indeed, Paul Sigmund has recently commented about the importance of Maritain in this development.[2] Kolnai, on the other hand, highlights and defends the aristocratic element in the tradition and points to some inconsistencies and weaknesses in the liberal position, however purified or elevated. A comparison and contrast may yield some very fruitful results, both for political theory and for political practice.

We shall examine Maritain, Simon, and Kolnai in order and, for each one, give a summary of his account of equality and any moderating or counter-tendency. That is, we shall look for their idea of equality, and consider also whether and to what degree equality is desirable and possible. At stake, ultimately, is the nature and meaning of contemporary democracy and its prospects for success.

I. Maritain: The "Realist" Approach to Equality

Maritain's key writing on the question of equality is the essay "Human Equality" (*RT* 1–32).[3] Maritain develops his notion of equality through his typical method of analysis; it involves an examination of two extremes and the virtuous middle position. The first approach to human equality outlined by Maritain is the nominalist/empiricist one, which denies the reality of a universal human nature: it permits the enslavement of one part of humanity by another. The second approach is the idealist one: it denies particularity, with its concomitant inequalities, and may be labeled egalitarianism. The third approach is called "realist": it allows for unity and diversity in the human species, for equality and inequality.

The nominalist or empiricist approach is so taken with concrete inequalities that it denies any validity to the idea of a common humanity. Instead it erects biological or social divisions into essential differences, dividing the truly human from the sub-human, constructing "False hierarchies of pseudo-specific gradation which establish between men inequalities in the same order as those which apply to a lion and an ass, an eagle and an ant" (*RT* 4–5). The divisions may correspond to social

---

[2]Paul Sigmund, "Maritain on Politics," in Deal Hudson and Matthew Mancini, eds., *Understanding Maritain* (Macon, GA: Mercer University Press, 1987) 153–55; see H. Rommen, *The State in Catholic Thought* (St. Louis: B. Herder, 1947), 483–503.

[3]See Donald Gallagher's introduction to the reissue of Maritain's *Christianity and Democracy and The Rights of Man and Natural Law*, xxviii–xxxii.

privilege, such as those of aristocratic birth or bourgeois wealth, or to supposed differences in race or ethnicity. The error lies in the rigid ideological posturing by which common humanity is denied of an entire segment of the species, and a group thereby "concentrates into itself" all the dignity and privileges of human nature. The lower group exists only for the higher group. But, as Maritain readily argues, the claimed superiority for a group or bloc is always undermined because of the aggregate nature of the excellence or inequality. That is, the values are on average or on the whole. Moreover, there may be overlapping from one group to the next. Aristotle uses a similar argument against conventional slavery and hereditary privilege.[4] The boundary separating the groups is usually so variable and fluid that it can be "broadened or contracted as the mind wishes." Finally, Maritain points out that an inferior group can improve; and in fact, both groups share "a common natural pattern which they more or less fully realize."

Maritain's critique of the nominalist approach makes the standard case against slavery or tyranny. It is critical of extreme forms of oligarchy, which Aristotle argues border on tyranny. But Maritain's argument only grazes the superior claims of the aristocrat or monarch. It does not touch them if their claims do not entail a superiority in essence or a reduction of the other to the status of slave. If the claim of superiority is detached from an ethnic and/or hereditary basis, and is rather claimed by an individual, its high reach is left open.

The relevance of this false "nominalist" approach was quite pressing in the face of National Socialism and its racist creed, and it remains so to challenge any form of racial exploitation. Also, if economic conditions of some segments of a regime are oppressive to the point of slave-like exploitation, the critique is operative. Maritain does not make the relevant applications in this essay.

The idealist approach to equality excludes empirical inequalities and treats the unity of mankind in the abstract. Maritain charges this approach with a "speculative denial" of natural inequality, because it considers inequalities as solely the result of the artificial stratification of social life. Hence, inequality is a "pure accident" suggesting no intelligible patterns for the mind. This leads further to a practical denial of inequality, because it is "an outrage against human dignity." The egalitarian idea of equality demands simple equality and uniformity. Its instinctive tendency, Maritain says, is hatred of superiority and a levelling spirit: "In mental pat-

---

[4]Aristotle, *Politics*, 1255b 1.

terns which correspond to this, there develops an uneasy touchiness regarding any possibility of a hierarchy of value among men" (*RT* 14).

Maritain's analysis of egalitarianism is very pointed; its major thrust runs counter to the claim of pure democracy. And it certainly allows no room for a democracy based upon value relativism. Maritain's critique of its abstract reduction of particularity resonates to some contemporary developments in the critique of democratic theory concerning the unencumbered self.[5] Maritain's critique of the two extreme approaches to equality comes down hardest on the egalitarian approach. Here, Maritain is more spirited and better aimed at real types. The nominalist approach is more hateful, he says, but the idealist approach is more treacherous and leads to worse forms of slavery, because it embodies a "bitter passion counterfeiting Christian charity" (*RT* 16; *TR* 130, 140, 145).

The realist approach to equality leads Maritain to eschew the idealist one in favor of an "existentialist one." Equality is found not in an abstract ideal, but in "the root energies and sources of being" that lead human beings to seek communication with each other. Rather than use the notion of equal nature, Maritain favors the notion of community in nature. He would found equality on the natural sociability of men, and specifically in a tendency to love one's own. It is similar, I would say, to Aristotle's notion of natural friendship, or philanthropy.[6]

Maritain adroitly develops a defense of inequality out of the same unity in nature that grounds equality. Sociality demands differentiation and differentiation demands inequality. Maritain gathers up and develops the various reasons for inequality in a human community. I refer to them as the metaphysical principle of variety, the principle of individual merit, and the social principle of differentiation. Maritain cites Thomas' argument that inequality, order, and hierarchy are part of divine creation.[7] As for individual merit, Maritain points to moral, psychological, and even biological origins. In *Art and Scholasticism*, Maritain refers to the "habitus" of virtue as a "metaphysical title to nobility" that makes for inequality among men (*AS* 11). Finally, diversity of internal structures in society and diversity of conditions result from social life itself; in fact, he says that inequalities testify to the "inconquerable originality and vitality of social life."

---

[5]Alasdair MacIntyre, *After Virtue* (Notre Dame: University of Notre Dame, 1981) and Michael Sandel, *Liberalism and Its Critics* (New York: New York University Press, 1984).

[6]Aristotle, *Nicomachean Ethics*, VIII, 1, 1155a 20.

[7]Thomas Aquinas, *Summa Theologiae*, I, 85, 7; I, 47, 2.

Maritain makes a strong affirmation of the necessity and value of inequality. He says further that Christianity does not iron out social inequalities, but brings them into "true proportion" (*RT* 23; *TR* 145–46). The true proportion of inequality is its two-fold subordination to equality. It must not obscure the foundational value of equality nor must it impede the progressive development of equality in society. Social inequality, he says, must not be a principle of exclusion but one of communication; the inequalities must not be erected into a state of social servitude, nor should the man in the lower condition be considered an inferior man without dignity. Maritain reminds the reader of his criticism of the nominalist approach to equality, which would "harden" the inequalities and become oppressive. The primordial unity of human nature is the basis for the inequalities—the latter are justified in terms of the community. But, as was noted above, this amounts to nothing more than strictures on tyranny or exploitation. The "true proportion of equality to inequality," however, also includes something more. Maritain now introduces his notion of progressive social equality as an aim and purpose of a just society.

Social equality, he writes, "rises up progressively in the midst of society, like a social flowering forth or fructifying of the equality of nature" (*RT* 26). For example, although fundamental rights of the person are anterior to society, the legal order must increasingly embody protection for them. Further, the rights of the person in the political and economic spheres require continual progress in awareness of the rights, conditions for fulfillment, and embodiment in law and fact. The inequalities in society must be compensated for by a "redistribution" of benefits such that the higher benefits are open to all and such that the dignity of lower level is acknowledged through a proportional equal opportunity for fulfillment. Further, Maritain states that all should "in so far as possible participate 'free of charge' in the elementary goods needed for human life" (*RT* 29). The *telos* of political community is equality, not the perpetuation of inequalities. Thus, through this second subordination of inequality to equality, Maritain surmounts the aristocratic orientation of the Aristotelian-Thomistic tradition from which he derives his basic concepts.

Of course, it is crucial to Maritain's own account that the principal qualities dominant in monarchical and aristocratic regimes are "preserved" in the democratic regime, even while being "transcended" (*RMNL* 51–52). How are these qualities preserved? Does it not require the presence of countervailing principles within the democratic regime? Has Maritain paid sufficient attention to the problem and the tensions inherent in the mixing of political principles?[8]

Maritain acknowledges the many obstacles that frustrate the ready achievement of the democratic principle of equality. Progress towards social equality is a long arduous road. The democratic principle of equality is marked by a "dynamism." It requires the "conquest of man over nature and over himself." It is "an end to struggle for, and with difficulty, and at the price of a constant tension of the energies of the spirit." The tensions are indeed real. For Maritain, by linking equality with his high idea of liberty, keeps an elevating tone to its progress. That is, excellence and standards are held firmly in place by his account of liberty. His is not a "levelling equality." Further, the qualification of social equality with the "proportion" to condition and function is bound to disappoint the contemporary egalitarian movement. Maritain states that identical opportunity, strict equal opportunity, is an illusion. What are the conditions, the merits, and functions that would limit proportionately equal opportunity? His remarks on equality for women are instructive on this point (*IH* 196–99).

Other tensions emerge from Maritain's account. Is the progress to the free participation in the goods needed for human life a call for state socialism, socialized health care for example? The problem is, of course, that this tendency, if centralized, can run counter to the principle of differentiation and pluralism. How is equality to be achieved? Maritain's metaphor of "flowering" is too vague: the hard question of means, such as affirmative action, quotas, and the like, are not treated in his account. It is hard to gauge his position given the dynamism towards equality on the one hand and the desire for pluralism and a high liberty on the other. Tocqueville saw this as the overriding tension and issue.[9] Maritain views the

---

[8]See criticisms of Edward Goerner, "Aristocracy and Natural Right," *The American Journal of Jurisprudence* 17 (1972): 1–13. See also John Hittinger, "Maritain and America," *This World* 3 (Fall, 1982): 113–23, and "Review of Maritain's 'Rights of Man and Natural Law' " in *Crisis* 5:7 (July/August, 1987): 50–52.

[9]A. de Tocqueville, *Democracy*, 690–705; see Whitney Pope, *Alexis de Tocqueville* (Beverly Hills: Sage Publications, 1986), 52–63.

two in tandem and therefore fails to acknowledge the deeper tension in democratic theory and practice.

Perhaps the greatest tension surrounds his notion of progress. Even though Maritain speaks about the law of twofold contrasting progress of good and evil in history, he often fails to acknowledge the presence of intrinsic limitations on progress, particularly in political life (*PH* 143–57).[10] Will progress overcome the tensions in political life or are we faced with inherent tensions whose resolution must be managed? Plato speaks about the paradox of philosopher-king, Aristotle of the incommensurable claims to rule, Madison of self-interest, faction, and common good, Tocqueville of glory and welfare; and thus they accommodate themselves accordingly, by means of the noble lie, the mixed regime, checks and balances, self-interest properly understood. These political thinkers would certainly not claim that democracy replicates the qualities of monarchy or aristocracy in any pure form, let alone would they claim that democracy transcends them to a superior level of achievement in their own line or according to their distinctive principle. The qualities are replicated in some analogous but less pure form, and only as the result of mixing in a principle that counteracts the pure democratic principle.

The polarity of individual and person plays a central role in Maritain's philosophy, but this polarity lends weight to the progressive resolution of the tensions themselves. The trajectory of realization is potentially unlimited, according to the "conquest" of man over nature and over himself, the conditions Maritain names as the engine or dynamism for the progress towards greater equality. Does his account give too much sail to the prospects for democratic achievement?

II. Simon: The Egalitarian Dynamism
And the Principle of Autonomy

Simon's political philosophy reflects a greater awareness of the inherent tensions of political life as such and he explicitly deals with the tension of equality and liberty. More specifically, he affirms Maritain's ideal of social equality, but he has a much better defined counter-tendency in the principle of autonomy (*PDG* 130). The latter principle is also important to Maritain (*MS* 24). But Simon carefully works through the tensions and arrives at well-defined principles of compromise. He does not speak of a brotherly city of the future; if anything, his concluding chapter on technol-

---

[10]See Thomas Flynn, "Time Redeemed: Maritain's Christian Philosophy of History," in Hudson and Mancini, *Understanding Maritain*, 307–24.

ogy carries an undertone of very limited expectations.

Simon begins his account of democratic equality with Maritain's idea of the notion of equality as a common human nature, rejecting the nominalist bias of doctrines of inequality. He excludes the doctrine that humankind can be divided essentially by race into higher and lower. Equality is grounded in potential for community life. He then turns the account more directly to the problem of equality and its tensions. The ideal of equality deriving from common humanity can be applied in a strict fashion and in the fashion of a tendency. For example, all men are covered by the norm prohibiting the killing of innocent life. Race, social standing, wealth, and so forth are irrelevant considerations here. Any excepting conditions are made on principle, like self-defense, not on an arbitrary basis. Simon, writing in 1950, prophetically mentions abortion and euthanasia as great violations of the ideal of equality and common humanity. Similarly, fair exchange demands a strict equality, for again race, wealth, and the like are not relevant factors. But, in other demands for equal consideration, limitations must be acknowledged. Hence, in some cases, equality must be adopted as a "progressive tendency" to greater realization. The two examples considered are health care and education. All human beings ought to be protected from disease and death. The desire for life is equal in all segments of society, Simon says. On this point, Simon claims that our conscience has improved (*PDG* 205).[11] But it does not follow, he says, that it is in our power to provide equal protection to all, nor is it "necessarily iniquitous that it [society] fails to do so." But society must be on a "track" leading to equal protection for all. This is "the equalitarian dynamism contained in the unity of human nature." But this dynamism, he says, is often lawfully restricted and delayed. Why? Its implementation may require "an enormously increased weight of bureaucratic organization [and a loss] of a considerable amount of liberty." He gives a similar account of education; society must be on track to greater opportunity, but the recognition of different abilities and conditions, and the problem of freedom and taxes, may restrict it.

Despite these "lawful restrictions and delays" in the realization of equality, Simon insists that democratic theory and practice be gauged above all in terms of progress in equality. Conservativism, he warns, simply seeks to maintain the advantages of small minorities. At best, Simon would allow for a form of "fiscal conservativism," from what he has said

---

[11]Cf. Leo Strauss, *What is Political Philosophy?* (New York: Greenwood Press, 1959), 309, and Aristotle, *Nicomachean Ethics*, 1117b 10.

about lawful restrictions. Does it follow, then, that democratic theory and practice must posit as a regulative ideal the eventual suppression of all advantage and privilege with the inequality that accompany them? That is, has Simon reduced the "conservative" objection to that of means and efficiency? Could greater power and technical prowess enhance progress in equality and pare down the conservative objections? Should democratic regimes be ever in search of greater power and take advantage of any possible advance in equality?

Simon argues very strenuously against this conclusion on the basis of the principle of autonomy or subsidiarity. Simon entertains the following proposition: "inequality should never be determined by any consideration foreign to individual merit." Simon says that this well-sounding vague notion has the "character of radicalism made inconspicuous" (*PDG* 223). Yet it would seem one is driven to this point by a certain logic in the equalitarian dynamism. For legal equality and open opportunity can neutralize aristocratic privilege. But then education, position, and other factors such as wealth can still leave great gaps in equal opportunity. Strict equal opportunity must eradicate "all privilege or handicap attaching to hazard of birth." If so, the right of inheritance and any family influence would stand in the way of equality. But the elimination of the family is a utopian scheme that would subject men to a far greater arbitrariness; hence Simon's fear of "radicalism made inconspicuous."

Simon backs off to a larger context in order to resolve the antinomy. The problem is biased by "an individualistic preconception." The family and social being is part of the good life desired for each citizen. Thus, "some of the things for which opportunity is sought are of such a nature as to balance and restrict the principle of equal opportunity." Equal opportunity is carried too far when "it threatens to dissolve the small communities from which men derive their best energies in the hard accomplishments of daily life." From the perspective of human flourishing, the principle of equality is limited not only by technical efficiency, but also by a positive notion of the good life.

Simon concludes with three principles pertaining to equal opportunity, thus gathering the various elements in tension: a democratic regime must strive for legal equality; it must take positive measures to avoid factual exclusion from any function, e.g., financial help for education; it must allow the greatest possible autonomy to prevail (*PDG* 229). The first principle reflects the strict equality of common humanity; the second principle reflects the equalitarian dynamism of a democratic regime; the third principle, Simon says, makes the principle of equal opportunity less absolute: without it, equal opportunity would be "a first class factor of atomization and a formidable wrecker of democratic communities."

Simon succinctly formulates the principle of autonomy or subsidiarity as

> the metaphysical law which demands ... that no task which can be satisfactorily fulfilled by the smaller unit should ever be assumed by the larger unit.... It is perfectly obvious that there is more life and, unqualifiedly, greater perfection in a community all parts of which are full of initiative than in a community whose parts act merely as instruments transmitting the initiative of the whole (*PDG* 129–30).

Simon does not denounce state intervention in principle—it could well serve freedom from exploitation and even strengthen autonomic institutions. Further, he does not want to suggest that the state is evil in essence or adopt the individualist preconception on the libertarian side that he sought to avoid on the egalitarian side. But, given the tendency of the modern state to expand, Simon cannot overemphasize the principle of autonomy. Concerning the problem of "free distribution" mentioned above, Simon also invokes the principle of autonomy, so as to rule out a socialist interpretation. The great problem, he says, is to make it "independent of the arbitrariness of individual whims without delivering it up to the arbitrariness of public powers and their bureaucracy." In all facets, the "absolutism of the state must be held in check by forces external to the state apparatus" (*PDG* 252, 137). Church, press, private school, labor unions, co-operatives of different sorts, and private property and free enterprise are all conditions of the principle of autonomy.

Simon's principle of autonomy leads him beyond the democratic regime to the idea of the mixed regime as the best. Any regime, he says, may need the operation of a principle distinct from and opposed to its own idea. The association of democracy with non-democratic, which must mean non-egalitarian, principles may be necessary to serve the common good and to check its own weaknesses. In fact, Simon's ultimate defense of democracy, universal suffrage, rests not upon the claim of the common man as such, but a "pessimistic" reason—resistance to the power of the state and elites (*PDG* 98). Thus, universal suffrage is but one of many devices necessary for the promotion of freedom.

In Simon, we find a more direct acknowledgement of the inherent tensions in the egalitarian claims of democracy. In his account, we find a statement of the equalitarian dynamism, but it is held in check by a counter-principle of autonomy. Simon, even more than Maritain, emphasizes the conservative element in political theory. But does his reading of the equalitarian dynamic set up a dialectic in which the citizens are always discontent and disappointed? Tocqueville observed that the idea of equality promotes envy precisely because the means for achieving equality are "constantly proving inadequate in the hands of those using them." Further, he says:

> Democratic institutions awaken and flatter the passion for equality without ever being able to satisfy it entirely.... [The people] are excited by the chance and irritated by the uncertainty of success; the excitement is followed by weariness and then by bitterness. In that state anything which in any way transcends the people seems an obstacle to their desires, and they are tired by the sight of any superiority, however legitimate.[12]

Concerning the problems of envy and mediocrity, Simon says simply that "these risks are well known and do not call for any elaboration" (*PDG* 214). But, without further elaborating, does Simon not run the risk of jeopardizing the principle of autonomy? By stressing the equalitarian tendency in contemporary democracy, he must then place the principle of subsidiarity/autonomy in the position of a check or a drag against the expansion of equality. Is it doomed to fight a rear-guard action and forever face the wrath of disappointed egalitarians?

III. Kolnai: Pluralism as a Conservative Principle

Aurel Kolnai was born in Budapest, Hungary in 1900. He studied philosophy at the University of Vienna, where he converted to Catholicism, in part due to the influence of the writings of G.K. Chesterton and the German Phenomenological School. Of Jewish extraction, Kolnai viewed the rise of National Socialism with particular alarm; he spent six years writing a critique of their doctrines, a book later published as *The War Against the West*.[13] His output was not as vast as Maritain or Simon, but he produced some very good essays in the fields of ethics and political philosophy. For the account of equality, we are interested in his review of

---

[12]A. de Tocqueville, *Democracy*, 198.

[13]Aurel Kolnai, *The War Against the West* (New York: Viking, 1939). For a biography and bibliography, see A. Kolnai, *Ethics, Value and Reality*, eds. Bernard Williams and David Wiggins, (Indianapolis: Hackett, 1978). See also Lee Congdon, "Aurel Kolnai: In Defense of Christian Europe," *The World and I* 3:9 (September 1988): 630–45. Articles to be examined include his review of Maritain's *Man and the State*—"The Synthesis of Christ and the Anti-Christ," *Integrity* V (1951): 40–45; "The Meaning of the Common Man," *Thomist* (1949): 272–335; and "Privilege and Liberty," *Université Laval Théologique et Philosophique* V (1949): 66–110.

Maritain's *Man and the State*, and two articles, "The Meaning of the Common Man," and "Privilege and Liberty."

Kolnai's criticism of Maritain is admittedly captious in tone and not entirely fair in representing the balanced sweep of Maritain's political philosophy as a whole.[14] On the other hand, *Man and the State*, with its democratic creed and its praise of shock troops like John Brown, is open to criticism. Kolnai identifies some critical weak points in Maritain's philosophy. Maritain does not recognize the tension between the "orderly life of democratic institutions" and the "spirit of mass subjectivism . . . which is the driving force of the democratic creed." Or, further, he clings to a dogma of "boundless terrestrial optimism." Maritain has a ready response to these charges. But there is something in his orientation that causes such an impression. Perhaps Kolnai scores the most direct hit in his praise of Maritain's concern for "pluralism." A pluralistic society, Kolnai says, "relies precisely upon given realities in their manifoldness, contingency and limitation," and is therefore "refractory" and opposed to a streamlined creation of social reality. "In other words," Kolnai says, "pluralism, if taken seriously, involves a conservative outlook."

Kolnai's claim is not simply a matter of labels. Russell Kirk outlines six principles of conservative thought as follows—a belief in a transcendent moral order, social continuity, prescription, prudence, variety, and imperfectibility.[15] Maritain and Simon affirm all of these principles in one way or another; and, indeed, they rely on them to structure the life of the city and to check and even brake the progressive spirit of social equality, as shown above. But does not this put the conservative value always in the rearguard, always catching up, and on the defensive? The position of Simon and Maritain would seem to encourage ardent hopes for equality that must then be dashed by the hidden conservative principle. Kolnai notices that, when conservative forces and conceptions serve as mere "brakes" on progress, an ambivalence and impatience is evoked towards them. Democratic society is faced, then, with an alternative: "maintenance of institutional freedoms and the full acceptation of the religion of the Common Man."[16]

---

[14]Kolnai, "Synthesis," 41. For a more temperate but incisive criticism of Maritain's project, see Ernest Fortin, "The New Rights Theory and the Natural Law," *Review of Politics* (October, 1982): 590–612.

[15]Russell Kirk, Introduction to *The Portable Conservative Reader* (New York: Viking, 1982), xv–xviii.

[16]Kolnai, "Privilege," 88–89.

Kolnai reveals an internal weakness in a philosophy of democratic government that emphasizes the principle of equality and aims at surpassing or neutralizing privilege. Liberal democracy, he says, will always appear in this light as insufficiently democratic, as insufficiently advanced "in its own direction." And this sets up a temptation to abandon "mere formal or political democracy" for real, substantial, or social democracy. The contradiction between formal equality and socioeconomic privilege leads to an attack upon privilege and the advocacy of a democracy of the common man. But Kolnai claims that this strikes at the very root of order and hastens its collapse.[17]

Kolnai's proposal is to approach the defense of democracy and equality from another perspective, stressing the principle of pluralism and autonomy as the leading idea. He says:

> What we have in mind is not, of course, a proposal to substitute for Western Democracy along with its ideological biases, a fancy system of Conservative Constitutionalism, nor a return to this or that specified stage of the past, but a suggestion to displace the spiritual stress from the "common man" aspect of democracy to its aspect of constitutionalism and of moral continuity with the high tradition of Antiquity, Christendom and the half-surviving Liberal cultures of yesterday.[18]

Kolnai wishes to emphasize rule of law, balance and limitation, responsible government, federalism, and the consent of the governed. He defends universal suffrage, as Simon does, as a check to the power of rule.[19] But checks and balances are not sufficient to maintain a regime of liberty, Kolnai argues. He calls it a "fallacy of federalism" to believe that "plurality of forms" and decentralization alone is sufficient to defend liberty. Administrative decentralization, he points out, could simply deal with a subsection of a still uniform whole. Moreover, equality as such

---

[17]*Ibid.*, 93.

[18]Kolnai, "Common Man," 274.

[19]"It is indubitably true that a system of government in which the 'plain man' as such 'has a say' is intrinsically better than government by an esoteric caste of public officials no matter how well bred, 'cultured' or 'public spirited.' This is what perennially validates Democracy in the sane sense of the term, as contrasted to its erection into a false religion of secular messianism. Democracy, in that same sense, means participation at various levels of the broad strata of the people in the shaping of public policy," *Ibid.*, 309.

tends to "centralization and uniformity." Tocqueville demonstrated this trend in democracy. In addition to federal or plural forms, an appreciation of difference and inequality is required. For the substance and savor of an intermediate group is constituted by "its particular structure of authority, of loyalty and allegiance, of tradition and formative power, of 'rulership' and obedience."[20] In short, vertical relationships with patterns of privilege within various groups and within society as a whole are essential to true autonomy and federalism.

Natural inequality, he argues, is "essentially inseparable" from artificial inequality. Further, natural distinction is a fruit of privilege and generative of new privilege.[21] The moderate equalitarian position, he says, fails to see this, and thus must remain hostile to privilege. The ideal of equality demands the elimination of privilege. Kolnai objects that not only does this approach to equality rest upon an individualist premise, but it is also an approach that tends to a reductionistic and uniform view of the good. And finally, the approach requires a centralized consciousness to administer and ensure equality. The equalitarian ideal may be opposed to any principle of autonomy.

The role of hierarchy and privilege must be understood in their full social valence and not simply as a "necessary evil." Kolnai defines privilege as: "a positional value in society relatively independent of the will of society."[22] Social hierarchy does not and is not meant to correspond univocally with the hierarchy of moral or intellectual values. Rather, hierarchy expresses the bondage of all men to what is intrinsically better than they.

---

[20]Kolnai, "Privilege," 97–98.

[21]Ibid., 86–87.

[22]"A society in which liberty is to thrive can only be a society rich in privileges, affording manifold means of redress and opportunities (not devised in the spirit bent upon effacing the framework of privileges) to the 'underprivileged': a society capitalistic in the sense of containing and recognizing finite power factors and formative influences in their own right, besides state power and the prevailing mood of the collective; a society ennobled and oriented by a plural system of 'hierarchies' pervading it with supra-social value references as contrasted with its totalitarian self-worship—hierarchies limited in their scope, but also sustained, by their mutual action and interpenetration, and again balanced by, but on their part helping to support and vitalize (as social realities), the constitutional design of public power, the validity of universal moral law, the protection of general human and civil rights, and the plane of Christian equality among men," Ibid., 96.

That is, social values are not good simply as an immanent unfolding of my volitions and needs, but objectively good.[23] The equalitarian tendency, in its objection to privilege, often masks a rejection of an objective order of values and the limited power of man. Kolnai sees here a metaphysical rebellion at the heart of the enterprise. And this is why a more radical assertion of human power in communism is a possible outcome of the trajectory of progressive democracy.

Kolnai thinks that liberty cannot be defended nor maintained without a vertical limitation on its use. He shares the concern of Solzhenitsyn about the abuse of liberty permitted within the context of its horizontal limitation by equal right alone. We need not only a theocentric humanism to provide the notion of liberty under God, but also the entire range of intermediary groups with their embodiment of high moral value and authority. The liberal conception of society, he argues, cannot support and protect liberty "except in a precarious and self-contradictory fashion." It must rely on conservative values such as autonomy, pluralism *et al*. But such values, while "unofficially tolerated," are "continually harassed and eaten away, by the immanent dialectic of liberal society as such." The university and the Church are perhaps the key intermediate groups to resist this harassment. It is the mission of these institutions, Kolnai urges, to "inoculate the national mind with the seeds of objective value reference, of a vision of things 'sub specie aeterni,' of intellectual independence and moral backbone."[24]

Kolnai thus would have us use the principle of pluralism and differentiation not in the rearguard as a mere check to equality, but as a vanguard in the promotion of excellence and the things that make a human life worth leading.

Conclusion

Maritain, Simon, and Kolnai have political philosophies and approaches to democracy that share the same essential elements. However, the stress within each approach is different. The former two stress the equalitarian tendency of modern democracy, which they check with the principle of autonomy or subsidiarity. Kolnai argues that this approach to autonomy and liberty, in a political perspective, appears as a mere brake or counterprogressive element. As a result, it seems like a reactionary position opposing the march of progress. Further, the use of autonomy as a

---

[23]Kolnai, "Common Man," 294; see also "Privilege," 72–73.
[24]*Ibid.*, 288–89.

principle of greater efficiency may prompt dreams of greater human power.

Kolnai's proposal to lead with the idea of virtue and pluralism allows political philosophy to be countercultural with respect to the democratic tendencies even in order to serve it well. That is, the principle of hierarchy can be adapted to a democratic regime defined in terms of rule of law and the society of free men and women. The ideal of equality can then be absorbed through the system of a balanced society in which each segment of society should be nourished but checked for a common good; that is, the idea of a mixed regime, in which all claims to rule are duly regarded, provides grounds for opposing oligarchical exploitation and a defense of equal rights. How far can we take this in establishing justice for all sectors and levels of society without invoking the progressive tendencies that lead to envy and disappointment?

The three thinkers together represent a remarkable philosophy of government with many fruitful tensions. Maritain and Simon offer the more comprehensive and daring applications of Thomistic philosophy to the problems of the day. But Kolnai offers an interesting corrective. The observations of Heinrich Rommen on the characteristics of Catholic political philosophy are quite apt in this case:

> Political philosophy in Catholic thought with its constitutive polar system will, through all of its eras, show a conservative and a liberal strain; it will depend upon the particular circumstances of an era which of them will be more outspoken. Furthermore, each of them keeps the other from falling into extremes. The continuous defense and attack that each needs and makes against the other prevents either from monopolizing political philosophy.[25]

---

[25]H. Rommen, *The State in Catholic Thought*, 500.

Raymond Dennehy

Being Is Better Than Freedom

I should like to unfold what is, for me, at any rate, an insight into Maritain's theory of freedom that I stumbled upon while engaged in my own investigations into the problem of reconciling the concept of a universal ideal for culture and progress with the uniqueness and autonomy of the person. Not only does this insight fully illuminate the rationale for this theory, but it also offers more evidence of how integral the notion of being is to the rest of his thought.

The title of this presentation slightly paraphrases a statement found in Maritain's essay "The Thomist Idea of Freedom":

> Truly and definitively speaking, being or actuality, according to all the analogical amplitude of the internal perfections which it bears, is best of all. *It is better than freedom.* [Emphasis added.] One does not die in the name of free will; one dies in the name of freedom of autonomy or exultation. And when a man dies in the name of freedom, although he sacrifices his existence to it, this sacrifice is made in the name of a better existence for his fellow-men. For this freedom, the freedom of exultation and of autonomy, is but another name for the plenitude and and superabundance of existence. God exists *necessarily.* He knows Himself and loves Himself *necessarily.* And this infinite necessity is an infinite *freedom of independence,* of exultation and of autonomy. It is *aseitas,* the freedom of independence subsistent by itself (*SP* 137).

In what precise sense is being better than freedom? Clearly, Maritain does not intend that seemingly paradoxical statement to mean that the fulfillment of the desire for the plenitude of being demands that one relinquish freedom; on the contrary, he insists that the exercise of freedom of the will is ordered to the higher freedom of exultation or freedom of autonomy. The answer is in the very nature of being.

I shall approach the topic of being by way of an overview of Maritain's theory of freedom.

He distinguishes two kinds of freedom: *freedom of choice* and *freedom of spontaneity and independence.* Because his position on freedom of choice is that of Thomas Aquinas and is thus well enough known, I shall proceed directly to the second kind of freedom. Although essentially a restatement of Aquinas' development of Aristotle's principle, "To live in a living thing is to be," into a theory of autonomy (*SP* 117–38), not only is this theory less known than the Thomistic theory of free will, but Maritain also adds his own distinctive interpretations to it.

By *freedom of spontaneity*, Maritain means the *absence of restraint*: it is a "freedom which is not a freedom of choice, not a free will, but which, however, deserves, in a quite different sense, the name of freedom" (*SP* 128). Freedom of spontaneity attains its fulfillment in *freedom of independence or autonomy*. Maritain emphasizes that he does not intend "freedom of autonomy" in the Kantian sense, but rather as "the expansion of and growing realization of human nature" (*SP* 132). The result of this freedom is *freedom of exultation* (*SP*). Although freedom of choice is freer than freedom of autonomy insofar as it is free from all necessity, as well as constraint, it is less perfect insofar as it is ordained to the latter (*SP* 137).

I. Freedom of Spontaneity

The unspoken operative principle in freedom of spontaneity is Aquinas' claim that ". . . the higher a nature, the more intimate to that nature is the activity that flows from it."[1] From plants to animals to human beings, material nature presents a spectrum of beings exhibiting the capacity to move themselves by a vital interior principle. The activities of subrational beings—growth, assimilation, propagation—although originating in a principle that is increasingly interiorized in proportion to the increase in sensory and neurological complexity, remain nevertheless the products of blind reflexive or, at best, instinctual powers, and for that reason are more characteristic of the species than of the individual member. *Intimate*, in the sense intended by Aquinas in the above statement refers not to what comes from within, where the word "within" has a spatial sense, but rather to what is *singular*, or better yet, *unique* to the individual agent.

II. Freedom of Autonomy or Independence:
The Domain of the Person

Of the above categories of living being, man alone acts from a genuinely unified center of unique being—the self or person. As a knower, he can judge the proportion between means and ends and thereby take respon-

---

[1] Thomas Aquinas, *Summa Contra Gentiles*, IV, 11.

sibility for his actions. Just as, on the level of knowing, it is the I, the unique self, who knows, so, on the level of practical activity, it is the self who chooses specific means for specific ends. Thus, at the level of man, ". . . freedom of spontaneity becomes freedom of independence, for at this point we are concerned with persons endowed with free will, and masters of their actions—persons, each of whom is as a whole or as a universe" (*SP* 129).

But if Maritain regards the freedom of the human person as his glory, he also regards it as his misery. His very being demands, " 'Let all my activity spring from myself as from its source, and be regulated by me; let me be sufficient unto myself in order to live' " (*SP* 129). This demand is, however, "an inefficacious metaphysical aspiration" (*SP* 129). Insofar as he is a person, he longs to rise to always higher degrees of freedom of spontaneity and independence; insofar as he is only a person "in embryo," this aspiration suffers constant frustration (*SP* 130–31).

As a composite of matter and spirit, he cannot be the source of all his activity. His actions do not flow entirely from a unique interiority; his inclinations and drives largely emanate from what he has in common with his species. In other words, much of his conduct is governed by *what* he is, by his essence. Not even his intellect and will—the two powers that are so much a part of himself, for is it not the I who knows and who takes responsibility for his conduct?—are unique to his selfhood, since they are characteristics of his human essence. Thus, man is not fully self-perfecting, because he is not fully the source of his own actions; he is not fully autonomous (*SP* 131).

Perfect autonomy belongs to God alone because, as absolutely perfect being, *Being itself*, He is absolutely self-identical. His activity is perfectly immanent and accordingly flows entirely from His unique selfhood; it is perfectly intimate to His unique being (*SP* 131).

III. The Dynamism of Freedom

If the human person cannot attain perfect autonomy and self-sufficiency of action, Maritain nonetheless sees a fruitful tension arising between his metaphysical aspiration and the constraints imposed upon it by his finitude. Through knowing and choosing, he can rise to ever higher levels of being. As an act of perfect immanence, knowing enables him to interiorize on the intentional level the *nonself; he thereby becomes the other as other* while retaining his own unique selfhood. Not dominated by matter, his composite nature of matter and spirit leaves him open not merely to other beings but also to the whole universe of spiritual being. This empowers him to become ever higher levels of being, thereby leading him closer to Being itself, God. His encounter with God in the beatific vision results in his becoming of the *divine other*, transforming freedom of independence or autonomy into *freedom of exultation*.

Through choosing, the agent creates realities in the world, to be sure, and, more importantly in his own being. Choice appropriates concrete realities to the being of the person choosing; for, in thus forming his character, he creates his being by transforming himself on the plane of existence into a unique concrete embodiment of the universal moral law. The happiness chosen by the virtuous man is genuine happiness, insofar as its progressive acquisition constitutes the ever more perfect actualization of the potencies contained in his essence to identify his being with that of the Absolute (*SP* 136).

This, then, is how Maritain sees the subordination of freedom of choice to freedom of independence or autonomy. In saying that ". . . freedom of choice is not an end in itself, but that one chooses in order, finally, not to have to choose" (*SP* 136), he means that the ultimate rationale of freedom of choice is the attainment of absolute being by the person's own capacity for self-perfection. The human person's choice of the Absolute could not, after all, be a choice at all unless he could have chosen what is not the Absolute.

I shall go no further in this explication of Maritain's theory of freedom. I advisedly omit aspects of it which, although important, such as his perceptive discussion of the non-being of evil choices, are unnecessary to the purpose of my presentation.

IV. How Being and Freedom Are the Same

We have seen that, following Aquinas, Maritain attributes freedom to a being in proportion to its degree of immanence. The proportion is implicit in Aquinas' principle, "The higher a being, the more intimate to it is the activity that flows from it." A consideration of the following points will help to establish the significance of this proportion.

First point: The statement "Being is better than freedom" draws upon basic metaphysical principles.

(a) all things are reducible to being, for however they may differ from each other, however unique their basic specificities, they remain, first and last, so many different *ways of being*.

(b) being is the object of all striving, including the exercise of free will; nonbeing cannot be a final cause. Aristotle's argument that the ultimate goal of all human striving is happiness supports this. For, by "happiness," he means the possession of the *good itself*. Since being and the good are convertible, the ultimate goal of our striving is *Being itself*. Approached from the perspective of Thomistic metaphysics, what we seek, first and last, is *existence itself*: "Existence is the act of all acts and the perfection of all perfections."

Second point: The absolute primacy of being can be expressed by the venerable principle, "Being is all there is; what is outside being is nonbeing." Thus, if one being is higher than another, *as being*, that can only be so because the former enjoys more being. Since being cannot be added to, higher beings must *be* more fully than lower beings.

Third point: Since what is outside being is nonbeing, it follows that being cannot be limited by what is outside it, for nonbeing cannot be a limiting principle. Being can be limited only by some limitation within itself. Now this inner limitation cannot be nonbeing in the absolute sense, for the reason just stated. The limitation must be *relative* nonbeing, which is to say, the being's potency *to be*. Because essence and existence are respectively the principles of potency and act in being, a being is lower in the hierarchy of being to the extent that its essence limits its act of existence and higher to the extent that its essence allows expression of its act of existence.

Fourth point: Being and unity are convertible. A thing has being to the extent that it has unity, which latter is one of the transcendentals. Unity, so construed, designates a thing's *oneness*, but in the strict and true sense of "oneness": identity with self.

This means that *uniqueness* is an inevitable consequence of unity because, just to the extent that a thing has unity, to that extent is it identical with itself. Now, because it is impossible for what is, by definition, unique to have an identical duplication, so is it impossible for a self-identical being to be duplicated. But since self-identity and unity go hand in hand, it is impossible to have a plurality of identical beings, for being and unity are convertible terms.

To summarize the argument thus far: (1) *To be* is to be *one*; (2) to be one is to be *self-identical*; (3) to be self-identical is to be *unique*; (4) therefore *to be* is to be unique.

Number three is the crucial step here. Why do self-identity and uniqueness go hand in hand? In other words, why do being (for a thing has being insofar as it has unity) and uniqueness go hand in hand? What about replications of the same brand and style of watch, toy soldiers, automobiles, etc., not to mention the possibility of identical grains of sand, redwood trees, field mice, etc.?

I would respond that such pluralities are possible only to the extent that the individuals in question lack *being*.

Consider: it is impossible, *in principle*, to replicate a person. If we could clone human beings, what we would have produced would be beings identical biologically and genetically, but not identical in personhood. To grasp this difference, imagine two substances for whom "I" meant the same thing. If such were possible, it would amount to two manifestations of the same substantial self, of one and the same person! (I shall return to this example shortly.) The capacity to think "I" requires a substance that is a *self*. The self-awareness implied in thinking "I" is the psychological manifestation of perfect self-identity—an ontological rather than a merely psychological self-identity.

Personhood, in other words, is simply the highest level of being. Because a thing has unity to the extent that it has being, the higher its place on the scale of being, the more perfect its unity. That is why the person is the perfection of being, and why, too, it is immaterial and unique. For the more fully a thing has being, the more fully does it have unity, and perfection of unity entails perfection of being.

Subpersonal things are dominated by matter and hence, to that extent, they lack being. Matter lacks a center; it consists of parts outside parts and thus, if it can be said to have an essence at all, it is that of extension. When an organism dies, the conspicuous features of its death are the cessation of respiration and motion. But these are only signs of its demise. To die is to corrupt, to go out of being; death is the separation of form from matter. The dissolution of the dead organism is caused by the absence of its form, which is its principle of unity and organization. Bereft of form, the organism loses its substantial being, although it is not thereby annihilated, for it assumes other, perhaps lower, forms of being. Without form, matter reverts to type, going to pieces, which is what "corruption" means.

Insofar as matter lacks a center, insofar as it is "parts outside parts," it lacks unity. And this is to say that it lacks being to that extent. Thus, if artifacts and natural entities can, in principle, be precisely duplicated, that is just because they are dominated by matter and lack unity—which is to lack identity with self, since matter is "parts outside parts"—and accordingly are, to the extent of that lack, *not being*.

Regarding the earlier observation that two substances for whom "I" meant the same thing would amount to two manifestations of the same substantial self, of one and the same person, I am not affirming the possibility of that kind of occurrence. What I am arguing is that the occurrence, absolutely and logically, could not mean that there were two identical selves; it would instead have to be explained as a simultaneous, spatially dual manifestation of the same self. Selfhood or personhood is substantial being that is immaterial. It is logically impossible for there to be a plurality of identical selves; but since place is a requirement of material substances, i.e., bodies, and not of immaterial substances, i.e., persons, the thought of a self bilocating does not seem to offend reason as much as the thought of two identical selves.

To conclude the argument concerning the fourth point: since, therefore, a thing is unique to the extent that it is identical with itself; and since it is identical with itself to the extent that it has unity; and since it has unity to the extent that it has being, it follows that a thing is unique to the extent that it has being: being entails uniqueness.

Fifth point: The action that flows from a thing will be intimate to it just to the extent that it flows from it insofar as it is being. To that extent the thing acts *autonomously*, for to that extent it acts from no principle but from what is unique to itself; in other words, its action is not determined by principles outside its identity with itself.

Sixth point: Because potency limits act, and because essence accordingly limits existence, anything less than perfect being, *Being itself*, does not enjoy perfect autonomy. Therefore, being is better than freedom of choice but not freedom of exultation or autonomy since the latter is precisely the action of a thing insofar as it is identical with itself: *being is being*.

Seventh point: In the hierarchy of being, the person shines forth as the only being that enjoys true self-identity. For it alone is capable of a truly *immanent* activity. We have seen that, unlike subrational beings, it acts—insofar as it *knows, chooses,* and *loves*—from a center unique to itself. This uniqueness of being, this genuine self-identity, is what it means to be a *self* and a *person*.

V. How Being as the Ground of Freedom Harmonizes The Universality and Absoluteness of Being Itself With the Uniqueness and Autonomy of the Person

Besides offering a fuller disclosure of the metaphysical and therefore ultimate rationale for freedom, the grounding of freedom in being also erases the apparently fundamental opposition between personal autonomy and the absolute, universal standards the conformity to which the survival and progress of a culture demands of its members. I emphasize the phrase "the apparently fundamental opposition" for the obvious reason that, given the imperfections of temporal political society, collisions between the human person and institutions will always be both abundant and inevitable. But, at all events, the pluralism that democratic society points to with pride must finally genuflect before common values. Otherwise, the centrifugal force of personal freedom and diversity of philosophies would burst the seams of its institutions.

An ideal for the created universe, and *a fortiori* for a culture, must be universal. But since the latter consists of persons, the only suitable ideal would be that which pertains at once to all human persons insofar as they are human and to each insofar as he is unique. How are universality and uniqueness to be reconciled? The question is but a variant formulation of the problem of universals—How are universal and particular to be reconciled?—which in turn is a variant of the problem of the one and the many: *How can being be both one and many?*

If being is taken as *univocal* in meaning, then, as Parmenides concluded, being is one and plurality is impossible; if being is taken as *equivocal*, then being is many and unity or oneness is impossible. Now, just as the problem of the one and the many finds its solution in the *analogy of being*, so does the problem of reconciling universality and uniqueness find its solution there.

We have noted that being *as being* is unique insofar as being and unity are convertible. We have also noted that the highest being, God, is absolutely unique because absolutely being. In God, therefore, do we have the ideal of all ideals and the standard of all standards.

Through the exercise of free choice, the human person can conform himself increasingly to the ideal of God. Yet, the closer he approaches the realization of that ideal, the more unique and autonomous he becomes. As *Being itself*, God is the absolute standard for all being *insofar as it is being*. Insofar as each creature is, God is its standard. But since it is impossible for two beings to be perfectly identical—*materially* so for subrational beings and *formally* so for rational beings—it follows, then, that the more a being actualizes its potencies *to be*, the more it becomes *itself*, i.e., the *more unique* it becomes. And the more unique it is as a source of activity, the more autonomous it is.

Thus, when Maritain describes the human person as overcoming the constraints on his freedom of independence or autonomy by interiorizing within himself the entire universe through knowing, by appropriating to himself the other *as other*, he has in mind here the human person's capacity to *become the other as other*, thereby enriching his own being and attaining increasingly higher levels of being, and all the while retaining his own unique selfhood. When Maritain describes the human person as overcoming those constraints by exercising free will in such a way as to choose increasingly to conform himself to the universal moral law, he has in mind the human person's capacity freely to become a unique, concrete embodiment of that law. In knowing and choosing, it is the unique self, the I, who identifies with the *other*.

VI. Conclusion

I have tried to show the sense in which Maritain is correct in saying that *being is better than freedom* by demonstrating that, far from being opposed, being and freedom—freedom of independence or autonomy—are one and the same reality. As I said at the outset, this demonstration discloses the ultimate rational ground for his theory of freedom as well as the latter's integral relationship with his metaphysics of being.

By implication, it also unmasks the poverty of current theories of personal freedom, at least as prevalent in Anglo-American circles, which represent freedom as a kind of vague undetermined, uncommitted—what shall I call it? *optionality?* Refusing to acknowledge any ontological determination for freedom, these theories foster a *de jure* incompatibility between person and political society. The demand that I conform my conduct to laws and institutions asks me to surrender the most important part of myself, my freedom to act as I see fit. We are no longer speaking of a tension arising from the imperfections of temporal life and the human situation, but rather one arising from an essential disaffinity.

Consider, for example, Hillary Putnam's recent attempt to reconcile individual freedom with the necessity of a "moral image" to guide society. Embracing a watered-down version of Kant's view of the community of rational beings as "a kingdom of ends," Putnam defends individual freedom by appealing to an equally watered-down notion of *equality.* "Watered-down" because he defends an agnostic realism that confesses the human intellect's inability to know reality *in itself;* he accordingly dismisses the "medieval" assurance that things have essences. As close as he can come, therefore, to grounding his notion of equality in the nature of man is to insist that we are *rational.* Each of us, then, is equally capable, potentially at least, of critically analyzing the assertions of others. This imposes on the political community the mandate of respecting each's freedom of inquiry and criticism.

Putnam defends the notion of a *moral image* for society by arguing that sociopolitical organization and harmony require it. The autonomy implied in the notion of individual equality and the standardization implied in the notion of moral image are reconciled in *epistemological agnosticism:* all theories and claims are open not only to criticism but to falsification.

Lest one suppose that such agnosticism robs the moral image of any compelling rationale for justifying the support of a community's individual members, Putnam appeals to the principle of *reasonableness:*

> The fact is that we have *underived,* a *primitive* obligation of some kind to be reasonable, not a "moral obligation" or an "ethical obligation," to be sure, but nevertheless a very real obligation to be reasonable which ... is *not* reducible to my expectations about the long run and my interest in the welfare of others or my own welfare at other times. I *also* believe that it will

work better in the long run for people to be reasonable, certainly; but when the question is *Why do you expect that, in this unrepeatable case, what is extremely likely to happen will happen?* here I have to say with Wittgenstein: "This is where my spade is turned. This is what I do, this is what I say." [Author's emphasis.][2]

The difference between the reconciliation of personal freedom and universal standards in Maritain's theory of freedom and Putnam's theory of equality is that the former is grounded in *being, in what is*, whereas the latter is grounded in *reasonableness*. I have tried to show why Maritain's theory is right. It should be equally evident why Putnam's theory is wrong. For Maritain, freedom of independence or autonomy is the action of an agent to the extent that *it is, has being*; freedom of choice, accordingly, has its ground and goal in what is not only real, but is the foundation of all intelligibility and hence rationality. For Putnam, freedom is a barren *optionality* whose ground is a rationality emptied of all content and foundation.

Writing in the aftermath of World War II, Maritain has underscored the shambles into which democratic institutions have been reduced by the illusion of the self-sufficiency of pure rationality, requiring nothing other than its own critical powers to guide mankind along the path of progress. Being *is* better than freedom.

---

[2]Hillary Putnam, *The Many Faces of Realism* (LaSalle, IL: Open Court Publishing Company, 1987), 84–85.

Michael D. Torre

The Freedoms of Man and
Their Relation to God

Jacques Maritain, Yves R. Simon, and Mortimer J. Adler are in nothing more united than in their appreciation of the rich dimensions of human freedom and in their luminous defense of its proper rights. Despite their varied writings on this subject,[1] they share a common vision of what freedom is and why it is good. Fundamental to that vision is the insistence that there are distinct human freedoms that cannot be reduced to one. I shall first attempt to make this truth plain. Following their doctrine throughout,[2] but in my own words, I shall present the essential features of man's diverse freedoms and indicate how they differ. Only this work, I believe, makes possible a just assessment of God's governance of man's freedom: it overcomes pseudo-problems and unveils the real drama of man's freedom before God. Just what that is I hope to indicate in my concluding reflections.

---

[1]This summary is primarily based on two works from each author: Maritain's "A Philosophy of Freedom," in *Freedom in the Modern World* (3–73) and chapter IV of *Existence and the Existent*, trans. Lewis Galantière and Gerald B. Phelan (New York: Doubleday, 1947), 85–122; Simon's *Freedom of Choice* and "On the Foreseeability of Free Acts," in *The New Scholasticism* XXII:4 (1948): 357–70; and Adler's two volumes on *The Idea of Freedom*, together with his trenchant comments in chapters 19 and 20 of *Six Great Ideas* (New York: Macmillan, 1981).

[2]Thus, the three freedoms discussed are easily recognizable as Adler's Circumstantial Freedom of Self-Realization, his Natural Freedom of Self-Determination, and his Acquired Freedom of Self-Perfection, respectively, recast in the language of "inclination." I have been guided principally by Adler in my discussion of the first freedom, by Simon in the second, and by Maritain in the third. My intention is to offer a synthetic view of freedom, one substantially shared by all three of them. In making their view mine, I have presented it in my own terms, while trying to be faithful to their common insights.

263

I. Freedom of Action

The most common freedom is the *freedom of action*, which may be defined as *the ability to act on one's inclinations*. This freedom is possessed by every degree of being, as our common speech indicates. We speak of the free fall of a stone, a vine spreading freely over a slope, the various animals moving freely in their native habitats; and we can also speak of the freedom of the angels to communicate with one another and to participate in the governance of the world, and of God's free creation and governance of that world. So, too, man is said to be free to act on his inclinations, whether they be rooted in the bodily or intellectual aspect of his nature: he is free to move about (with the other animals) and free to govern and transform his world (with the other intelligences).

This freedom is defined in relation to *another* being. One is free in one's action to the extent that one can operate in and upon an external reality, and to the extent that this reality does not limit one's independence. Thus, it is the freedom of one whole in relation to another (or others): it is an *external* freedom. Because the other being is so often recalcitrant to one's desires or inclinations, this freedom is primarily conceived *negatively*; that is, one is free insofar as one is *not* restrained in one's action by other agents. For man, this means that this freedom is primarily conceived in relation to *material* causes. He is generally seen and said to be free if he is not restrained in and through his *body*.

Every agent is in fact limited by other agents; thus, this freedom is never absolute, and its limited success must generally be fought for. The greater the power of a being, the greater its likely victory and freedom; for the same reason, the more immaterial the being, the greater its freedom. Thus, if it rains, salt will dissolve, and it is not free to protect itself from this dissolution. A flower can at least close its petals, and an animal is free to seek cover. The angels go much further, their nature freeing them from all material interference in their operations. Yet, even with God (and *a fortiori* with the angels), this freedom is not absolute. For His will is truly (if relatively) *resisted* by the sins of His spiritual creatures (be they angels or men): the good inclinations caused in them by His will are frustrated and limited by their sins.

Man experiences a limitation on his freedom of action both by the material and the intellectual world. His physical environment limits him, as does his body: no man is free to live without oxygen; a man with polio is not free to set track records. Man is equally (if not more) enslaved, however, by other intelligences, most obviously his fellow men. He is limited by his social and political environment. It is in this sphere that he especially seeks to win his freedom. And, again, this freedom is primarily conceived negatively, as a freedom from outside restraint or coercion. Thus, one will speak of free trade (freedom from governmental regulation) or free speech (freedom from governmental censorship).

Here, at the very outset of our analysis, we discover the essentially *analogous* nature of freedom. This is so not merely because freedom is formally participated in by different degrees of being and thus in different ways. It is evident even in the case of man alone. On the one hand, man's freedom of action is a freedom to *make* things and to transform his world. Thus, we speak of the freedom of his labor, free trade, a free press, and artistic freedom. In each case, man is held to be free to act on an external reality; these are examples of *transitive* action and are rightly placed in the category of action. On the other hand, man's freedom of action is a freedom to *do* things and to express himself. Thus, we speak of his freedom of movement, or his freedom of assembly, or of speech, or even of thought. Here, his freedom of action is not to go outside himself to transform another; rather, these are examples of actions that primarily perfect the agent. They are *immanent* acts that are rightly placed in the category of quality. Freedom is a mode of action; it is as analogous in its nature as action itself.[3] Nonetheless, this freedom seems to be predicated primarily of actions in and upon the world: transitive acts. Thus, even God is said to be free in this sense of freedom insofar as He can create and shape beings external to Himself.

This freedom is the most obvious one and the one most universally recognized. It is our first conception of freedom as children. As a matter of fact, when I told my eight-year-old daughter that I was struggling with a paper on freedom, she looked at me with some surprise and explained to me that this was a simple matter: "Freedom," she matter-of-factly declared, "is being able to do what I want!" Nor is it surprising that this should be a child's first conception of freedom. Her first freedom was one of controlling her body, of being able to walk, climb, and so on. And that freedom of movement is curbed and limited by parental authority: an external agent. Similarly, my students, who are defining themselves over against the authority of parents, teachers, and society, usually conceive of freedom this way, albeit with a little more sophistication. "I ought to be free," they confidentially assert, "to do whatever I want, so long as I don't curtail someone else's freedom." Law and authority are thus conceived as restraints upon freedom; they are external agencies limiting the ability to

---

[3]For the analogous nature of action, see Yves R. Simon's "An Essay on the Classification of Action and the Understanding of Act," *Revue de l'Université d'Ottawa* 41 (1971): 518–41.

act on one's inclinations.

One who gratuitously asserts an absolute right to act as he pleases can justly be accused of having confused the legitimate rights of freedom with mere license. Nonetheless, he defends a vital truth when he asserts that human freedom requires external action. For man is an embodied being. His need to grow and move are intrinsic to his nature. To violate his physical freedom is to do violence to his very person. This is why the natural image of freedom *denied* is immobility, whether frozen in ice or impaled on a cross. Furthermore, man naturally seeks to express himself through his body. To deny him the opportunity to speak the truth or to express his love, or to deny him that greatest external good, the communion of friends, is to strike at his very heart. Indeed, his spirit not only can be limited by denying him physical freedom; it can also be profoundly altered through his body. Perhaps the ultimate case of this is feral children. The unfortunately more common case of children brutalized by their parents indicates how deeply one can strike the spirit through the body. Again, one can affect man's inner self through his body chemistry. Or one can coerce him through pain or fear, either for his own safety or that of his loved ones. In these various ways, to strike at man's freedom of action is to tyrannize his very soul.

II. Freedom of Choice

When we distinguish acts freely undertaken from ones that have been coerced through violence or fear, we have begun to speak of a different sort of freedom. For a man who acts under duress may possess an equal freedom of action as one who does not: his ability to act on his inclination may be identical. He differs in the way he arrives at that inclination: by duress, not freely. Here we are speaking of a freedom prior to that of action: the freedom to form the very inclination upon which he acts. This freedom may be defined as *the ability to incline or not to a known good*. The man under duress is being more or less compelled to incline to one course of action, and is more or less unable to incline to its opposite. Substituting "to choose" for "to incline" (as we easily can do), we see that this freedom is the one usually spoken of as man's *freedom of choice*.

Man's freedom of choice is rooted in his intellectual nature. As the given definition indicates, this freedom comes from knowledge. Thus, it is a freedom man shares only with other intellectual beings: with angels and God. This freedom is an *internal* one: man's ability relates to known options he has in mind, that he possesses. It concerns the *formal* cause: the *known good.* His love is solicited by various known goods, or just by one. He may be initially attracted to one or several, but to which will he definitively give himself? In what will he place his happiness? This is the question he faces, and he faces it freely insofar as he is able to choose or not choose the object before him. Such a freedom can be conceived either positively or negatively with equal weight: it is a freedom for or from the good at hand.

This freedom corresponds to the freedom we experience in ourselves as we deliberate about what decision to make. Indeed, it is our internal experience that first leads us to identify this freedom. And it is by virtue of this freedom that we declare ourselves responsible for the external acts we go on to commit. We accept responsibility for them because we were free to choose to do them or not to do them. We determined our course of action, did not have it determined for us. Because this experience of ourselves is common, and because a sense of responsibility is fundamental to social intercourse, this second freedom is commonly admitted.

Yet the existence of this freedom is controversial. The chief difficulty is that it seems to violate the principle of causality; that is, it looks as though affirming a freedom to choose is equally affirming that nothing causes one to choose. But this is absurd. If there is no cause of one's choice, it will proceed from nothing; but from nothing nothing comes. Thus, some have been led to assert a determinism that denies free choice. And, since this freedom is defined in relation to the known good, this determinism is commonly one of motive: that is, one chooses as one does because one good is seen to be better than another. The posited indifference before the known good is illusory: one's choice is necessarily determined by a previous judgment that choosing *this* good is one's best option.

There is a basic truth behind this objection. To make a free choice be an uncaused choice (in the manner of the Epicurean "swerve") is to make it contradictory and senseless.[4] It is true that the will cannot move to make the known good its own unless it is moved to act. Ultimately, this means that the will does not incline freely to *all* its acts. By its nature and of necessity, it is moved to its proper object: the comprehensive good, the *bonum in communi*, goodness in all its extent and intensity. Put more plainly, of necessity man wants to be fulfilled, to be happy. About this orientation, he

---

[4]For an excellent discussion of the Epicurean *clinamen*, see Simon's Introduction to *Freedom*.

is not free to choose.

And yet, precisely in admitting this necessary act, one grounds the freedom of man's other acts. For while man is not free in relation to his ultimate end of being happy, he is free in relation to the means that may lead to this end. Only were he presented with a means that fulfilled his natural inclination to the comprehensive good would he choose it of necessity. Again, put plainly, were man to see God, he would love Him. Every other object falls short of man's standard of judging: it measures up to the good and is satisfying in one respect, but it fails to do so in another. Considering my honor and love of country, it is good to do battle; considering the risk to my life and my family's welfare, it is not good. Faced with these diverse considerations, neither course of action dominates my desire. On the contrary, my will possesses a dominating indifference to the motives at hand: one is finally judged to be right only because I give myself to it.

Nor does this determination, which makes the known good the one finally judged right, come from nothing. On the contrary, the cause of the determination is man's *active* will of the comprehensive good. One's free choice of a particular good is caused by one's natural love of the universal good. The active power of choosing or not choosing lies in one's own will, in one's own power. Rightly, then, is man's freedom of choice said to be an active and dominating indifference to the known good.[5] This definition does equal justice to our internal experience and to the principle of causality.

Freedom of choice, like freedom of action, is not absolute. The will of

---

[5]Maritain uses this language of "active and dominating indifference" from his very first work (1914). He gets it from Reginald Garrigou-Lagrange, O.P., who, in his turn, is here depending upon John of St. Thomas (in his *de Anima*, q. xii, a. 2). Maritain expressly refers us to Garrigou-Lagrange's first work on freedom, to which he says he is "especially indebted" (*Bergsonian Philosophy and Thomism*, trans. Mabelle L. Andison in collaboration with J. Gordon Andison [New York: Philosophical Library, 1955], 266, n. 2). Garrigou-Lagrange's study is "Intellectualisme et Liberté chez Saint Thomas," in *Revue des Sciences philosophiques et théologiques* 1 (1907): 649–73 and 2 (1908): 5–32.

the angel, as well as man, of necessity seeks happiness, and God Himself cannot but love Himself and be blessed. Unlike freedom of action, this freedom is restricted to intellectual beings. Yet, because it is natural to them, it can never be lost as long as they exist. It can be more or less impeded in man's case, because he is an embodied intellect, but it cannot be lost. Thus, it is present in the good and the wicked alike, even if they have irrevocably committed themselves to a final end.[6] Whether this end be good or evil, a man is free to choose various good or evil means, as ways of loving and serving his end. Indeed, he is free to choose a means even if it is the only one presently available to attain his end.[7] Provided he recognizes that it is only a partial good, he remains free to choose it or not. The known disproportion between particular and universal goodness is the sufficient foundation of man's freedom of choice.

III. Freedom of Spirit

The natural desire for the comprehensive good is, in the practical order, what the principle of non-contradiction is in the speculative order.[8] As with that principle, it pervades its entire order: it is implicit to all desires or inclinations. Yet, just as one cannot *deduce* other speculative principles from the principle of non-contradiction (say, the principle that the whole is greater than its part), so one cannot *order* one's inclinations on the basis of this desire. For the fulfillment of each of those inclinations in one way meets the desire for the comprehensive good and in another way does not. It does not provide an adequate guide for choosing among them.

Yet man finds himself in need of an ordering principle. For, by nature, he inclines to diverse and potentially conflicting goods: he desires to live, to procreate and look after his young, to seek the truth, to enjoy the friendship of others, and in general to enjoy the pleasures of his sensitive nature. Without a guide to reconciling these diverse desires, he will remain in a state of self-division, torn between various goods, indecisive and perplexed about which to choose. Or, worse, he will enslave himself to one of his desires at the expense of others and of his overall well-being. Various

---

[6]Maritain is explicit about this, at least for the blessed: "freedom of choice . . . remains of course, for it is the privilege of a spiritual nature, and it continues to manifest the lofty independence of this nature in face of all that is means or intermediate end: but not in face of that which is the End" (*Freedom*, 35).

[7]Simon insists on this point in "Foreseeability," 362–63.

[8]For Maritain's most extensive treatment of this parallel, see the sixth *leçon* of his posthumously published *La loi naturelle ou loi non ecrite* (Editions Universitaires Fribourg Suisse: Fribourg, 1986), particularly 134–35.

forms of this enslavement are commonly acknowledged: bodily addictions of various sorts (e.g., drugs), emotional phobias and manias (e.g., claustrophobia, kleptomania), domination by a passion ("a slave to lust") or to an unreasonable pursuit of truth (e.g., the mad scientist). The more a person becomes attached to one of these partial goods, the less free he becomes to choose any other.

Fortunately, man possesses an intrinsic principle of order: his practical intelligence. It is the nature of the intellect to order, and man possesses a natural inclination to the good of his reason, to the *bonum honestum* or to the moral good. If he follows this inclination, he can give due weight to each of his various desires: he can master his passions and provide for the well-being of his entire person. He can thereby avoid self-division and achieve a stable peace within himself: he can become a man of integrity. We recognize an analogous situation in the realm of art: the master craftsman is one whose entire talent is placed at the service of his art. Through discipline and hard work, his art is at the disposal of his creative inspiration. He is free to use his talent as he chooses.

This sort of freedom is obviously different from the previous ones. It is not a freedom of the whole self set over against others, as is the freedom of action, but a freedom achieved *within* the self: with this freedom, a person becomes an *ordered* whole. Nor is this freedom something natural, inborn, as is the freedom of choice; rather, it is something usually gained through a succession of free choices. By them, a person *attains* self-mastery. He places his lower self at the service of his better self: his passions do not war with his reason, but serve it. Such a freedom may be defined as *the ready inclination to love and do the true good*[9] and might be called a *freedom of spirit*. If man's freedom of action principally concerns his body, and his freedom of choice his will, his freedom of spirit relates to his entire *person*: by it, he is able to give his entire being to a chosen good and to a course of action.

Some have refused to admit that there are true goods for man, that he possesses real needs whose fulfillment perfect him, as opposed to merely apparent needs and goods. They deny natural and objective goods and hence deny the existence of spiritual freedom. Yet, they are rarely consistent in their position. For, with most sane people, they admit that phobias, manias, and addictions are sicknesses, forms of enslavement. Now this absence of freedom is due to a person's state, his entire condition; it is not due to an inability to determine his inclination or act on it. One can freely choose to become an addict, and one may freely act on one's addiction. To

---

[9]I am here obviously recasting Simon's felicitous use of "readiness" to describe moral virtue. See *The Definition of Moral Virtue*, 71ff.

admit, then, that an addict lacks freedom is to concede that there is another form of freedom beyond the ones previously given. In any case, as Aristotle remarked long ago, whatever certain people may *say* about all goods being equal, they never *act* as though this were so; instead, they live their lives as though one course of action were better than another.[10] Implicit in all they do is an affirmation of the existence of spiritual freedom.

Such a freedom is not an ability for opposites; rather, it is a stable inclination of the will towards one goal: the true, moral good. In possessing it, a person possesses a spontaneous and ready attraction to the honest good. Such a freedom is primarily *positive* in import. True, it can be described as a freedom from moral evil. Such a liberation, however, does not leave the subject on some neutral ground; on the contrary, being so liberated frees him *for* the opposite order that he now wants to serve.

Spiritual freedom is even narrower in extent than freedom of choice. Indeed, it is natural and necessary to God's will alone to incline to the true good. For angels and men, this is something that must be achieved through the operation of their free choice. And it is an achievement ever at risk unless and until they see God Himself, for only then will they infallibly exercise their freedom for the moral order rather than against it. To possess an inclination exclusively for the true good is to will in a divine way, not a creaturely way. "Freedom" is a holy name principally on the basis of this freedom, for it is proper to God alone.

IV. The Freedoms Compared

This freedom is illumined by a comparison to the other two. Its most important contrast to a freedom of action comes in relation to law. If one accepts only the latter freedom, one will usually conceive authority and law as restraints, perhaps necessary, but regrettable: limits on one's freedom of movement and expression. Order is here opposed to freedom. In a freedom of spirit, on the other hand, true law is something essentially liberating. For example, placing the passions under the authority of reason frees one to accomplish the other goals proper to man's nature. Thus, a man possessing spiritual freedom readily embraces any law worthy of its name.

A similar difference is seen in relation to other agents. If one accepts only a freedom of action, another person is a potential enemy, someone who may restrict one's own agency. The person is here an object to be reckoned with. A freedom of spirit, on the other hand, places one at the disposal of the other. Free from being absorbed in self-conflict, the person is

---

[10] Aristotle, *Metaphysics*, 1008b 10–30.

ready to go out to the other and give him his proper respect and even love. The other is a potential friend, another self. He is viewed as a subject, not as an object. Love of one's own good becomes identified with a love of his good.

More significant for my purposes here is the comparison to man's freedom of choice. Recall that the latter is rooted in the *intellect* and in a *formal* cause—the known disproportion between particular and universal goodness; freedom of spirit, on the other hand, is rooted in the *will* and in an *efficient* cause—the ready inclination to the true good. Note, also, that the basis of a freedom of choice is an inclination to the comprehensive good or *bonum in communi*, whereas the basis of a freedom of spirit is an inclination to the moral good or *bonum honestum*. Note, finally, that freedom of choice is based on a dominating *indifference* towards a known good; a freedom of spirit, on the other hand, is hardly indifferent in the face of various goods, but *firmly inclines* away from the apparent good and to the true good. A consequence of this difference is that man's freedom of choice, in itself, will always be fallible in relation to the moral good: a person is free to choose it or to fail to choose it. On the contrary, a freedom of spirit tends toward infallibility in relation to the moral good: at its term, a person possessing this freedom perfectly cannot fail to choose the true good.

Although man's several freedoms are distinct, there is an evident order between them. In the order of genesis, they follow one another as examined. Thus, a freedom of action conditions and makes possible the exercise of a freedom of choice. It is hard to imagine a person who could live with *no* freedom of action; such extreme brutalization, barring the intervention of divine aid, would so dehumanize anyone as to render his free choice practically impossible. Free choice, for its part, is the condition of spiritual freedom: one becomes rooted in the true good because one has freely placed one's happiness in it, rather than somewhere else. In the order of ends, however, the order between the freedoms is reversed. Freedom of action is valuable because it conditions freedom of choice and makes possible its natural expression; and freedom of choice is good because it makes possible the perfection of the entire self achieved in spiritual freedom. Man's freedom is most valuable because, through it, he can become like God.

Such a subordination of one freedom to another, however, cannot be made absolute. From the perspective of spiritual freedom, law is salutary and necessary to educate man's passions and will. Yet it would be wrong to impose the moral law in all its detail, either upon an individual or the body politic. For man, in possessing his freedom of choice, possesses the freedom to err; and restricting his freedom to express error can be to strike illegitimately at that freedom. Thus, the state, for example, should restrict freedom of action only where it would harm the common good of society. Conversely, one seeking spiritual freedom may have to forfeit certain freedoms of action in themselves good. For example, brotherly love may require that one become a prisoner on behalf of one's neighbor. In fact, because our body is not subservient to our will, nor our will to its true good, there are inevitable conflicts between the demands of these different freedoms as we discover them in ourselves.

V. Man's Freedom in Relation to God

Forgive me for having gone over largely common ground that is no doubt familiar to most. Having done so, however, puts us in a position properly to relate man's freedom to God (as traditionally conceived: the creator and governor of the world). In effect, we can now see that certain difficulties in this area are really false problems, based on an inadequate appreciation of man's diverse freedoms. And we can also see the great question posed to man by his freedom before God. It is to these matters that my concluding reflections turn.

If someone only affirms man's freedom of action, God almost certainly will be conceived as an enemy of it. He will be seen as the ultimate external agent set over against man. By His law and by His punishment against those who transgress it, He denies man freedom of action. Such a narrow and false view of God's dealing with man is based on a narrow and false view of man's freedom. To dispel it, one need only recall that man possesses a real freedom of choice. He does so because of his very nature. Thus, far from being a denier of man's freedom, God is the cause of it, by creating him an intelligent and voluntary being. Not only does He give him freedom of choice, but He also gives him a world in which that freedom of choice can freely act.

Truth to tell, it is difficult to posit only a freedom of action. For, in this case, man's actions turn out to be only the expression of un-free inclinations determined by previous causes. Nor can it even be termed a freedom of self-expression, without equivocation. For what sort of self is it that cannot freely respond to the attraction of various goods? Such a being does not perdure, but is constantly changing given the agents acting on it: one is faced with a series of "phenomenal" selves but no real *self*. Furthermore, why should one become exercised over the rightful freedoms of such a series of beings, who seem little better, ontologically, than inert matter? As a consequence, it is far more common to find people who assert both freedom of action and of choice.

Seemingly, it is from such a perspective that many Catholics speak when they strenuously advocate the proper rights of academic freedom on

Catholic campuses of higher learning: the dignity of man as student and teacher requires that he be free to determine the curricular requirements and educational goals of the institute. Scholars should be free, that is, for their intellectual pursuits and from the outside authority of the Church and the mandates of Her faith. Such a brouhaha, however, is another false problem. For the Church, in calling Her sons and daughters to place their faith at the heart of their educational enterprise, is precisely seeking to orient man towards his true freedom as a child of God. Presumably, Catholics still believe that, in knowing the truth of their faith, they shall be set free. No doubt, this still leaves much room for discussing how that authority is best served on the present campus. But to cast the debate simply in terms of academic freedom versus ecclesial authority is to present a false dilemma: it is to forget that man's freedom of choice is at the service of a spiritual freedom that is his final end.

Even when man's diverse freedoms are recognized, false debates can arise from not keeping their differences clearly in view. This seems in part to have happened in the famous argument between the Jesuits and Dominicans at the beginning of the seventeenth century. The Jesuits never tired of insisting that man's freedom gave him the power to choose the good or *not* to choose it. He could fail to choose as he ought, and therefore God could justly hold him accountable for his fault. And this is true: the mode proper to man's freedom of choice is a fallible one. For their part, the Dominicans held that man could not choose the moral good unless God moved him to it. And this likewise is true: man's spiritual freedom is made possible because God inclines him to the *bonum honestum*. Each of the parties in a sense speaks past the legitimate concerns of the other, failing to see that man's freedom of choice and his spiritual freedom have diverse bases. Once this is recognized, it is possible to untie their Gordian knot, by affirming that man is moved by God to the honest good in a way that can be resisted. Thus, he only chooses well because God *moves* him to do so, yet his *failure* to do so is in his own hands and is his responsibility.[11]

We are thus led to recognize the true dilemma of freedom and the magnitude of the choice before God that a free creature must make. On the one hand, being endowed with free choice, he sees that he possesses a real ability to create his destiny. He can be the author of his own moral order. He can place his happiness in his own free will, a depth of himself seen

---

[11]It is thus that Maritain offers his way out of the "Molinist-Bañezian" impasse, save that he speaks of a resistible motion as a "shatterable" one: a purely verbal difference. See *God and the Permission of Evil*, trans. Joseph W. Evans (Milwaukee: Bruce Publishing Company, 1966), chapters I and II, especially 38ff.

and naturally loved. God has placed within his hands a certain autonomy, a certain independence that mimics His own sovereign independence (*aseitas*). On the other hand, being moved towards a spiritual freedom, he sees that he possesses the real ability to be whole, to be at peace. He discovers in himself a certain order, one not created by himself. Its author is unseen. In following it, he moves towards an unseen goal. He thereby relinquishes the opportunity to be the first cause of his moral life, implicitly subordinating his will to God. Yet, in doing so, he keeps the possibility of seeing Him and being happy.

God is radically independent and absolutely blessed. It is not possible for a free creature to be both of these. He must choose. He can be independent, insofar as this is possible to a creature. To do so means turning away from God and His order, thereby relinquishing any right to see the Absolute Good and the happiness that goes with that sight. Or he can follow the order towards the true good found in himself. To do so means subordinating his will to the author of that order and to His will. The price of glory is the sacrifice of his self-will. A creature can be his own master and lose happiness or he can be the servant of God and gain happiness; he cannot, however, be his own master and be happy. That is the privilege of God alone.

We can see, then, that it is not absurdly paradoxical to say that man must give up his freedom in order to find his freedom, or that he must lose himself in order to gain himself. For, by committing himself to the pursuit of spiritual freedom, he gives up a certain possibility contained in his freedom of choice. As his will becomes rooted in the true good, he becomes less and less indifferent to the goods before him. The more he places God first in his life, the more his destiny is outside the control of his will. The self-mastery that comes with spiritual freedom is achieved by the sacrifice of his possible independence.

Thus, the conclusion to which our entire analysis leads is that the true drama of freedom is a drama of love. In governing His free creatures according to their fallible freedom, God gives them an awful opportunity: to love Him enough to offer up their own independence to Him. They give this up to Him sight unseen. There is a self-emptying here that is the true creaturely image of God's creative love. The risk is that they will refuse Him their love. That is their privilege as free creatures. They can decide that the price of a possible glory is not worth it: they can prefer their own seen will to His unseen one.

I cannot fail to add, finally, that this natural structure and the choice it provokes are not destroyed, but deepened, under the present conditions in which man finds himself. Now, he discovers in himself not merely the possibility of not following the moral order, but also actual inclinations against it. Now, in following the true good, he must therefore sacrifice even more of himself, for he is in part identified with those tendencies. And he also comes to realize, in making this attempt, that he no longer possesses the capacity to succeed on his own. If he is to become spiritually free, he must admit his own relative impotence to accomplish this. Someone must help free him from his self-division. Thus, the submission of his will must be even greater, the sacrifice and the love demanded even deeper. For the Christian, this work is undertaken in the full knowledge that it is crucifying, that great sacrifices will be asked of him. Certainly, a Catholic can never forget this, for the one sacrifice that makes his possible is daily offered up on the altars of his Church. In the light of that sacrificial love, forever set against the enslavement of sin and death, there is hardly any word more sacred to him than freedom.

Donald A. Gallagher

Appendix

Message to the American Maritain
Association and the Canadian
Jacques Maritain Association

This message to my fellow members of the American Maritain Association and my colleagues in the Canadian Jacques Maritain Association
comes to you from Rome, where I am a press representative at the Epis-
copal Synod. With regret, I note that this is the first meeting of the AMA I
have missed since its founding in 1977. I wish to say a few words on the
question: what path should we as Associations, or as "little flocks," pursue in the years to come?

The pathways are various. One path is an obvious dead-end: that of
following Maritain literally and almost slavishly, a path leading to idoliza-
tion. Our decade of work shows that this poses no danger to us, but it must
be borne in mind as a temptation. At the other extreme is the path of merely honoring the name of Maritain, but treating current trends of thought
with little or no reference to his principles and methodology. Again, there
is no real danger to us in this, but it is a more insidious path.

A praiseworthy pathway is one of being a relatively small professional
society dedicated to the study and propagation of Maritain's thought. In
effect, this is what we have been and are, but we should aim at something
more. It may well be what we do best, but we should constantly re-examine this objective and judge whether it suffices.

Sometimes I reflect that, in this age of intellectual crisis, we are called
upon to be prophets as well as strict philosophers. Maritain was a prophet
as well as a philosopher; rather, his Christian philosophy embraces a
prophetic dimension. There is an affinity between Maritain the youthful in
Antimoderne and Maritain the elder in *Le Paysan de la Garonne*. We all know
that he recognized the historic gains in our present age, but did not
hesitate to expose and criticize its failings. Are we not called upon to be
prophets and not merely academics?

In this brief message, I would not dream of presenting my idea of what the right pathway for us to tread is. I wish to hint at something, following the lead of Maritain. He speaks of the need of Ontosophy, embracing the ethical and metaphysical orders. (His word, "ontosophy," if I may borrow an expression from Charles S. Peirce, is one safe enough from kidnappers. It signifies Maritain's determination to break out of old formats and to express something new.)

Jacques Maritain teaches us to ascend to and embark upon the High Road, as well as to pursue the little way.

The High Road, as I use the expression, signifies the immense task of reconstructing the social order and building a New Christendom (Integral Humanism) and of the renewal and development of Christian Philosophy. Sometimes, Maritain speaks as though almost nothing has been done regarding these objectives, the accomplishment of which he recognizes is bound to take generations. However, he does not disdain the little way or ways, the path of doing our best in our own local setting. Indeed, he praises the little way; it is what his own Little Brothers of Jesus do. Is it not what his own "little groups" or "little flocks" do?

Who is to say that the little way most if not all of us follow does not, in some obscure way, lead to what I called the High Road? These paths are not exclusive of one another. Our question remains: what should our task or our path be as a group or as a society? What can and should we do that would effect more than our own individual efforts?

As I said above, I would not presume to answer such a question in a short allocution. Let me adopt a lesson or formula I learned long ago in high-school mathematics. Even the little group bears within itself enormous potentialities for dialogue or encounter. If every person in a group of 100 members met one-on-one or formed a pair with every other member, there would be 4,950 pairings and thus potential authentic dialogal one-on-one encounters. Out of this stunning potential, something actual, something actually splendid, should be enacted. I put the matter this way because we are so often discouraged in the face of gigantic difficulties involved, in the task of renewal on a global basis—for example, in coping with entrenched errors and in laboring at reconstruction or at what I call instauration. It is encouraging to reflect that even the "little flock" (again, as Maritain is fond of calling it) is capable of achieving something of lasting importance. No doubt, we intend more than we are able to accomplish, but we also accomplish more at times than we intend.

Best wishes to my friends in the CJMA and the AMA!

Rome, Italy: October 31, 1987

Contributors

Mortimer J. Adler is Chairman of the Board of Editors of the *Encyclopaedia Britannica*, Director of the Institute for Philosophical Research, and author of over forty books: from *Dialectic* through *The Idea of Freedom* to *Intellect: Mind over Matter* and *The Plurality of Religions and the Unity of Truth* (tentative title), both forthcoming from Macmillan.

George Anastaplo, subject of the celebrated Supreme Court decision *In re Anastaplo* (1950–1961), is Professor of Law at Loyola University of Chicago and longtime member of the Liberal Arts Adult Education Program at the University of Chicago. His most recent book is *The Constitution of 1787*.

Otto Bird is founder and former Director of the Liberal Studies Program at the University of Notre Dame, former Editor of *Great Ideas Today*, and author of *The Idea of Justice*.

Joseph J. Califano is Professor of Philosophy at Saint John's University (Jamaica, NY), and has published articles in the *Thomist*, Asian and European scientific journals, and for the Department of Energy.

Raymond Dennehy is Professor of Philosophy at the University of San Francisco and the present President of the American Maritain Association. Author of *Reason and Dignity*, he has written widely on ethics and metaphysics, and has frequently participated in televised debates on abortion and related matters.

Desmond J. FitzGerald is Professor of Philosophy at the University of San Francisco and a former Research Fellow for *The Idea of Freedom*. He assisted in editing Yves R. Simon's *Freedom of Choice*.

Donald A. Gallagher is President of the De Rance Foundation, President Emeritus of the American Maritain Association, and co-author, with his wife Idella, of the definitive Maritain bibliography, *The Achievement of Jacques and Raïssa Maritain*.

Catherine Green is author of "The Nature of Moral Action: An Examination of Yves R. Simon's Metaphysics of Morals" (M.A. thesis, Catholic University of America, 1987) and is presently completing her doctoral work on Simon's ontology of knowledge.

John A. Gueguen is Professor of Political Science at Illinois State University. He has published various articles dealing with the applications of political science to contemporary issues, and is editor of the recently released *The Good Man and Society; Active Contemplation: Essays in Honor of Gerhart Niemeyer*.

John Hellman, Professor of History at McGill University, has authored books on Simone Weil and Emmanuel Mounier and the introduction to the revised edition of Yves. R. Simon's *The Road to Vichy*.

John P. Hittinger, Associate Professor of Philosophy at the College of Saint Francis (Joliet, IL), has published articles in *This World* and *Social Justice Review*, and is presently working on a book on twentieth century Catholic philosophers.

David T. Koyzis is Assistant Professor of Political Science at Redeemer College (Ancaster, Ontario), and author of "Towards a Christian Democratic Pluralism. A Comparative Study of Neo-Thomist and Neo-Calvinist Political Theories" (Ph.D. dissertation, University of Notre Dame, 1986).

Marianne Mahoney, Adjunct Associate Professor of Political Science at Elmhurst College and Lecturer in Philosophy at Loyola University of Chicago, is currently doing research for a book on contemporary democratic theory based on the Thomistic notion of prudence.

Matthew J. Mancini, Associate Professor of History and Philosophy at Mercer University, has published articles and reviews in *The Journal of Negro History*, *The Journal of Southern History*, and *Notes et Documents*, and is the co-editor of *Understanding Maritain: Philosopher and Friend*.

Ralph McInerny is Professor of Philosophy at the University of Notre Dame, Director of the Jacques Maritain Center there, and Editor of *The New Scholasticism*. One of his most recent books is *Art and Prudence: Studies in the Thought of Jacques Maritain*.

Robert J. Mulvaney is Professor of Philosophy at the University of South Carolina and editor of Yves R. Simon's *Practical Knowledge*, forth-coming from Fordham University Press.

Ralph Nelson, Professor of Political Science at the University of Windsor, is presently co-translating Jacques Maritain's *Neuf leçons sur les notions premières de la philosophie morale*.

Michael Novak is George F. Jewett Scholar in Religion, Philosophy, and Public Policy at the American Enterprise Institute (Washington, DC), and was Professor of American Studies at the University of Notre Dame in the fall of 1987 and of 1988. Among his most recent books is *Free Persons and the Common Good*.

Robert Royal is Director of Catholic Studies at the Ethics and Public Policy Center (Washington, DC). His articles and reviews have appeared in various publications, among them *The National Review* and *The American Spectator*.

Michael D. Torre, a former instructor in the Great Books program of Saint Mary's College (Moraga, CA) and a contributor to the American Maritain Association's previous volume on Maritain, is an Assistant Professor of Philosophy at the University of San Francisco.

S. Iniobong Udoidem is Professor of Philosophy at the University of Port Harcourt, Nigeria, and author of *Authority and the Common Good in Social and Political Philosophy*.

John Van Doren is Executive Editor of *The Great Ideas Today* and Fellow of the Institute for Philosophical Research.

Select Bibliography[1]

Mortimer J. Adler

The Common Sense of Politics. New York: Holt, Rinehart and Winston, 1971.

The Idea of Freedom. 2 vols. Garden City, New York: Doubleday and Company, 1958–61.

Philosopher at Large: An Intellectual Autobiography. New York: Macmillan, 1977.

Ten Philosophical Mistakes. New York: Macmillan, 1985.

Jacques Maritain

Art and Scholasticism and The Frontiers of Poetry. Trans. by Joseph W. Evans. New York: Scribner's, 1962.

Creative Intuition in Art and Poetry. New York: Pantheon Books, 1953.

Distinguish to Unite or The Degrees of Knowledge. Trans. under the supervision of Gerald B. Phelan. New York: Scribner's, 1959.

Freedom in the Modern World. Trans. by Richard O'Sullivan. New York: Scribner's, 1936.

Integral Humanism: Temporal and Spiritual Problems of a New Christendom. Trans. by Joseph W. Evans. New York: Scribner's, 1968.

Man and the State. Chicago: University of Chicago Press, 1951.

On the Philosophy of History. Ed. by Joseph W. Evans. New York: Scribner's, 1957.

The Range of Reason. New York: Scribner's, 1952.

Ransoming the Time. Trans. by Harry Lorin Binsse. New York: Scribner's, 1941.

Reflections on America. New York: Scribner's, 1958.

Religion and Culture. Trans. by J.F. Scanlan, with an intro. by Christopher Dawson. London: Sheed and Ward, 1931.

The Responsibility of the Artist. New York: Scribner's, 1960.

---

[1]This bibliography includes only those books abbreviated in the text.

283

The Rights of Man and Natural Law. Trans. by Doris C. Anson. New York: Scribner's, 1943. Reissued in *Christianity and Democracy and The Rights of Man and Natural Law*. Intro. by Donald A. Gallagher. San Francisco: Ignatius Press, 1986.

Three Reformers: Luther, Descartes, Rousseau. New York: Scribner's, 1929.

Yves R. Simon

"Charles Dunoyer, mémoire." Thesis for the *Diplôme d'Études Supérieur de Philosophie*, University of Paris, Sorbonne, 1923. Copy available at the University of Notre Dame Hesburgh Library.

The Community of the Free. Trans. by Willard R. Trask. Revised edition. Lanham, Maryland: University Press of America, 1984.

Freedom and Community. Ed. by Charles P. O'Donnell. New York: Fordham University Press, 1968.

Freedom of Choice. Ed. by Peter Wolff. Foreword by Mortimer J. Adler. New York: Fordham University Press, 1969.

A General Theory of Authority. Revised edition. Intro. by Vukan Kuic. Notre Dame: University of Notre Dame Press, 1980.

The Definition of Moral Virtue. Ed. by Vukan Kuic. Bio-Bibliography by M.V. Leroy. New York: Fordham University Press, 1986.

Nature and Functions of Authority. Milwaukee: Marquette University Press, 1940.

Philosophy of Democratic Government. Foreword by Jerome G. Kerwin. Chicago: University of Chicago Press, 1951.

Trois leçons sur le travail. Collection "Cours et Documents de Philosophie." Paris: Pierre Tequi, 1938.

Work, Society, and Culture. Ed. by Vukan Kuic. New York: Fordham University Press, 1971. Revised edition. "Yves R. Simon: A Bibliography, 1923–1970," by Anthony O. Simon. New York: Fordham University Press, 1986.

Index

The text of this book was set in Palatino, and the
titles in Helvetica. Pages were prepared with
Ventura and typeset with a Postscript laser printer.
Book design and layout by Mike Mollerus, 2515B
McAllister, San Francisco, California 94118.